Adventure Education for the Classroom Community:

Over 90 Activities for Developing Character, Responsibility, and the Courage to Achieve

LAURIE S. FRANK
AMBROSE PANICO

Solution Tree

Copyright © 2000, 2007 by Solution Tree
(formerly National Educational Service)
304 West Kirkwood Avenue
Bloomington, Indiana 47404
(812) 336-7700
(800) 733-6786 (toll free)
FAX: (812) 336-7790
email: info@solution-tree.com
www.solution-tree.com

Cover art by Dave Coverly
Cover design by Grannan Graphic Design Ltd.
Text design and composition by Karla Dunn

Printed in the United States of America

ISBN 978-1-934009-00-0

Dedication

In memory of Marcia Hiller, 1963–2002. Your music lives on.

—Laurie

To my wife Debbie and sons Bo and Andrew—what a community we four have made.

To my guru "The Vic" for being "The Vic."

In memory of Douglas H. Long, July 22, 1945–January 28, 2006.

—Ambrose

Contents

Part III: Going Further

Appendices

Foreword

Adventure Education for the Classroom Community is about nurturing a healthy learning environment where students feel connected, safe, and empowered. While the two issues of school safety and standards currently compete for national attention, one might ask, "Is there a place for a book about the classroom community?" I assure you that, now more than ever before, there is not only a place for this resource, but also good reasons to read and rely on it. Safe schools and improved academic achievement begin with the classroom community.

All children, young adolescents, and teenagers need to feel connected, valued, and significant. Their very nature as social beings calls out for it. Those of us who work and live with children and youth know this firsthand. We see reminders of their need to be connected and belong every day, from the first-graders who compete to sit beside the teacher at circle time to the cliques of high school. The school environment holds an important key to unlocking the way to safety in our schools and communities. School is where young people learn how to make friends and interact with peers, how to fit in or avoid others, how to shine or become invisible. When we transform our classrooms into communities, we have the opportunity to help students develop healthy relationships and lifelong skills and to help them learn the skills of conflict management, setting goals, giving affirmations, and solving problems.

Yet improving school safety through increasing our students' sense of connection is just one of the possible benefits of developing classroom communities. The trust and security these communities provide create learning environments that are vital for intellectual development. The human brain's ability to create meaning and gain new knowledge depends in part on the environment. If the surrounding environment is safe and supportive, the brain can do its job. It learns. To the extent that students feel connected to each other and to their teachers in the learning environment, they can learn new skills, develop greater competencies, and more effectively apply new knowledge. To neglect the development and health of the learning community is to jeopardize the very reason that groups of children and youth are gathered together in schools—to learn. Nurturing the classroom community improves results in the very outcome that standards-based assessment demands—improved academic achievement.

In *Adventure Education for the Classroom Community,* Laurie Frank and Ambrose Panico present a rationale and methodology for building the kind of learning community that helps students learn. If you are new to the notions of classroom community and adventure learning, you will appreciate the authors' inviting style, easy-to-read activities, and practical and realistic guidelines for implementation. If you are a seasoned experiential teacher, you will appreciate the new activities along with the redesign and new applications of adventure activity "classics." As in all good resources, *Adventure Education for the Classroom Community* provides good explanations, helpful examples, and easy-to-follow directions and suggestions for extension and further application.

Please join with teachers who, like yourself, are committed to the healthy growth, development, and achievement of their students by including *Adventure Education for the Classroom Community* among your teaching essentials.

—Mary Henton
Author of *Adventure in the Classroom*
Director of Professional Development, National Middle School Association

About the Authors

Laurie S. Frank is a public school teacher who has worked in the adventure field for more than 20 years. She began her career as a special education teacher in emotional disabilities, working with students of all ages. Her path diverged upon the discovery of adventure education and experiential methodologies. The need to develop community within the school setting was apparent to her, and the adventure philosophy seemed the perfect vehicle to achieve that goal.

Laurie was a leader in designing the nationally recognized Stress/Challenge adventure program for Madison (Wisconsin) Metropolitan School District. She wrote their curriculum, *Adventure in the Classroom*, in 1988. Currently, she is the owner and director of GOAL Consulting, working with school districts, camps, and nonprofit organizations throughout the country to create environments where students, faculty, staff, and families are invited into the educational process. She also helps schools develop experiential education curricula for children and young adults.

Laurie wrote the *Camp Manito-wish (Collaborative) Leadership Manual* in 1997. Her book *Journey Toward the Caring Classroom: Using Adventure to Create Community* (2004) is an expanded version of *The Caring Classroom*, which was published in 2001. She also collaborated on another book, *Games (& Other Stuff) for Teachers* (1999). She is working with the Wisconsin Leadership Institute to develop a collaborative leadership curriculum for high school students, and with the city of Chicago to develop and implement standards for youth programming.

Laurie has been a certified trainer with Project Adventure and is a recipient of the Michael Stratton Practitioner of the Year award from the Association for Experiential Education. She currently serves on the boards of the Association for Experiential Education, Wisconsin Youth Company, Wil-Mar Neighborhood Center, and the Hancock Center for Movement Arts and Therapies.

Ambrose "Broz" Panico is a veteran educator and change agent whose work includes 30 years in public education. He has worked as a teacher, coach, dean, principal, State Due Process Hearing Officer, and central office administrator. Ambrose began his career as a teacher in a Chicago Public School behavior disorders classroom and currently is the Assistant Director of the ECHO Joint Agreement located in South Holland, Illinois. As a local school district administrator, he has developed alternative education environments for behavior disordered, emotionally disturbed, disruptive, and at-risk students.

As a consultant, he has supported the efforts of like-minded educators nationally. In addition to his public school career, he is a private staff development specialist, consultant, and trainer. He believes in focusing less on externally controlling student behavior and more on creating learning environments that meet student needs to belong, be competent, exercise independence, and have fun. He challenges teachers to acknowledge and accept that they are the most important variable in the classroom. His book, *Discipline and the Classroom Community Model: Recapturing Control of Our Schools* (1999), and articles, "The Classroom Community Model: Teaching Responsibility" (1997) and "Service Learning as a Community Initiation" (1998), evidence his professional commitment to responsibility education and experiential education. Ambrose's alternative education programs have won the prestigious JC Penney Golden Rule Award for Outstanding Community Service and designations as National Service-Learning Schools from the Corporation for National and Community Service and as National Schools of Character from the Character Education Partnership.

Acknowledgments

This work was created through partnership. Although our names are on the cover, the book was refined by colleagues who share our passion for turning schools into learning communities where everyone is not just tolerated, but valued as human beings.

A sincere thank you to everyone who took the time to review this book—educators all, but unique individuals for sure. Your willingness to apply your knowledge and years of experience working with and for youth has added much to what we believe will be a valuable resource. Reviewers include:

Steve Bennett, Guidance Counselor, Sauk Prairie High School

Tom Donausky, Principal, Rich South High School

Sylvia Dresser, Executive Director, Association for Challenge Course Technology (ACCT)

Dorothea Fitzgerald, Superintendent, Dolton School District 148

Bill García, Principal Consultant, Illinois State Board of Education

Diana Grossi, Director, South Cook Intermediate Service Center #4

Vinni M. Hall, Chair, Special Education, Chicago State University

Douglas C. Hamilton, Superintendent, South Holland School District 151

Lynn Jones, Teacher, Athens, Georgia

Sally Kaminski, Director of Special Education, Dolton District 148

Barbara Kwit, Assistant Director, School Association for Special Education in DuPage County

Lucy Neuenschwander, Yoga Instructor, Former Teacher in the Kenosha Unified School District

Russell F. Retterer, Executive Director, ECHO Joint Agreement

James R. Sorensen, Teacher, Chippewa Middle School

Robert K. Wilhite, Assistant Superintendent, Thornton Fractional Township High School District 215

A special thank you to Suemarie Gonzalez whose skill and attention to detail helped to ensure the quality of this resource.

We also wish to thank those who have gone before us in the field of adventure/ experiential education. Many of the activities were originally documented by Karl Rohnke, Steve Butler, Faith Evans, Chris Cavert, and others. We have simply adapted many of these activities to help further the notion of classroom communities. This is not to exclude those activities we have been privileged to experience during workshops, conferences, and sharing sessions. As poet Maya Angelou has said, "[we] stand on the shoulders of those who come before us, and those who come after stand on ours."

—Laurie Frank and Ambrose Panico

Introduction

America is great because she is good; but if America
ceases to be good, she will cease to be great.

> —Alexis de Tocqueville, French political leader, historian, and
> writer

We must remember that intelligence is not enough.
Intelligence plus character—that is the goal of true
education.

> —Martin Luther King, Jr., American clergyman and civil rights
> leader

When considering the importance of character education in our classrooms, we need not look further than the current statistics on youth violence:

- It is estimated that 30% of sixth to tenth graders in the United States are involved in bullying as either a bully or as the target of a bully—or both (Nansel et al., 2001).

- In a nationwide study of high school students (CDC, 2004), 33% of students reported being in a physical fight one or more times in the previous year and 17% reported carrying a weapon in the month preceding the survey.

- In 2003, juveniles were involved in 1 in 12 arrests for murder, 1 in 9 arrests for drug abuse violations, and 1 in 4 arrests for weapons violations and for robbery (U.S. Department of Justice, Federal Bureau of Investigation, 2004).

- In 2003, an average of 15 young people aged 10 to 24 were murdered each day (CDC, 2004).

The statistics are staggering, and the consequences of this violence are enormous—both for the youths involved, for their families, and for their communities. According to the Surgeon General (2006), we have come to understand that young people in every community—cities, small towns, suburbs, and rural regions—can be involved in violence. As Lickona noted more than a decade ago, teenagers involved in violence often carry out their crimes with "new lows of brutality with a seeming total lack of conscience or remorse" (1992, p. 4). Murphy (1998) underscores the seriousness of the problem in her research and suggests that schools can and must be part of the solution. She examines a question originally posed by Socrates: Can virtue be taught? The answer is yes.

The teaching of human virtue and the subsequent shaping of good character are critical tasks in education today. Research has found that there is a need to return to the moral purpose of teaching (Fenstermacher, 1990). Character education programs are one way schools can teach students to value themselves and each other. This is crucial because as Lewis (1998) states, "history has shown that societies tend to self-destruct when their people don't possess a core group of positive character traits" (p.1).

The Association for Supervision and Curriculum Development (ASCD) brought together experts in moral education to form a panel to draft a document ("Moral Education in the Life of the School," 1998) in which they list six characteristics of a morally mature person. According to the document, the morally mature person habitually

1. Respects human dignity

2. Cares about the welfare of others

3. Integrates individual interest and social responsibilities

4. Demonstrates integrity

5. Reflects on moral choices

6. Seeks peaceful resolution of conflict

Schools have responded to the need for moral education. In their *Character Education Curriculum*, the Chicago Public Schools (2002) identify 11 traits as critical to moral development: caring, courage, courtesy, fairness, family pride, honesty and truthfulness, kindness, helpfulness, respect, responsibility, and work ethic. It is very common now to find schools that include some form of character education as part of their standard curriculum. Some schools purchase and implement published curriculum, while others prefer to use teacher-made materials that help to develop identified student outcomes. Typical character education programs differ from traditional obedience-based discipline programs in many ways. However, the primary difference is that they attempt to empower students to choose to control themselves instead of coercing them to behave through punishments and/or external rewards. Some character education programs provide direct instruction in core values and virtues. Some teach decision-making and problem-solving strategies. Many focus on conflict-resolution paradigms. Programs often include units on social and communication skills, and some emphasize the development of self-esteem. There are even programs that encourage students to examine their belief systems.

Teaching methodologies vary greatly and include direct instruction, role plays, conversation groups, literature that deals with moral and citizenship issues, puppet shows that model conflict-resolution strategies, school awards, school mottoes, motivational assemblies, and community service. Some schools deliver their character education via a specific class or program, while others weave it into the curriculum. Some of the best efforts attempt to create classrooms and even entire schools that function as communities that encourage their members to practice the skills and aspire to the virtues of the school's character education program.

Many schools address the three components of character education, defined by Thomas Lickona (1992) as the combination of moral knowing, moral feeling, and moral action.

—Adapted from *Educating for Character* (Lickona, 1992)

Although much emphasis has been placed on training children to know right from wrong (moral knowing), we believe too little thoughtful effort has been made to help children want to do right (moral feeling). We also believe that there should be more structured efforts to encourage children to actually do right (moral action).

BUILDING A CLASSROOM COMMUNITY

We believe that, more than any other single variable, a sense of community will motivate children to want to do the right thing. This book is our effort to provide teachers with simple but potent experiential education tools for building classroom and school communities. *Adventure Education for the Classroom Community* is a stand-alone curriculum to teach students to

1. Get to know and trust each other

2. Build and nurture lasting relationships

3. Master communication, planning, decision-making, problem-solving, and conflict-resolution skills

This book provides teachers who are seriously interested in empowering their students with a structure for doing so: the classroom community meeting. The meeting format helps a teacher transform his or her classroom into the students' community in which students become shareholders and decision makers. Once students are enfranchised and empowered to help conduct community (classroom) affairs, make community decisions, manage community discipline, and mediate community conflicts, they have reasons to put limits on their own behavior, and they do!

The book can also be used with and as a supplement to other character education or good citizenship programs. It is especially recommended for use with curricula and programs that focus on skills (as opposed to those that focus on processes). Many teachers we have spoken with report that although their students seem to know right from wrong and have mastered the communication and social skills curriculum, they seem to choose not to apply these skills to life in the classroom. We usually find the following three issues in these situations:

1. A lack of the all-important sense of community

2. Scarcity of meaningful student-to-student relationships

3. A lack of structure that provides the opportunity for students to practice and apply the desired skills

The first two of these three issues are addressed through the book's experiential education activities in chapters 5 through 10; the third is remedied through the classroom community meeting process described in chapter 11.

Another way to use the book is for teachers to simply select individual activities or groups of activities that make sense for their students in their situations.

At its heart, this book is an experiential education resource especially formatted for use in the traditional school setting by a traditional classroom teacher. It does not assume that the teacher has access to experiential education environments, such as adventure camps, nor does it assume that the teacher has special training, such as a degree in adventure or experiential education. It does make one assumption, however—it assumes that teachers are adventurers!

HOW TO BEGIN

Rather than assuming your students would benefit from exposure to all the activities we provide (or pretending we think you could actually find time to do them all), we suggest the following strategies.

Read the entire book, paying particular attention to four key points:

1. The importance of building a community and forming relationships

2. The format of the Experiential Learning Cycle

3. The dynamics of the Adventure Wave

4. The life cycle of the group

Keep in mind the possibility of changing your role from knowledge-giver to facilitator to gradually empower your students to accept control of and responsibility for their learning experience. As you read, take time to reflect on your class, the current class climate, and individual students to whom you may want to offer a little extra support. You are now ready to decide to use the materials in this book in one of three ways:

1. Implement the entire program—helping your students get to know and trust each other, teaching communication and goal-writing skills, and facilitating problem solving and conflict resolution through the classroom community meeting process.

Or

2. Use the experiential education activities to enhance and support skills and processes taught through another character-education or life-skills education program.

Or

3. Implement selected activities that make sense for your students.

Once you have decided how you want to implement the program, it is time to select specific activities. Even if you intend to implement the entire program, we suggest you pre-select specific activities because you probably will not have time to do them all. The activities we offer have wide appeal and are by nature flexible and easily adapted to accommodate differences in age, maturity, and ability levels.

The activities in chapter 5 ("Getting Acquainted") and chapter 6 ("Learning to Trust and Depend on Each Other") are designed to create a foundation from which students can master the skills and processes presented in subsequent chapters. Experience has taught us the importance of building this foundation. It will support the development of the skills and processes in this book and other like-minded curricula. It will also enhance academic excellence and help limit nonproductive and antisocial behavior. While we invite you to pick and choose among the other chapters, we strongly suggest you include chapters 5 and 6. If you do, everything else will come more easily.

Finally and perhaps most important, never forget that you are involved in a dynamic endeavor. Let your heart and good teacher instincts be your guide. Pay careful attention to your students' feedback. Experiment, be aggressive, and take some chances—you have little to lose and much to gain.

CHAPTER OVERVIEWS

CHAPTER 1: CLASSROOM COMMUNITIES

This chapter presents the concept of and rationale for viewing the classroom as a community. We explore the idea that young people learn to act responsibly only if they are given the opportunity to have responsibility, and we ask you to reflect on your personal paradigms and evaluate the possibility of relinquishing some control to students. The chapter also provides background information, including definitions of "community," a comparison of nonproductive classroom paradigms and classroom community paradigms, and the benefits to students. Teachers implementing the entire program are encouraged to share this background information with their students; young people learn better when they know *why* they are learning what they are.

CHAPTER 2: ADVENTURE EDUCATION IS EXPERIENTIAL

This chapter reviews and discusses experiential education as a methodology, addressing several basic questions: what is it, why does it work, and is it sound education?

CHAPTER 3: THE EXPERIENTIAL LEARNING CYCLE

This chapter is an experiential education primer for the classroom teacher who has no previous experiential education knowledge or training. It presents the Experiential Learning Cycle, which is the format for all experiential education lessons. The Experiential Learning Cycle components—experiencing, reflecting, generalizing, and applying—are discussed from an instructional point of view. The chapter reviews the teacher's role as a facilitator of learning and shares strategies for assuming this role. Also included are practical guidelines and helpful hints, such as knowing when it is time to step in, using metaphors to focus the experience, discussing safety issues, and making debriefing sessions successful.

CHAPTER 4: UNDERSTANDING THE LIFE CYCLE OF THE GROUP

This chapter explores the concept of viewing the group or class as a living entity. Because each group is made up of different individuals, each group is unique. Despite this uniqueness, however, there are some consistent, general processes at work in every group situation. Knowledge of these processes positions a teacher (facilitator) to better observe and understand the dynamics of the group. Also important to the teacher's ability to facilitate is a basic knowledge of group development. Predictable stages of development are discussed, and strategies for addressing growth issues are presented.

CHAPTER 5: GETTING ACQUAINTED

This chapter offers 15 different activities designed to accelerate and direct the process of getting to know each other. It explains the many benefits of providing structure to this very basic human process. Also explored is the idea that everything that happens or fails to happen in a classroom community is, to some degree, related to a teacher's ability to build relationships with and among students.

CHAPTER 6: LEARNING TO TRUST AND DEPEND ON EACH OTHER

This chapter builds on the work done in the chapter 5 activities. We examine the belief that students do better socially, emotionally, behaviorally, and academically when they trust and depend on each other. The chapter's 17 activities have been designed to further this trust.

CHAPTER 7: SETTING GOALS

Goals give direction to behavior. By teaching students to identify goals and write plans for their attainment, you help them focus on and evaluate their behavior. This chapter provides two introductory activities: a strategy for writing short-term goals and a strategy for writing long-term goals. You will want to include one or both of these activities unless you are already teaching another goal-writing strategy. You should conduct at least one of these goal-writing activities initially before using the chapter's other eight activities.

CHAPTER 8: USING COMMUNICATION SKILLS: THE BIG PICTURE

This chapter emphasizes the importance of not assuming students already have the communication skills and processes necessary in a shared-responsibility classroom. It presents a developmental sequence for teaching basic communication skills and complex communication processes, which will position students to learn and apply a decision-making/problem-solving process. Skill definitions and process models are provided, conflict resolution is introduced, and the concept of win-win solutions is defined and discussed.

CHAPTER 9: ACTIVE LISTENING, TAKING TURNS, AND USING "I" MESSAGES

The introductory activity in chapter 9, "Communication Skills Introduction," gives students a basic understanding of the three key communication skills: active listening, taking turns, and using "I" messages. The chapter's remaining 21 activities build on and support these three skills.

CHAPTER 10: PROBLEM SOLVING AND CONFLICT RESOLUTION

This chapter presents two introductory activities ("Decision-Making/Problem-Solving Process Introduction" and "Conflict-Resolution Process Introduction") intended to provide students with a basic understanding of these rather involved endeavors. These two skills are supported by the chapter's 20 remaining activities.

CHAPTER 11: PUTTING IT ALL TOGETHER: COMMUNITY MEETINGS AND ACTIVITIES THAT MAKE THEM PRODUCTIVE

Chapter 11 takes you right to the heart of the classroom community. Classroom community meetings are where you will offer your students the opportunity to use and develop their newly acquired communication, decision-making, problem-solving, and conflict-resolution skills. The chapter discusses the importance of providing this opportunity to your students and offers ideas for schedules, setup, and formats. Specific steps for holding productive meetings are outlined, and an implementation process is provided to help you successfully implement the classroom community meeting process. The chapter's six activities have been designed to improve your students' teamwork and leadership skills.

CHAPTER 12: MAKING THE CORE CURRICULUM RELEVANT: COMMUNITY SERVICE AND SERVICE LEARNING AS EXPERIENTIAL EDUCATION

In this chapter, we suggest that community service and service learning are really forms of experiential education taught in the local community. The chapter is written for a teacher new to community service and service learning, and includes definitions and comparisons of the two. Also included are service learning principles, reflection concepts, a student interest survey, two adventure activities, and examples of service learning lessons and activities that make the core curriculum relevant through experiential education methodology.

TAKING THE FIRST STEP

We know of no better tool for building communities and relationships. If talking, lecturing, and preaching worked, we would have had no need to write *Adventure Education for the Classroom Community*. The best strategy we have found for building a classroom community is to stop talking at the students and start experiencing with them! We present this curriculum with an invitation to join your students in developing a classroom community.

Part I

Getting Started

Chapter 1

Classroom Communities

Discipline is not a simple device for securing superficial peace in the classroom; it is the morality of the classroom as a small society.

—Émile Durkheim, French sociologist

Chapter 1

Classroom Communities

In today's world, we can no longer view schools as a kind of factory designed to mold students into a one-size-fits-all shape. Technology and a global community are transforming our society into one in which information has become the means of survival. Through school, television, and the Internet, we are often in contact with people outside of our own culture who may or may not share our values and with whom we may be expected to work. As our society changes, the goal of education must change along with it. We have a responsibility to prepare students for life in this ever-changing landscape. We can do this by teaching them skills of collaboration and providing a safe place in which they can make sense of their expanding roles.

Traditional education is built upon a static worldview. In this traditional paradigm, students sit at desks, taking in information that has been deemed necessary for survival. Yet that same information can become obsolete within moments of its acquisition. Education today must be built upon the principle that the world is a dynamic place—ever changing and ever growing. To prepare a young person for life in this dynamic society, we need to mirror that society in our schools. In order for people to learn to live in a democracy, they must *experience* democracy. By creating a healthy community in school, students learn how to create a healthy sense of community in their own lives. Practicing peaceful conflict resolution in our classrooms teaches youngsters how to resolve conflicts peacefully outside of the school environment.

Creating this microcosm of a peaceful, democratic community requires us to change our basic concepts of what education is all about. The dynamic worldview rests upon the premise that people are whole beings, connected to the larger environment and to each other. Creating a community where people have common interests and where there is common ownership begins with an environment that values and celebrates the contributions of each member. It is a safe place where conflicts can be settled without violence or abuse and where collaboration thrives.

Collaboration can be described as developing and encouraging relationships in which people can complete a variety of tasks and achieve a variety of goals over an extended period of time (Frank, Christ, & Carlin, in press). Collaborating individuals go beyond mere cooperation; they share ideas, occasionally argue over concepts, and develop solutions that are greater than those the individuals could have devised on their own. In a collaborative group, all individuals are equals who work together to create solutions that allow everyone to swim . . . or cause everyone to sink. Given the stakes, these group members must operate with respect and trust while working toward common goals.

> In genuine community there are no sides. It is not always easy, but by the time they reach community, the members have learned how to give up cliques and factions. They have learned how to listen to each other and how not to reject each other. Sometimes consensus in community is reached with miraculous rapidity. But at other times it is arrived at only after lengthy struggle. Just because it is a safe place does not mean community is a place without conflict. It is, however, a place where conflict can be resolved without physical or emotional bloodshed and with wisdom as well as grace. A community is a group that can fight gracefully.
>
> —M. Scott Peck (Schoel & Stratton, 1995, p. 19)

True classroom communities honor the importance of positioning community members to

- Feel valued as individuals

- Feel connected to the community and to each other

- Believe their needs to belong, be competent, experience some independence, and have some fun can be met in the community

- Believe they have something of value to offer to the community

Alfie Kohn (1996, p. 101) has described such a community as a

> place in which students feel cared about and are encouraged to care about each other. They experience a sense of being valued and respected; the children matter to one another and to the teacher. They have come to think in the plural; they feel connected to each other; they are part of an "us."

In communities such as these, individuals are willing to work hard and to practice reasonable self-denial in order to support the group, its purpose, and its values. These types of communities encourage students to build what Stephen Covey (1989) refers to as "emotional bank accounts" with each other. An emotional bank account is a metaphor that describes the amount of trust that has been built up in a relationship.

Deposits into an emotional bank account can take the form of kindnesses, thoughtful deeds, following through on commitments, and honest communications. Students who build emotional bank accounts with each other tend to

- Feel good about each other and their relationships

- Work to protect relationships

- Give each other the benefit of the doubt

- Solve conflict in a nonviolent manner

- Support each other to achieve at high levels

Membership in the classroom community motivates a student to attend regularly, work hard, and live by the rules. It also makes a student receptive to all of the wonderful things good teachers want to teach. Everything that happens or fails to happen in a classroom is, to some degree, predicated on this membership. Every classroom success or failure is, to some degree, dependent upon building a classroom with the classroom community–based paradigms found in the chart on page 8.

CLASSROOM COMMUNITY = PRODUCTIVE PARADIGMS

We can only achieve quantum improvements in our lives as we quit hacking at the leaves of attitude and behavior and get to work on the root, the paradigms from which our attitudes and behaviors flow.

—Stephen Covey, *The Seven Habits of Highly Effective People* (1989, p. 31)

ESTABLISHING A CLASSROOM COMMUNITY

The best teachers intuitively know that time spent establishing a classroom community is time spent building the foundation for student success. These teachers understand that for some children school is full of excitement, and for others it is the cause of much anxiety. Some students cannot wait to demonstrate how smart they are, while others think of new strategies to avoid being embarrassed. The popular students are happy to see their friends; those who struggle socially just hope to blend into the background to avoid being the brunt of jokes or the target of bullies. The best teachers have a plan—a curriculum for establishing a classroom community.

The best teachers begin to establish a classroom community on the very first day of the school year—a crucial time for the overall success of the school year (Wong & Wong, 2001). They also share with students their vision of this classroom community. This is particularly important with adventure education because this vision gives meaning and importance to the unique experiences students will encounter. Rather than attempting to coerce or trick students into participating in adventure education

Nonproductive Classroom Paradigms	Classroom Community Paradigms
1. Competition.	1. Cooperation.
2. There is not enough to go around.	2. Together, we can make more than ever.
3. It is the teacher against the students.	3. We are all in this together.
4. I want to know about and associate with people that are like me.	4. I want to know about and associate with all kinds of people. I never know who my next best friend might be.
5. My need to belong, be competent, be independent, and have fun cannot be met in school.	5. My need to belong, be competent, be independent, and have fun is met in school.
6. Showing up every day and working hard does not necessarily equal success.	6. Showing up every day and working hard equals success.
7. The teacher is responsible for controlling student behavior.	7. The students are responsible for behaving and controlling their own outcomes.
8. The students are responsible for knowing how to be responsible community members.	8. The teacher teaches what the students need to know.
9. The power is the principal's or dean's office.	9. The power is in the community.
10. Find someone or something to blame.	10. Find a solution.
11. You made me do it.	11. I chose to do it, and I had other choices.
12. What I choose to do or not to do is my business.	12. What I choose to do or not to do affects my community.
13. Needs justify behaviors.	13. Needs justify needs; behaviors must be adaptive and fair.
14. Teaching focuses on deficits.	14. Teaching focuses on strengths.
15. Teachers teach subjects.	15. Teachers teach students.

activities, teachers must help them *see* the benefits of building and living in a classroom community; they must help teach students collaboration by being collaborative with them. Engaging our students in this manner empowers them to build a learning environment where each individual is positioned to achieve at his or her highest level of competence.

You cannot assume that students will naturally *see* and *feel* a sense of community. In fact, students will most often immediately separate and sort themselves into cliques. The classroom community offers students a healthy alternative to this divisive dynamic. Students will begin to realize that only in a true community will they be able to relax, feel safe physically and psychologically, take the academic risks necessary to succeed, build and maintain meaningful relationships, and acknowledge and address personal challenges.

Building a classroom community is one of the many strategies efficient and effective teachers use to help their students survive and thrive in an era of standards-based reform. Wong and Wong (2001) define "efficiency" as doing things right and "effectiveness" as doing the right thing. Adventure education is an efficient way to be effective. The best teachers always remember the standards students must reach, but they never forget that they teach more than reading, writing, and arithmetic: They teach people. As Mary Henton instructs us in her foreword, "The human brain's ability to create meaning and gain new knowledge depends in part on the environment. If the surrounding environment is safe and supportive, the brain can do its job" (p. vii).

In addition, research indicates that educators spend more time dealing with behavior than they spend delivering instruction (Van Acker, Potterton, & Boreson, 2003). The extra time spent building community significantly reduces time off task, time lost to discipline issues, and time spent on conflict resolution. This recaptured time can then be spent on teaching and learning the academic curriculum.

Considering that most of us grew up in traditional classrooms, learned traditional teaching techniques from traditional professors in traditional universities, and teach in an environment of standards-based reform, we understandably struggle to

- Take time from academic instruction and reallocate it to community building

- Employ a nontraditional methodology such as adventure education

- Actually tell students why we do what we do—let them start with the "end in mind"

- Relinquish some control and empower students to take control

It may be difficult to make classroom culture a priority in these stressful times, but the payoff can be immense for students. The skills they gain will help them to learn and succeed in our collaborative global society, and in the meantime, the classroom will become a place of greater learning, a model of democracy, and a very fun place to be.

Chapter 2

Adventure Education Is Experiential

I hear and I forget. I see and I remember. I do and I understand.

—Confucius, Chinese philosopher

Chapter 2

Adventure Education Is Experiential

Adventure education is an approach that uses experiential education as its theoretical base. Adventure is just one of the many experiential methodologies and is a form of teaching and learning based on the belief that people learn best by doing. It provides people with the opportunity to actively participate in their own learning. Lessons begin with students engaging in a physical activity. This activity may be as simple as asking students to step on their partners' toes before being stepped on themselves, or as complex as getting the entire class across an imaginary river.

What—that doesn't sound too complex? What if the river is teeming with piranhas, a tornado is coming, and the only resources available are some plywood disks the teacher insists can form a floating bridge—and, of course, the human resource of each other? To succeed, students must create a plan for accomplishing the task that includes everyone, decide who will do what, and follow through with the plan. If someone accidentally "falls" into the river, they must start all over again. Still not tough enough? They must complete the task without diminishing their resources: If they do not use a disk, it will "float" away and they will lose it.

Get the idea?

Experiential education stresses the process over the product or outcome. What happens during the activity is more important to the students' learning than any result they may achieve. The students actually create the lesson with their interaction and cause the learning to occur. The activity alone carries no meaning. In the river example, students are simply walking on plywood disks. They create the meaning through their interactions, their choices, and, ultimately, how they work together.

This concept of using the environment as teacher is not new, but it is too seldom applied in the school setting. The idea of first providing an activity and then allowing time for processing seems simple. However, it is rarely done in traditional education, unless one considers listening to a lecture or watching a video an activity. For true adventure education, an activity must be participatory in nature. Students first do and then process—they play first and talk later. Enjoy the game, and then figure out the important lessons. Adventure education provides students with continuous opportunities to learn while maximizing cooperation and minimizing competition. The bedrock of all experiential education methods—the Experiential Learning Cycle—is presented in chapter 3, along with specific teaching strategies and predictable challenges.

A typical adventure education lesson follows the pattern below (also see the Adventure Wave on page 23):

1. Briefing: Provide the rules and object of the challenge or activity.

2. Experience: Have the students do the activity.

3. Debriefing: Process the activity.

WHY DOES IT WORK?

First and foremost, adventure education works because it is fun! It allows you to actually capitalize on the natural curiosity, unrestricted imagination, and boundless energy of children and young people. Rather than fighting to keep them in their seats, you can invite them to get up and "just do it!" Rather than directing them to arrive at a lesson's predetermined outcome, you can help them create their own learning and arrive at an outcome that is relevant to the experience they created. Rather than giving them the answer and forcing or bribing them to regurgitate it, you can provide them with the problem or challenge and encourage them to discern the solution. In the process, your students will learn more than specific answers to specific problems. They will learn to think for themselves. They will consider and evaluate assumptions they have about themselves and their classmates. They will learn to communicate with and rely on each other. Most important, they will learn to relax and have fun with each other!

Learning through experience is friendly to all learners because it has both right- and left-brain components. Each lesson's introduction is logical and language-based— and therefore left-brain friendly. The problem or challenge is presented, information is provided, and conditions are explained. The challenge itself relies heavily on right-brain processing because creativity and active involvement are stressed. The ability to manage the emotional or interaction phase of the lesson also taps the right brain. The activity is always followed by a processing session, where the logical left brain is once again important. Students discuss what happened and why. They look for ways that their patterns of interaction were helpful or hurtful to successfully completing the challenge and to building and maintaining relationships. They find ways to apply what they learned to life in their classroom community and to other communities in which they belong.

Experiential methodology also acknowledges the reality that in any classroom there will be some visual, some auditory, and some kinesthetic learners. Eric Jensen (1988) estimates that 40% of the general population are visual learners, 40% are auditory learners, and 20% are kinesthetic learners (p. 22). The very nature of experiential education presents all learners with at least some information in their preferred learning or processing style.

Traditional teaching methods honor a limited view of intelligence based on mathematical and linguistic strengths. Adventure education taps into a range, or spectrum, of intelligences. These multiple intelligences were identified by Howard Gardner (2000). They include bodily-kinesthetic, interpersonal, intrapersonal, linguistic, logical-mathematical, musical, naturalist, spatial, and possibly existential.

In addition to using verbal communication and logic for problem solving, adventure activities are frequently physical (bodily-kinesthetic), require spatial awareness, and call for a high degree of interpersonal skill to solve problems together. During processing, participants are encouraged to reflect, which makes use of intrapersonal and existential intelligence. Adventure education can appeal to the musical learner with the use of songs. And although much of what adventure education has to offer can take place in the classroom, it has its roots in the wilderness and can take place as easily in the woods and on the trail as it can inside the school, which utilizes naturalist intelligence. Multiple intelligence theory pays tribute to the whole person, and adventure education attends to the unique spectrum of intelligences in all of us.

Adventure Education lessons are presented as group challenges, and productive groups learn quickly how to tap individuals' areas of strength and compensate for relative areas of weakness. Students learn that there are many different ways to serve the group and to contribute to successfully completing a challenge. Leadership becomes fluid, dependent upon such variables as the nature of the specific challenge, the match between the specific challenge and individual group members' strengths and weaknesses, the situational interest and motivation of individuals, and a general concept of fairness. Too often our classrooms have too few leaders. Adventure education enables a teacher to offer every student the chance to lead. It also asks those who are used to leading to learn to be good followers.

Finally, adventure education acknowledges that as families and communities become increasingly diverse, it is risky to assume that any group of students share a common set of experiences or background. The worldview (perspectives and assumptions) each student uses to make sense of and process events can vary greatly. By holding an experience constant and sharing perceptions of it, students begin to see that they are different, that they process things differently, and that it is okay to do so. Understanding that two people may experience reality differently, process it differently, and ultimately arrive at different but valid conclusions forms the basis for accepting and often celebrating differences. There is no doubt that the ability to see the issue through the other person's eyes is the first step to finding solutions rather than simply fixing blame. Adventure education is diversity education.

WHAT MAKES ADVENTURE EDUCATION SOUND EDUCATION?

A number of characteristics support the soundness of adventure education. Adventure education

- Is fun, so children like it, and motivation is high.

- Involves everyone, while allowing individuals the opportunity to participate at different levels—from leader to follower and everything in between.

- Is friendly to a variety of learning styles. This can be very important to our kinesthetic learners, because most traditional lessons and teaching methodologies rely heavily on auditory and visual channels for presenting information.

- Speaks to both sides of the brain. Its lesson components present material in ways that are appealing to right- and left-brain learners.

- Honors the whole person by focusing on a variety of learning styles and intelligences.

- Provides a constructive outlet for natural energy in addition to physical education and recess.

- Does not assume that all members of the class have had a particular experience—it provides the experience. Holding the experience constant makes processing much more productive.

- Focuses on process rather than outcome.

- Shifts the responsibility for learning from the teacher to the student, allowing the teacher to become a learning facilitator instead of knowledge giver. Thus, it empowers students to become active, lifelong learners. It helps students accept and embrace more rigorous academic standards.

- Shifts the focus from learning the results of someone else's reasoning to mastering the skills of reasoning, testing, evaluating, and ultimately arriving at self-discerned solutions. Thus, it empowers students to become confident problem solvers and decision makers.

- Serves as a vehicle for students to get to know and trust each other. It allows the teacher to facilitate development of a classroom community while protecting against the formation of counterproductive cliques. It helps all kids to feel included by their peers and connected to their school. It is a violence prevention strategy.

- Serves as a vehicle for teachers and students to examine patterns of interaction—to reinforce those that are productive and caring and change those that are counterproductive and harmful.

- Provides a model of "fluid leadership."

- Stresses cooperation over competition.

Chapter 3

The Experiential Learning Cycle

Exclusive study of the products of prior work looks back, disempowering students; conducting creative investigations looks forward, empowering students.

—Spencer Kagan, American cooperative learning writer and authority

The Experiential Learning Cycle

There are many forms of experiential education. Adventure education, outdoor education, and service learning are a few. There is adventure-based counseling for the therapeutic realm and experience-based training and development for the corporate world. Project Adventure has created Adventure in the Classroom, and Outward Bound offers Expeditionary Learning as a model for schools. Although each of these models may look different, they are all based on the use of the Experiential Learning Cycle. This cycle offers a structure in which to create experiential lessons for your students.

EXPERIENTIAL LEARNING CYCLE

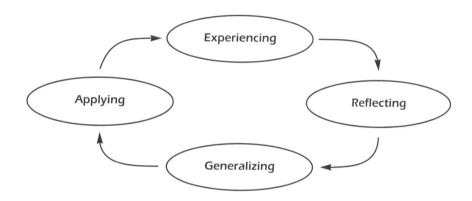

Because experiential education relies on the process rather than the product or outcome, this cycle helps keep that process going. Each phase of the cycle is important to learning. If we focus on only one part of the cycle, learning is incomplete. In adventure education, learning does not occur simply by having an experience; learning occurs after the individual or group has had an experience and then has the opportunity to process it (sometimes called "debriefing") by reflecting, generalizing, and applying their new learning.

The first two phases of the cycle, "experiencing" and "reflecting," focus on the *present*. Students have an experience and then reflect upon what has just happened. The experience engages them in the concepts to be learned by offering a shared involvement. Reflecting upon the experience personalizes it, allowing each person to draw upon his or her own background, values, and frame of reference in relation to the shared experience.

The "generalizing" phase of the cycle lets students expand their learning from a simple shared experience to the larger world. The focus in this phase is on the *past*: "What have we learned before that connects to the experience we just had?" "Have others written or shared information that can help us learn about the concepts we are exploring?" Generalizing is about drawing meaning from the experience and making connections between our own experiences and the larger world.

The next phase, "applying," lets students determine which of the new information and insights they have generated can be applied to the next activity or to their lives, both inside and outside of the classroom. This phase focuses on the future. In essence, the question answered here is, "How can we use what we have learned?" Sometimes students can apply the new learning immediately, while other times it is tucked away for later use.

THE EXPERIENTIAL LEARNING CYCLE IN ACTION

The phases of the cycle do not require equal time. For example, one reflecting session might take the form of a journal-writing activity that takes 15 minutes. The next reflecting session might take only 2 minutes of class discussion. It all depends upon the needs of the class at that moment, and there is much room for teacher discretion. Remember that we do not engage in this process to fill time; it is important that it makes sense within the context of your class. More than anything else, this process must have meaning.

When engaged in creating a community, a lesson using the experiential learning cycle may look like this:

Experiencing: For the first day of school, you choose the Name Game Circle activity (chapter 5, page 51), so the class can learn names. The students throw Nerf® balls to each other in order to learn one another's names.

Reflecting: After the activity, you lead a discussion about the activity. You might ask why it was important to have eye contact during the activity or why it might be important to learn the names of our classmates. You might ask if anyone dropped a ball, made a bad throw, or committed any other type of mistake.

Generalizing: You lead a class discussion on other ways people have learned about people they do not know and on how they have made an effort to get to know everyone in the class better. Alternatively, you might have the students brainstorm a list of mistakes that are commonly made in class and ask how it feels to make a mistake.

Applying: You have the class create ways to get to know each other better. For example, the class may choose to have teach-ins, where a student can teach about a personal interest. If the focus is on making mistakes, you might create a way to encourage students when they make errors, thus taking advantage of these teachable moments.

Once the cycle is complete, it flows into the next lesson. For example, the next activity you choose might be similar, except that you focus on how many times the ball dropped, and then set a goal of fewer drops. Making a mistake, then, would have a higher consequence, because a dropped ball affects the group goal. How would the class use what they learned from the last activity to help keep the new activity emotionally safe? How might we use our skills to work toward a group goal together? As the cycles continue, students become better at reflecting and begin to make connections without prompting. They are on their way to taking responsibility for their own learning, rather than waiting for you to pour the information into their heads.

MAKING THE CYCLE WORK: FACILITATING THE PROCESS

Leading activities designed to create community in the classroom requires you to assume the role of facilitator. To "facilitate" means to "make easy" or to "assist." In this case, you are assisting the students in creating a community. This cannot be taught in a lecture format, but must be experienced. Each activity is a learning experience.

Presenting an activity involves three steps. This process is sometimes called the "Adventure Wave," a concept developed by Project Adventure, Inc. (Schoel, Prouty, & Radcliffe, 1988):

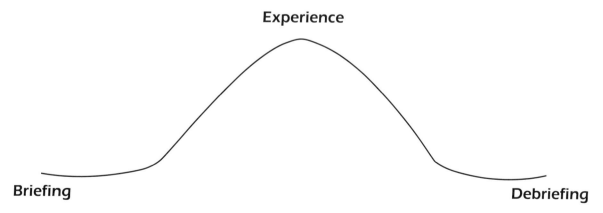

Experience

Briefing

Debriefing

The Adventure Wave takes into account the Experiential Learning Cycle by making sure that there is an experience and that reflection takes place during the debriefing. Further discussion or extension activities can be used to help students generalize and apply new insights and information they gain from the activity.

BRIEFING

A briefing session consists of four steps:

1. **Give the rules and object of the activity.** Keep the directions as concise as possible. At first, it may be easier for you to read them in order to make your presentation clear. Many students benefit from a visual demonstration of what is expected, in addition to the verbal directions.

2. **Teach the safety guidelines.** Some activities require students to put themselves in a position where they must trust others in the group, both physically and emotionally (see "Hang Together to Hang Extreme," chapter 5, page 68, as an example). It is your responsibility to cover and demonstrate all safety guidelines before these activities begin:

   - Teach how to spot individuals and how to use the "bumpers up" (hands up in front of face) position for blindfolded activities.

   - Discuss how a person might feel if his or her trust was broken by another.

   - Look around the activity area and point out any safety hazards.

   - Establish agreed-upon boundaries, both physical and emotional, for the activity. For example, it is important to discuss how to appropriately touch one another when guiding classmates during a blindfold walk.

3. **Answer questions from students.** Invariably, students will have questions about what to expect. Sometimes you will want everything to be very clear, such as when you are discussing safety issues. Other times, however, it is preferable to leave things rather hazy, so that students must figure out how to solve a given problem.

4. **Frontload metaphors or previous information.** "Frontloading" is a way to help set the stage for an activity. Sometimes we use metaphors to help frame the experience. For example, in the Name Game Circle (chapter 5, page 51), you can label the items that are thrown as "communication." You can talk about different types of communication and how people can miscommunicate. Then, every time an item is dropped, it can be considered a miscommunication. During the debriefing, you can discuss how a class might work if it were filled with miscommunication, and how one might work if it

were filled with clear communication. Another use of frontloading is to bring in previous learning and information. If the class has explored the issue of making mistakes in a previous activity, for example, reminding them of that before the next activity can help them apply what they have previously learned.

Activities need not be frontloaded. Sometimes an activity "speaks for itself." If this is the case, students are simply asked to glean any insights and learning from it. Other times, we participate in an activity for the sole purpose of having fun. Enjoying each other's company is a sure way to help a community grow.

EXPERIENCE

The actual experience can take place just about anywhere—in the classroom, hallway, gym, front lawn, all-purpose room, parking lot, library, or atrium. If space is an issue (which is almost always the case in a school), activities can be chosen or modified to fit the available space. Directing students to walk instead of run can make even tag games feasible in small spaces. Where you do the activity is not as important as how you do it.

As the teacher, your role is ambiguous at this point. At times you will be a participant in the activity, and at times you will choose to observe. Because you, too, are a member of the community, it is important for you to participate in the activities at the beginning of the community's life. So get in there and throw the Nerf balls, stand in the middle of the circle and say, "bumpity bump bump bump," and play games with the students. You serve as a model for your students, and your participation speaks volumes.

As the students become more comfortable and willing to take risks, your role will change from participant to observer. You will brief the activity, then stand back to watch how the action unfolds. You may step in at times if you see safety concerns or if the process breaks down. Determining when to step in and when to let things go is one of the most difficult decisions to make. You must ask yourself, "Are they able to learn from this struggle, or is it harmful in some way?" Struggle in itself is not harmful—it is an excellent opportunity to learn. However, when students' frustration gets the best of them, and their physical or emotional safety is at risk, then it is time to step in. Look for the following signs:

- Blaming

- Checking out—One or more students pulling out of the process and standing apart from the group

- Everyone talking at once so that the "rule of loud" takes over—whoever is the loudest gets heard

- Students threatening each other verbally or physically

- Put-downs ("You're stupid." "Shut up.")

- Students physically struggling over props or over who gets to go next

- Suddenly hearing students say, "This is boring," or, "This is stupid."

At first, you will have to be the one who steps in to deal with these situations and provide a model for how to intervene in conflicts. As time goes on, however, you may want to teach students that they also have the power to step in and remedy a situation. Ask the class to come up with a signal that means "Freeze!" and make it clear that anyone can use this signal to stop the process when they notice a safety issue or are confused. This signal is most effective when it is both verbal and visual. For example, use a timeout signal, holding the hands in a "T" while saying the words "team stop!"

Another decision you will have to make is when to change an activity because it presents an inappropriate level of challenge for the class—either too difficult or too easy. Unless students are experiencing an overabundance of frustration, it is best to let the situation play itself out, process the activity, and then change the level of challenge for a second round. If the activity is too easy, it will be accomplished quickly, and then students can try it again at the "graduate school level." If the activity is too difficult, students can learn from the frustration and then attempt the activity again at an easier level that guarantees a measure of success. Whatever happens in an activity, the debriefing session offers time to reflect upon what worked and what did not work. Effective processing focuses on what actually happened, not on what you as the teacher thought should happen.

STRATEGIES FOR PAIRING STUDENTS

Depending upon the age and maturity level of your class, you can use a variety of techniques to have students pair up for activities. The following are a few suggestions:

- Ask everyone to find a partner.

- Have students find someone who has the same (or different) size thumb or eye color than them. (Thanks to Pete Albert for this strategy.)

- Instruct students to find someone who was born in a different season than them.

- Identify each person as either a spoon or a fork. Those that are "forks" put their hands over their heads at shoulder length apart. "Spoons" put their hands over their heads with hands clasped. When you say "Spork," everyone finds a partner by joining with someone who is the opposite (that is, a fork finds a spoon). (Thanks to Mark Roark for this strategy.)

- Direct the group to line up, and then fold the line in half. The person each student is facing is his or her partner.

- Keep a can of tongue depressors, with the name of each student written on one depressor. Choose two randomly to make partners.

- Keep a deck of cards with pairs that number the size of your class. Give one card to each person, and have students match up their cards to find their partners.

- Take index cards and cut them in half creatively, so that they are like puzzle pieces. Give each person one half of a piece, and direct students to find their matching halves.

- Have different songs (that everyone knows) written on scraps of paper. Write each song on two scraps of paper. Throw the scraps into the air, and ask each student to pick one and hum until he or she finds the other student humming the same song.

Sometimes it is important to split up friends, while other times it may be helpful to let people who know each other well work together. Mixing up student pairs is beneficial because it gives students a chance to experience a variety of scenarios. At times you may decide to pair students who do not get along. When doing so, make sure to frontload the activity by explaining your intention: "You two are having difficulty getting along. It is a distraction to our community. This is a chance for you to work it out. Do your best. If you really need to, call 'team stop' to stop the activity." Experiential education is a potent tool for ensuring that everyone learns to work with everyone else.

DEBRIEFING

Debriefing is sometimes called processing because it allows students to take a look at the process that was used to accomplish the task. This act of processing offers an opportunity to learn from experience and actually covers three fourths of the

Experiential Learning Cycle by asking students to reflect upon the activity, generalize by blending the present experience with past learning, and choose useful information to apply to future situations.

EXPERIENTIAL LEARNING CYCLE

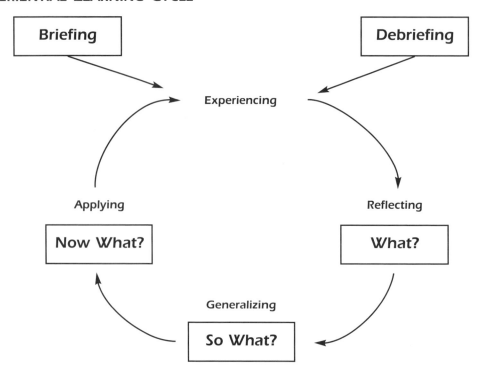

A well-crafted debriefing session consists of three parts: What? So What? and Now What? These three parts were first described in *Islands of Healing* (Schoel, Prouty, & Radcliffe, 1988, pp. 170–181).

What?

After an experience is the perfect time to ask, "What just happened?" This gives students an opportunity to reflect upon their own roles, thoughts, feelings, and observations during the activity. Activities are planned with a particular theme or skill in mind, such as listening, trust building, goal setting, and getting to know each other. During the "what?" stage of processing, you might ask questions that get at this theme. Sometimes, however, the theme you choose is lost in a larger issue. Whether planned or unplanned, this issue usually comes out in the "what?" stage.

Beginning a debriefing session can be a real challenge. Sometimes students are reluctant to share feelings or are unsure where to start. Others have difficulty verbalizing their thoughts. Quieter students may also be drowned out by those who are more assertive about sharing their thoughts. The following strategies can help make a debriefing session work:

- Make sure students are comfortable. Sit on the ground, floor, chairs, or carpet squares. Students can even stand if it is a short session.

- Make sure everyone can see and be seen. A circle is the best configuration for this. If you are meeting in a lecture hall or a science room with fixed tables, encourage students to stand up when talking so everyone can see and hear the speaker.

- Encourage students to speak directly to each other rather than to you. At first, you will be the focal point for discussion. Students will look at you, address questions to you, and speak to you. Sit with the group, and tell them that you are a group member like everyone else. You may even need to avoid making eye contact with speakers so that they will look at others.

It is also helpful to have a toolbox of strategies for getting the conversation started. The following are a few conversation starters:

Round robin. Ask students to think of a word or phrase that describes a thought or feeling they had during the activity. Then "whip" around the group, allowing each person to share his or her word or phrase.

Journals. Take some quiet time to write or draw in a journal about the activity. This is especially useful for documenting progress over time. It is also handy when you run out of time but want to keep the thoughts fresh to discuss during the next session, which may be a day or even a week later.

Crumpled paper. Hand a piece of paper to each student. Ask students to write a comment about the activity on their paper, crumple it up, and throw it into the middle of the circle. Have everyone then choose a paper and read it to the class. Because this reflection strategy is anonymous, it can be a useful tool for allowing people to share more freely. The anonymity factor can also cause some to be blunt or tactless with their language, so caution students to make constructive, rather than destructive, comments.

Talking circle. Select an item that can be passed from person to person—such as a rock, pencil, or marble. It is nice if the item has special meaning for the class. Then ask the students to form a circle and pass the item from person to person around the circle. Whenever someone has the item, he or she is the speaker. The others are the listeners. If someone has something to share, he or she says it and passes the item on. If someone wishes to pass, he or she simply passes the item to the next person. A talking circle is a nice ritual to begin or end a class or day. It is a quiet time where everyone has an opportunity to speak if they wish. If used consistently, students become freer to share thoughts and feelings with the class.

Object pass. Use a soft, throwable object like a Nerf ball or bean bag. Ask a question about the activity. When someone wishes to respond, he or she signals to you to throw him the object. After finishing, he or she waits until someone else signals and then throws it to that person. This strategy controls the talking by indicating who has the floor, and allows each person to choose when she or he is ready to speak.

Goals/contracts. If students have developed a community contract or set some group goals, this is a perfect time to refer to them. Ask students to look at their contract or goals and identify which ones have been met and which ones need more work.

Feelings cards. There are some sets of cards available that depict a large array of human emotions, such as confidence, anger, embarrassment, boredom, and so on. Purchase a set of these cards or lead students in making a set for the class. Spread them out on the floor, and ask students to pick some that describe how the activity went for them. Give each student a chance to show the cards to the class and explain why he or she picked them.

Postcards. Collect a variety of postcards and use them like the feeling cards.

Processing prompts. Ask students specific questions about the activity. This is especially helpful for younger students or for those who have a difficult time responding to general questions.

Play food. Most toy stores stock play food, which is great for using as a reflection tool. Spread the food out, and ask students to choose the kind of food that best describes the activity for them. For example, someone may choose the chicken leg and say, "I felt like a chicken because. . . ." Others may choose the makings for a sandwich to show how everyone worked together to create something.

Rating scales. Ask students to rate the activity on a scale of 1 to 10 or 1 to 5. Then give them a chance to share their ratings and their reasons for choosing those particular ratings. You can use the same method with thumbs (for example, thumbs up, thumbs down, or in between). You can also try the "fist to five" method, with a closed fist equaling 0 and five fingers equaling 5.

Pick a photo. Spread out imaginary photos on the floor. Ask students to sift through the imaginary photos and choose one to hang on their refrigerator as a keepsake. Then give everyone an opportunity to describe the picture he or she has chosen.

Video review. Tell the class that you are going to view an imaginary video of the activity. Have someone start relating what happened at the beginning from memory. That person continues until someone says, "Stop!" The person who said "stop" then continues the story until the next person says, "Stop!"

Creations. Supply the class with clay or pipe cleaners or markers and paper. Ask each student to produce a sculpture or drawing that depicts the experience for him or her. Give everyone an opportunity to share with the class.

Dyads and triads. Divide students into groups of two or three. Give them time to talk in their small groups about the activity. You can then either continue to the next activity or have the small groups share out loud to the class.

WHEN FACILITATING A CLASSROOM DISCUSSION, THE TEACHER MAY PLAY MANY ROLES:

Encourager. Encourage students to use "I" messages. Using the pronoun "I" personalizes the statement so that people talk about their own thoughts, rather than telling other people what to think. This makes the difference between "You didn't listen to what was said" and "I felt like people weren't listening to each other."

Model. Model active listening during the discussion by looking at the person who is talking and by making sounds or motions that indicate you are listening. Paraphrase a comment or ask clarifying questions. Teach these skills to the students, and ask them to use active listening when others are speaking.

Safety expert. Although you ask students to share the responsibility for safety, you are the ultimate safety expert for the group. Keep track of physical and emotional safety issues. If students gang up on one person during a discussion, step in to deflect or defend that person, even if you feel he or she is encouraging it. If there is conflict, it must be handled fairly. Look for win-win solutions.

Referee. Make sure students are taking turns when talking. Sometimes when a conflict escalates, people begin interrupting or monopolizing the discussion. If necessary, take control of the order in which people speak. Use an object (a pencil, book, or Nerf ball) to show who has the floor.

Mediator. There may be times when students blame each other for a frustrating situation. In these cases, it can be necessary to step in and mediate. You may need to involve the whole class or to discuss the issue privately with a few people.

Mirror. Act as a mirror for the group. If many students are talking at once, hold up an imaginary mirror and say, "I see five people talking at the same time. Is this working?"

Chooser. The more people we bring together, the more issues arise. Usually, there are many issues that come up during a debriefing session. Use your discretion about what to discuss. It is generally enough to focus on one issue per debriefing session, so choose one and go with it. A general rule is that if something is not addressed now, it will always come back later. To keep track of all the issues that arise, you might use a "parking lot" approach. A parking lot is a posted list of issues, questions, or concerns that cannot be dealt with at the moment. Write issues on the parking lot for later discussion.

Reflecting ("What?") Questions

- What happened during the activity?

- How did it feel when . . . ?

- How did it work when . . . ?

- Did everyone get a chance to be heard?

- What was your plan? How did you make it?

- Who were the leaders? Who were the followers?

- What happened when things got challenging?

- Was there any frustration in the group? How could you tell?

So What?

The "so what?" stage of a debriefing can be a challenging time for the teacher. Students will have identified issues from the "what?" stage, yet where do you start the "so what?" stage?

The "so what?" stage allows students to examine how this experience affected them, and then to look at how it fits in with past experiences. Although a large class discussion is necessary at times, it is also possible to use a variety of strategies to explore the "so what?" stage. Some examples include the following.

Brainstorming. Brainstorm similar instances or ways that the situation in the activity could have been handled differently. For example, you might brainstorm mistakes that are often made in the classroom, situations that make students feel threatened or frustrated, or things that help ease conflict. Do this in small groups, and share with the class.

Readings. Collect readings that have some connection with community-building issues. For example, all group situations involve issues of commitment, conflict, leadership, and values. If the class is involved in a conflict, read *The Different Drum: Community Making and Peace* (1988) by M. Scott Peck. A reading at the right time can offer an outside view that puts your group's struggles into perspective. A wonderful resource for readings is *Gold Nuggets: Readings for Experiential Education,* edited by Jim Schoel and Mike Stratton (1995; available from Project Adventure, Inc., www.pa.org). Also refer to the Character Education Literature List in the Additional Resources Appendix, page 357 (thanks to Shannon Horton for compiling this list).

Stories. Children's books and short stories are wonderful tools to bring in at this time and are appreciated by students of all ages. Dr. Seuss offers a wide range of stories that deal with conflict, such as *The Sneetches* and *The Butter Battle Book.* Another fine resource is *Teaching Conflict Resolution Through Children's Literature* by William J. Kreidler (available from Educators for Social Responsibility, www.esrnational.org). After reading the book or excerpt, offer up the larger concepts for discussion, and make the connection with the personal issues your class is facing.

Another use of stories is to ask students to write a story about their experiences with the issue under consideration. The stories can be true or fictional. Students may share the stories with one or more people or keep them in a private journal.

Role play. Ask students to role-play the experience as it happened. Then ask them to role-play it again so that it has a different outcome. Discuss what they did differently to produce the different outcome.

Historical content. Bring in historical instances of similar struggles. If, for example, your students are struggling with cliques, gender, or race segregation, bring in writings from Dr. Martin Luther King, Jr., or newspaper articles about the civil rights movement.

Whether you lead a short class discussion or choose another strategy, this stage helps students place the experience within a larger context by finding answers to the question, "So what does this mean to me/us in the larger picture?"

Generalizing ("So What?") Questions

- How is this like . . . ? (what happened yesterday; how you have been treated in the past; the civil rights movement)

- When have you experienced this/these feelings before?

- Have you ever been in a group where . . . ?

- What do you think it would be like if we acted like this every day?

- How is this connected to . . . ? (the way people communicate; the way we work together; how people can show support for each other)

Now What?

All of this reflection is much more powerful if students actually apply it to future experiences. After bringing up an issue during an activity, discussing it, and putting it into a larger context, it is necessary to ask, "What have we learned from this experience that can be applied to future situations?" Here are some strategies to enter the "now what?" stage:

Action plans. Ask individuals or small groups to create an action plan for using their new knowledge or skills. This is especially helpful if the class has been struggling with a long-term conflict or an issue that continues to surface.

Goal setting. Challenge students to set individual and group goals and use them to determine if they are applying their new learning/skills.

Other activities. Use another activity to test the students' new skills right away. For example, if the class is working on taking turns talking instead of everyone talking at once, you might follow the first activity with an activity that lets them practice the skill.

Ask for gems of learning/insight. Be sure to ask for gems of learning before moving on. Invite students to share them with the class.

Contracts. Create contracts for individuals and for the class as a whole. Like goal setting, this offers a timeline in which to apply learning, but also asks students to make a written or verbal commitment.

Check ins. Check in periodically with the class: "How are we doing with the idea of taking turns when talking?" This can occur any time during an activity or an unrelated class.

Visual reminders. Post reminders around the room to help everyone in the classroom community remember to apply what they have learned.

Applying ("Now What?") Questions

- What did we learn?

- How can we use this information?

- How would we do the activity the same/differently?

- What can we do to make sure . . . ?

- Where can you use this in your own life?

The three phases of the Adventure Wave—briefing, experience, and debriefing—gives us a structure for the Experiential Learning Cycle. Each trip around the cycle builds on the one before, creating a spiral to a greater depth of understanding. As students become better at processing, the "what?" "so what?" and "now what?" begin to blend together. They will begin to internalize this process and engage in self-reflection without prompting. By consciously focusing on the whole process, you can make the classroom community a reality.

Chapter 4

Understanding the Life Cycle of the Group

To understand life is to understand ourselves, and that is both the beginning and end of education.

—Jiddu Krishnamurti, Indian mystic and philosopher

Chapter 4

Understanding the Life Cycle of the Group

Every group of individuals that comes together for a purpose takes on a life of its own. It becomes, in essence, a living entity. And because the individuals comprising a group are people with unique and dynamic personalities, every group has a chemistry all its own.

Although each group is unique, there are some general, universal processes at work. Like other living entities, groups grow and mature. There is a definite life cycle in every group, and your class is no different. Your awareness of this cycle can be your best friend when you are observing group dynamics. Just as you would treat a 3-year-old child differently than a 13-year-old adolescent, your interactions with your class will change over time.

The life cycle of a group consists of the following stages: birth/childhood, adolescence, adulthood, elderhood, and death. Your group of students will exhibit certain behaviors and must deal with certain issues at each stage. If the issues are addressed and worked through, the group will be prepared to enter the next stage. To facilitate a group's passage through each stage, you must choose appropriate activities and help students process the issues that arise.

BIRTH/CHILDHOOD

Think back to the last time you joined a new group. Maybe it was a university class, a social group, or a volunteer organization. Remember the feelings of anxiety as you made your way to your seat? You probably wondered if you would feel comfortable with these people or if you would like them. You may have been concerned that you would do something to embarrass yourself. You may have wondered if they would like you.

These feelings are common for people entering into new situations. At the beginning of a new endeavor, everything is unfamiliar, and it is difficult to ascertain the rules (or norms) for this group of people. The newness and ambiguity increase our anxiety levels. Whether they show it or not, your students are full of apprehension on the first day of school, and they are watching to see what will happen next. Will they be included in this new group or pushed out?

There is much you can do to ease their anxiety levels. Because the main issue of this stage is *inclusion,* you can begin with activities that help students get to know each other. Spend time on name games, activities that allow people to share a little bit about themselves, and discussions of how important it is to create a place where everyone is included. Set the stage by reinforcing your belief that *everyone* is a valuable member of this classroom community. Just as a child needs direction, this forming group needs your leadership and guidance.

Once the students know each other better, you can gradually move to activities that help build trust, which is the foundation of a true community. By consciously working to build trust, you will be able to establish a safe place in which students feel free to take risks. If students are willing to risk making mistakes, for example, they have the opportunity to learn from those mistakes. Trust enables students to risk, learn, and grow, paving the way for the group to move into the next stage.

ADOLESCENCE

As students gain a high degree of comfort and trust, they move into a stormy phase that is usually marked by conflict. Just like youngsters entering their teenage years, your students will begin to assert their need for independence. You will likely see signs of power struggles between students and with you.

The main issue at this stage is *influence.* Power and control are up for grabs. Without the atmosphere of inclusion that was developed in the first stage of the group's life, this stage could be very painful. Fortunately, the foundation of trust you have built allows for discussion of the power and control issues that arise.

To help students work through these issues, you can offer activities that require the class to solve problems together. At this point, you are no longer the sole leader of the group, but have become a process observer. Your role is to mentor this group in its adolescence. The processing phase of each activity takes on an added importance, because students have real conflicts to resolve. Successfully resolving these conflicts allows the group to mature to the next stage.

ADULTHOOD

As the classroom community works through its various issues, it develops new operating norms. The following example illustrates this shift:

You have been working with your class for a month on activities to create an inclusive and safe environment. You have been focusing on trust for a while and are confident that your students are ready for a more complicated activity—one that will be challenging, but not too difficult. You choose the Moon Ball activity (*see chapter 7, page 136*). As students hit the beach ball in the air, you notice that some students have their hands down and are not participating. During the debriefing session, students raise the issue that "some people were hogging the ball."

As you continue the debriefing session, the students accused of "hogging" the ball assert that they were just trying to help the group and that some people were not really trying. Although simplistic, this is an issue of sharing leadership. Some people are naturally more aggressive than others, and in a community situation, they must learn to step back once in a while to make room for others. Those who are naturally more passive must learn to step up once in a while and take the initiative. After discussing these issues with the class, you ask, "What can we do the next time a situation like this comes up?" The students decide to set a goal of making sure everyone is included. They determine to check in periodically to make sure everyone feels that he or she is part of what is happening. The more passive students agree to take the initiative to inform others when they are feeling left out.

Some norms have now been established. The main issue at this stage is gaining *understanding.* Your mentoring role has allowed the group to work through the conflict and establish operative group norms. This group of individuals has finally come into its own, allowing it to progress to the next stage of group development.

ELDERHOOD

As the group enters elderhood, the struggles and rough times of adolescence and adulthood have helped the students define what this particular group is about. The main issue of this stage is *belonging.* In the beginning of the group's life, people worried about being included. In the elderhood stage, everyone in the group is accepted as an important member of the community and feels safe to be a unique individual. Individual strengths are valued, and leadership is shared.

Because conflict is a hallmark of growth, it will continue to be present at this stage. However, it is handled with understanding and an underlying acceptance of those in conflict. The true nature of conflict now is not to exercise power, but to reach ever-deeper levels of understanding.

Your role is now one of consultant. Because group members are showing a fair amount of interdependence, you bring in an outside perspective. You continue to monitor safety issues and offer suggestions or advice to help students accomplish their tasks. Because there is always more to learn, you also continue to offer problem-solving activities and challenges for both the class and individuals. The individual challenges are attempted with the support of the classroom community, and there is a true family-feel to the classroom.

DEATH

Like any living entity, every group dies. In the case of your classroom, the school year inevitably comes to an end, and the class disbands. The main issue at this stage is *transition.* Many students will grieve for the loss of this unique group that can never be repeated. Your role is to help them end the school year and make the transition into the next one. A number of strategies will help you do this. You can provide activities that give students the opportunity to say goodbye and offer thank-yous and hopes for the future. Spend time reminiscing about your shared history, and even offer a memento of the year in the form of a class picture or other item that has special meaning for this group. One way to lend closure to the year is to have each student write a letter to him- or herself, which you can then mail to the students during the summer.

THE GROUP CYCLE IN ACTION

Unlike a true living entity, the group's stages of life are not consistently marked by chronological time. Because every group is different, each will progress at a different pace. Some classes stagnate at a given stage for a long period of time, while others fly through the stages almost overnight. There are a number of dynamics that can affect the pace of the group's life cycle:

• The group's needs at each stage must be addressed in order for it to move on. If a group of students comes together, and you never address the need for inclusion, it is possible that the class will remain in the childhood stage all year. In many college classrooms people do not know the name of anyone else in the class at the end of a semester. Likewise, a group can become locked in the power struggles of the adolescence stage unless issues are discussed and resolved. Once the class has talked through the issues and developed norms, however, the path is cleared to move on.

• When students enter or leave the community, the chemistry of the group changes. When a student transfers out or a new student arrives, it is as if the group is starting over again. You may even see a community that has been operating at a high level regress to adolescence until new norms are established to include the new person or address the void created by a student who has left. When this happens, no matter how late in the year, it is important to use several "get to know you" activities to help the group get back on track. This is very important in schools and districts that experience high rates of mobility.

- If the classroom community reaches elderhood, it will cycle through the life stages again. As a community evolves, the group reaches for higher levels of understanding. This means that once a group reaches elderhood, it is ready to become a "new" group again and to deal with issues at a deeper level. The underlying themes remain the same, but the depth of understanding will be greater.

The life cycle of the group is a force to be reckoned with. It cannot be manipulated or controlled, and if you ignore it, your class will take on the persona of a child without direction. Recognizing its existence allows you to work with it—and provide the necessary guidance at each life stage to help your classroom community reach its true potential.

The first four chapters of this book have provided you with the tools you need to serve as the architect for a classroom community—to oversee the project and keep an eye on the big picture. The experiential education activities in the following six chapters provide your students with the tools they need to build their own unique classroom community.

Part II

Activities

Chapter 5

Getting Acquainted

The most important observation you can make is when you become a glimmer in the child's eyes and he becomes a glimmer in yours.

—Albert E. Trieschman, American educator, psychologist, and writer

Chapter 5

Getting Acquainted

The challenges and activities in this chapter are designed to help you get to know your students and to help your students get to know each other. Most teachers understand the importance of getting to know their students and make a conscious effort to do so. Some plan specific activities and set aside designated times to make sure this happens. Others do it a little less formally, but they do it all the same.

Far fewer teachers understand the tremendous importance of helping their students get to know each other. Fewer still actually schedule activities and set aside time to encourage students to build relationships with each other.

While it is entirely possible to teach a class of students who do not know each other, it can be much more effective and much more enjoyable to teach a class of students who have built relationships with each other. Whether they know it or not, most teachers (ourselves included) have suffered the following effects of teaching in a classroom where the students are unfamiliar with each other:

- Little positive risk taking occurs, and learning is stiff and stifled.

- There is less chance of collective energy, or synergy, taking place.

- It is harder to rebound from classroom disagreements or tensions, because there are no existing relationships to fall back on.

- There is an absence of fun.

No community can exist without the commitment of its individual members. Teachers can begin to establish commitment to their classroom communities by helping their students get to know one another and ultimately build and maintain meaningful relationships. The following challenges and activities will help you do just that. They will enable you to

- Accelerate the natural process of becoming comfortable with new people.

- Ensure that *everyone* gets to know *everyone,* avoiding the formation of counterproductive cliques.

- Lay the groundwork for the acceptance and celebration of individual and cultural differences.

- Begin creating a climate where trust can grow, students can take positive risks, and nonviolent conflict resolution can occur.

- Allow your students to simply have fun together.

Activity 1
NAME GAME CIRCLE

FOCUS POINTS

- Have fun.

- Learn each other's names and discuss the importance of using them.

- Introduce the idea that everyone makes mistakes sometimes.

PREPARATION AND MATERIALS

5–8 soft objects (Nerf balls, wadded-up pieces of paper, stuffed animals, and so on)

DIRECTIONS

Invite everyone to stand in a circle. Tell students that this activity is designed to help them learn the names of their classmates. Tell them that you are going to pass around one of the objects. When the students get the object, they are to say their names and one thing that happened to them during the past year. Start by saying your own name and something that happened to you.

When the object returns to you, tell students they can now throw the object to anyone in the group, but must first call out that person's name and make eye contact before throwing. Anyone can get the object, and each person can get the object more than once. Then begin the game by calling out a student's name, making eye contact, and throwing him or her the object. He or she will do the same to someone else. Once this has gone on for a short while, introduce another item into the game. Keep introducing more items until many are flying around, and most of the class is involved in either throwing or catching.

After a few minutes of this controlled chaos (good thing you have soft objects!), stop the action to see if anyone would like to name everyone in the class.

PROCESSING PROMPTS

- Why is it important to learn each other's names?

- What does using your classmates' names tell them? What does calling a classmate names tell him or her?

- Why was *eye contact* important when playing the Name Game Circle? How will it be important in class?

- How do you feel when someone makes eye contact with you? What does it tell you?

- Did anyone miss the ball? Make a bad throw? How did it feel? How does it feel when you make a mistake in class?

- What types of mistakes can we expect to make in class?

EXTENDING ACTIVITIES

- Ask the class to work in groups of four to six to brainstorm a list of mistakes they can expect to make in class. Have the small groups report their lists back to the whole class and record one composite list. It can be fun to add some common teacher mistakes that you might expect to make. Lead the class in a discussion of how you can help people feel comfortable enough to take positive risks and make mistakes. Talk about how the class can support someone who makes a mistake. Let them know that anyone who never makes a mistake *just can't be trying hard enough.*

- Play the game again, but this time substitute tennis balls for the Nerf balls. Explain that because the tennis balls are harder, safety is now a factor. Ask for suggestions on how to adapt the game to make it a little safer. Look for suggestions like (1) make sure you have eye contact before you throw the ball, (2) only throw underhanded, or (3) use bounce passes. If these suggestions are not offered, offer them yourself.

PROCESSING PROMPTS

- Was it tougher with tennis balls? Why?

- In the game, were the throwers trying to help the catchers catch the ball or trying to make them miss it?

- How can we help each other "catch" an education?

- Making *eye contact* and throwing in a way that made it easy to catch the ball positioned your classmates to be successful. How can we position each other to be successful in class and in school?

Activity 2
LET ME INTRODUCE MYSELF

FOCUS POINTS

- Have fun.

- Help students get to know each other.

- Help students see that people who know each other are able to work together better.

- Help students see that we are alike in some ways and different in others—and that it's OK.

PREPARATION AND MATERIALS

One "Let Me Introduce Myself" worksheet for each student (page 54)

DIRECTIONS

Form students into pairs. If there is an uneven number of people, you can be a partner with the extra student. Have your pairs sit together. Give students approximately 15 minutes to complete the "Let Me Introduce Myself" worksheet (page 54). Ask students to take turns explaining their answers to their partners. (This usually takes about 10 minutes altogether.) Students then take turns introducing their partners to the whole class. If time is short, you can instruct students to share only their favorite answer for each category.

You may wish to display the completed worksheets. If so, you might consider giving students time to look at their classmates' work and learn more about them.

PROCESSING PROMPTS

- Was the activity fun?

- Why did we do it?

- Why is it important for us to get to know each other?

- How will getting to know each other help us do a better job in class?

- Did we have a lot of similarities? How about a lot of differences? Is that OK?

LET ME INTRODUCE MYSELF

Three things I really like are . . .

1. _____

2. _____

3. _____

Three of my heroes are . . .

1. _____

2. _____

3. _____

My name: _____

My nickname: _____

My favorite animal: _____

Three things I really dislike are . . .

1. _____

2. _____

3. _____

Three action words describing me are . . .

1. _____

2. _____

3. _____

Activity 3

HANDS AROUND THE COMMUNITY, PART 1

FOCUS POINTS

- Have fun.

- Begin to help students understand that the class is, or should be, a community.

- Introduce the idea that, as members of the same class, we are interrelated. What one person does or does not do affects the others.

- Introduce the idea that people who know each other are better able to solve differences when they encounter them.

PREPARATION AND MATERIALS

Decide if you want to have your class work as one group, or if it would be better to divide into smaller groups. There is no limit on group size, but groups of fewer than eight tend not to be as much fun.

If you choose to have the class work as a single group, you will need one large piece of roll paper (butcher's paper). If you plan to break the class into smaller groups, you will need a piece of roll paper for each group. You will also need an assortment of colored markers (washable are recommended). It is preferable to have at least one marker for each participant.

DIRECTIONS

Explain to the class that you are a group just because the principal put your names on the same class list. Tell them it is possible, however, to go beyond being merely a group and become a community. You may wish to leave it at that or to ask for (1) a definition of community, (2) examples of communities, or (3) examples of communities your students belong to. Tell the students that whether or not the class becomes a community is up to them. However, because they will be in the same place, at the same time, sharing the same resources, and working toward the same purpose, they are all connected to each other. Explain that you are going to do a fun art project called "Hands Around the Community" that will represent this "connectedness." Direct your students to trace their handprints (both left and right) on the top and bottom of the paper, as shown in the following diagram.

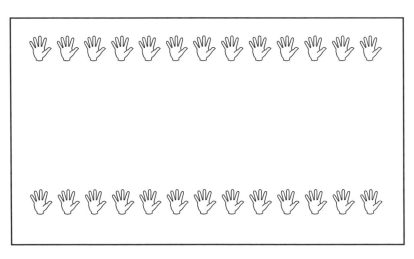

 Students' outline of their hands

The paper's long dimension should run horizontally. The hands signify where the students should position their handprints.

Students are to write their names in their left-hand outlines, and one thing they like about school in their right-hand outlines. It can also be fun to challenge students to decorate their hands (paint the fingernails, add rings and bracelets, and so on). Some teachers like to provide art supplies for this purpose (such as glitter, glitter glue, paints, watercolors, stamps, and so on). If you chose to divide the class into smaller groups, the groups should now join their individual banners together using masking tape.

You will probably notice that your border is incomplete; it needs ends. This is where the teacher's handprints go. You will probably need to draw more than one set of handprints to complete the border. Inside the outlines, write your name, the names of your spouse, children, or pets, and other things you want to share about yourself (students love to hear your nickname). Hang the finished banner in a prominent place. Instruct your students to take turns going to the banner, pointing to their hands, introducing themselves by name, and sharing what they like about school. Make sure that the banner is low enough for your students to reach the top of the paper. They will need to do so if you choose to do part two of this activity. We recommend doing part two on a second day; the days do not necessarily need to be consecutive.

PROCESSING PROMPTS

- Did you have fun?

- Was it messy?

- Is our class a community? What is a community? Should our class be a community?

- What does the continuous border symbolize?

- Why do we share information about ourselves?

- Are you better able to solve differences with people you know? With friends? What differences might we have in our class? What problems might people have with each other?

Activity 4
HANDS AROUND THE COMMUNITY, PART 2

FOCUS POINTS

- Have fun.

- Begin to help students understand that the class is, or should be, a community.

- Introduce the idea that, as members of the same class, we are interrelated. What one person does or does not do affects the others.

- Introduce the idea that people who know each other are better able to solve differences when they encounter them.

PREPARATION AND MATERIALS

Scissors; pencils; glue; and half sheets of construction paper (You may wish to provide young children with actual hand cutouts.)

DIRECTIONS

Ask students to trace the outline of one of their hands on a half sheet of construction paper and then cut the outline out. Ask them to print their name and one goal they have for this year inside the cutout. You may choose to have students decorate their hands. When the cutouts are completed, invite each student to go to the banner, introduce him or herself, and share his or her goal with the class. He or she can then glue the hand cutout somewhere in the center of the banner. Display your banner for future reference. It is an artifact of your classroom community and can be used to remind the class that they should act as a community.

PROCESSING PROMPTS

- Was it fun?

- What do you think of our banner?

- How did you feel getting up in front of the class? Anyone feel a little nervous? Would you like to be more comfortable?

- If we were all comfortable with each other, how would it affect our school year?

- What would make you more comfortable?

- What do you think about leaving our banner up to remind us that we are a community?

EXTENDING ACTIVITY

You may want to do the activity again, this time inviting your students to write different information in the cutouts, such as (1) something they really dislike about school, (2) something about their family, or (3) their favorite sport or activity. You may also want to repeat this activity later in the year once your students are ready to share more. At that point, you might ask them to share such information as (1) a problem they have, (2) a secret, (3) something they want to be better at, or (4) something they want to change.

Note: You may choose to peel off the original cutouts and replace them with new cutouts, put the new ones up over the old ones, or create a new banner. If students create a new banner, start with the outline of handprints presented in "Hands Around the Community, Part 1." Displaying more than one banner can be a fun way to prompt a discussion on the life cycle of the group (see chapter 4, "Understanding the Life Cycle of the Group").

Activity 5
GET THE POINT

FOCUS POINTS

- Have fun.

- Underscore the importance of having fun together.

- Initiate discussion of issues of personal space and safety (optional).

PREPARATION AND MATERIALS

None

DIRECTIONS

Ask the class to stand in a circle and put their left hands out, palms facing up to the ceiling. Then ask them to put the pointer finger of their right hand in the upturned palm of the person on their right. The students should now be standing with their right index finger in the palm of their neighbor's left hand.

Tell students that the object of the activity is to catch the finger of their neighbor without allowing their own finger to get caught. Say "1-2-3 Go!" After the laughing and chatter dies down, ask students to reset the game and try again. After a few attempts, switch hands.

Once everyone has become used to "1-2-3 Go!," shake things up a bit. Try saying "1-2 Go!" or "1-2-3 (pause) Go!" Another option is to use a nonverbal signal instead of a verbal one, or to combine a verbal and nonverbal signal.

PROCESSING PROMPTS

- Why might it be important for us to have fun together?

- Will our school year be easier or harder if we learn to have fun together?

- What things might we do to make working with each other more enjoyable?

- What things might we agree not to do?

- Optional: Was it easier or harder to do the activity with (verbal/nonverbal) communication? How do we use verbal and nonverbal communication in class? How could we communicate better?

- Optional: Was anyone nervous about putting your finger in someone else's hand? Why? Could we hurt each other if we played the game wrong? Squeezed too hard? How can we relax, have fun, and keep each other safe in the classroom?

Activity 6
ON THE MOVE

FOCUS POINTS

- Have fun.

- Identify similarities and differences.

- Demonstrate that there are similarities among classmates that they might not have predicted.

PREPARATION AND MATERIALS

A list of similarities and differences (You may use the list provided, create your own, or have students create one.)

DIRECTIONS

Explain that in most groups of people as large as your class, there are both similarities and differences among individuals. Use the following example:

"If I took a poll of the class on favorite ice cream flavors, I bet I'd find that some of you like chocolate ice cream, some vanilla, and some both chocolate and vanilla. Those of you who have the same preference in ice cream might not necessarily share similar tastes in fast food. However, you would probably find other classmates who do share your preferences for fast food. What this shows is that you have things in common with . . . and things different from . . . everyone."

Establish three gathering areas and ask your students to demonstrate their answers to the following questions by physically going to the appropriate gathering area.

SIMILARITIES AND DIFFERENCES

1. Do you (1) like McDonald's best? (2) like Burger King best? or (3) not like either McDonald's or Burger King?

2. Do you (1) have a brother? (2) have a sister? or (3) are you an only child?

3. Are you (1) the youngest in your family? (2) the oldest in your family? or (3) somewhere in the middle?

4. Do you (1) have a grandmother or grandfather who lives with or near you? (2) have both a grandmother *and* a grandfather who lives with or near you? or (3) have neither a grandmother or grandfather who lives with or near you?

5. Do you (1) like roller-blading best? (2) like ice-skating best? or (3) not like either one?

6. Do you (1) like spiders? (2) hate spiders? or (3) feel neutral about spiders?

7. Do you (1) like baseball best? (2) like basketball best? or (3) like another sport best?

8. Do you (1) like your middle name? (2) dislike your middle name? or (3) not have a middle name?

9. Do you (1) like sausage on your pizza? (2) like mushrooms on your pizza? or (3) like something else on your pizza or don't like pizza at all?

10. Do you (1) really like school? (2) really dislike school? or (3) like school OK?

PROCESSING PROMPTS

- Was it fun?

- Were you ever surprised by who was in your group? When?

- Did anyone have at least one other person who made all of the same choices?

- Could this activity help anyone make a new friend or two? How?

- Why did we do this activity? How might it help us be better classmates?

EXTENDING ACTIVITY

Tell the class you would like to play the game again later in the week, but this time using questions that the class has made up. Divide students into groups of four to eight and give them some time to develop lists. When they are finished, make up a composite list and play the game again.

Activity 7
CIRCLE THE CIRCLE

FOCUS POINTS

- Have fun.

- Relax and become comfortable with each other.

- Practice working in close proximity to others.

PREPARATION AND MATERIALS

Two Hula-Hoops™

DIRECTIONS

Instruct everyone to stand in a circle and hold hands. Have two students unclasp hands, place a Hula-Hoop between them, and then rejoin hands through the middle of the hoop. Tell students they are to attempt to pass the hoop around the circle without letting go of each others' hands.

After students have figured out one or more strategies, try timing how long it takes to get the hoop around the group. Try adding more hoops going in opposite directions.

As the students become better at this task, add a challenge by asking them to talk to the person they are working with about something completely unrelated (such as something that happened to them recently or a goal they might have for school).

Another option is for students to offer a compliment to the person they are working with at the moment.

PROCESSING PROMPTS

- Was it fun?

- How does it feel to hold hands?

- How did you work together to accomplish the challenge?

- What would have happened if someone refused to hold hands with the person next to him or her? How would that person feel?

- Do we ever refuse to work with people in class? Should we? How would you feel if someone refused to work or play with you?

Activity 8
CIRCULATION CIRCLES

FOCUS POINTS

- Have fun.

- Make sure everyone is getting to know everyone else; help the kids to connect.

- Break down any developing barriers.

PREPARATION AND MATERIALS

Radio, record player, tape player, or CD player (If you do not wish to use the conversation prompts below, you will need to develop your own before the activity.)

DIRECTIONS

Divide students into two equal groups and direct them to form two circles, one within the other. Students in the outer circle should face inward and students in the inner circle should face outward, so students are face-to-face. Tell them that when the music is playing, the outer circle is to rotate clockwise, and the inner circle is to rotate counterclockwise. When the music stops, the rotation should stop. Explain that you will then provide a topic for conversation, and the students who end up facing each other are simply to talk to each other.

Suggested conversation topics are as follows:

1. Talk about your favorite subject in school.

2. Talk about your least favorite subject in school.

3. Talk about a goal you have for yourself in school.

4. Talk about a goal you have for yourself outside of school.

5. Talk about a hobby you have.

6. Talk about a family member.

7. Talk about an illness or injury you have had.

8. Talk about whatever you want to.

PROCESSING PROMPTS

- Was it fun?

- Did you learn anything interesting about your partners?

- Why might it be important for all of us to talk and work with everyone else?

- Have you ever had a classmate react positively/negatively when he or she is assigned to work with you? How does this type of experience feel?

Activity 9
HANG TOGETHER TO HANG EXTREME

FOCUS POINTS

- We are interrelated as part of a circle or community. What one person does or does not do affects everyone else.

- We can choose to either support each other or drag each other down.

- Working together, we can achieve much more than we can individually.

PREPARATION AND MATERIALS

Flip chart and marker or chalkboard and chalk

DIRECTIONS

On the flip chart or chalkboard, draw the following illustration:

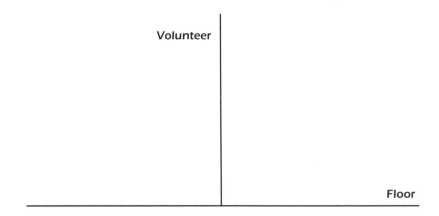

Introduce the concept of gravity and demonstrate it by dropping an object. Explain that gravity will allow a person only so much freedom before it takes over. Ask for a volunteer, and tell the student you want him or her to see just how far gravity will let him or her go before it takes over.

Explain that you want the student to pretend his or her body is a board and, without bending at the knees or the waist, to lean backward and defy gravity. Before performing the experiment, ask your volunteer to draw a broken line on the illustration indicating how far he or she thinks he or she will be able to lean before losing his or her balance and giving in to gravity.

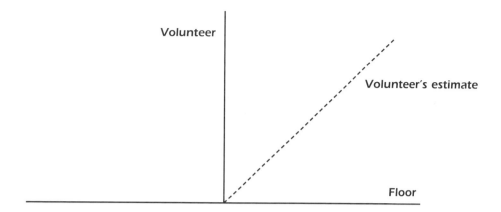

Volunteer

Volunteer's estimate

Floor

Explain to the volunteer that you will stand behind him and catch him when he falls. Do the experiment. Ask the individual how he thinks he did in relationship to his estimate. Ask the class. Explain that, as an individual, the volunteer did a good job of beating gravity. Tell the class that the only way you know to do a better job is to work as a supportive group or community.

Tell the class you would like to work together to beat gravity. You will need an even number of people; if your class is not an even number, you can join in to make it so. Instruct students to stand in a circle and count off by twos (one/two, one/two). Ask all the "ones" to raise their hands; then ask them to turn around and face away from the middle or center of the circle. Have the students hold hands around the circle, and take a step or two away from the center. Tell them it is important for everyone to maintain a good grip and to not let go. Explain that, through tension, everyone will be holding and supporting everyone else. Suggest that to really beat gravity, everyone needs to listen to you give the signals, move slowly and in concert, and communicate with each other. Explain that bending at the waist or knees is not allowed and that if students start to lose their balance, they should simply put a foot out in front of themselves.

Agree on a signal to start leaning and a signal to come back out of the lean. Explain that on your signal, everyone should lean forward. Give the signal. After trying the lean a couple of times, switch directions. You might also try having students switch directions without stopping, in a sort of a wave action. This makes communication more interesting and important.

If you are not already part of the circle, join it now. Explain that as a classroom community, you are all connected. What one person does affects the others. Put a little of your weight on the students you are holding hands with; most people will instinctively hold you up. Thank them for supporting you. Tell students that there will be days when you will not be 100% your best (you might be a little sick, a little tired, and so on), and that you would appreciate it if they would help support you on those days. Offer to do the same for them, and invite them to do the same for each other.

PROCESSING PROMPTS

- How did you feel about the people around you in the leaning experiment?

- Did you feel safe? If so, why? If not, why?

- What did it take to beat gravity? Was communication important? Was trust important?

- How important are communication and trust to a group? A community? A classroom community?

EXTENDING ACTIVITIES

- Break the class into small groups and lead the groups in developing lists of times when individuals may need the community's support. Have them discuss ways the community could offer support. Ask them to share their ideas with the whole class.

- Lead the class in a brainstorming activity to suggest ways that community members can support each other.

- The leaning activity can be challenging, and some groups really enjoy working on it until they can do the wave motion. Challenge your students by offering 10 minutes at the start or end of the day for a week or so to work on it. A lot of learning may occur.

Activity 10
COMMUNITY, COMMUNITY, COMMUNITY

FOCUS POINTS

- Have fun.

- Learn each other's names.

- Break down barriers.

PREPARATION AND MATERIALS

None

DIRECTIONS

Tell the class to form a circle, and inform them that this is a name reminder activity. Ask them to make sure they know the names of the people on the left and right of them. Stand in the middle of the circle. Tell students that when you point to them and say "left" or "right," they are to say the name of the person standing beside them. Practice a few times.

Now tell them you are going to add something that will mix up their brains. Explain that when you point and say "left" or "right," you will add the three words "Community, Community, Community." Point at someone and say "Left Community, Community, Community!" That person's task is to try to say the student's name on his or her left before you finish the phrase. If he or she is successful, you continue. If not, he or she takes your place in the circle.

After you have practiced this for a while, add two new designations: "You" (if you point at someone and say "you," that person must say his or her own name) and "Me" (if you point at someone and say "me," that person must say your name).

PROCESSING PROMPTS

- Was it fun?

- Did anyone feel anxious or nervous during this activity? How did you handle it?

- When do you feel nervous in class? In school? How do you handle it?

- Is being put on the spot good or bad? Always?

- Do you ever feel put on the spot in class? Is it good or bad? Do I put you on the spot? What would you like me to do differently?

Activity 11

LINE UP LIKE THIS—NO, LINE UP LIKE *THAT*

FOCUS POINTS

- Have fun.

- Begin to explore leadership and inclusion issues.

- Stress the importance of communication.

PREPARATION AND MATERIALS

Stopwatch, wristwatch, or room clock with a second hand

DIRECTIONS

Explain that in this activity, students will be challenged to line up according to a certain criterion while being timed. For example, they may be asked to line up in alphabetical order by first name. When finished, they are to signal the timer, who will then stop the watch. The students will then be asked to say their names in order to check their work. If they are out of order, they are assessed a 5-second penalty.

Try having students line up according to different criteria, such as last name, middle name, mother's first name, birthday, shoe size, hair length or color, or height. Try doing some of these with no talking.

PROCESSING PROMPTS

- Was it fun?

- Was it frustrating? Are there things that frustrate you in school?

- What communication strategies did you use? Could these strategies be helpful in class? How?

- Did everyone feel included? Did everyone feel like their ideas were taken seriously? Do we try to make everyone feel included in our class? How can we do a better job?

- In the activity, did you direct the action or hold back to see how things developed? Why did you choose your role?

- Are there times in school when you want to lead? To follow?

- Should the same people always be the leaders? Do you have any suggestions for how we can give more people opportunities to be leaders in class?

- Do you have any suggestions for helping people feel like they are a part of our classroom community?

Activity 12
A PRESENT FOR ME—FROM ME?

FOCUS POINTS

- Have fun.

- Encourage everyone to talk to everyone else. Prevent cliques and barriers from forming.

- Help students get to know something important about each other.

PREPARATION AND MATERIALS

One index card for each student; optional: art supplies, such as art paper, markers, crayons, glitter, glue, ribbon, and so on.

DIRECTIONS

Ask each student to give careful thought to what three objects he or she would most like to have. Tell students that in this game they can give themselves the objects as presents. If you are using index cards, simply have each student print (clearly) his or her three choices. If you are providing art supplies, have each student decorate his or her piece of art paper to look like a wrapped-up present and then print the three choices on the back. When everyone is finished, direct them to mill around a designated area until you signal them to stop (you might want to play music as the cue to mingle and then turn it off as the cue to stop). When they stop, they are to pair up with the person closest to them and discuss why they made the choices they did. Instruct students to continue doing this, making sure that they pair up with different people each time.

PROCESSING PROMPTS

- Was it fun?

- How many of you talked to at least one person who had chosen at least one of the same "presents" that you chose?

- What do a person's choices say about him or her?

Activity 13
MAKING CONNECTIONS

FOCUS POINTS

- Have fun.

- Break down barriers.

- Consider how laughing *with* each other helps us not laugh *at* each other.

PREPARATION AND MATERIALS

None

DIRECTIONS

Ask the class to stand in a circle. Explain that we all pass people in the halls and on the street every day without even noticing they are there. Tell students this activity will help them practice making connections with other people by making eye contact.

Ask everyone to look down at someone else's feet. When you say "look up," they are to look at that person. If he or she is looking at someone else, nothing happens. If, however, two people make eye contact, they are to put their hands on their hearts and say "oh my." After the initial surprise, they are to recover, greet each other in the middle of the circle, high-five, and change places.

Try this for a while, then change the rules to encourage more connections. Ask each person to identify a partner across the circle. If there is an odd number of people, you can join in to make it even. Ask everyone to point at his or her partner (partners should be pointing at each other). Now, tell students they may look either at the feet of their partners, or at the feet of the person on their **own** right or **own** left. Because the choices have been narrowed, when students look up, there will be more surprises and more movement.

PROCESSING PROMPTS

- Was it fun?

- Was it risky? Why or why not?

- Why might it be important for us to be able to laugh together as a class?

- Do you think laughing together as a class will help us not want to laugh at each other?

- What is the difference between laughing *at* a classmate and laughing *with* him or her?

- What about being able to laugh at yourself? How does that fit in?

- How will being able to laugh with each other help us take risks in class?

- What kinds of risks can we take in class? Will taking risks help us learn more? Grow more? How?

Activity 14
STUDENT TO STUDENT

FOCUS POINTS

- Have fun.

- Begin to discuss issues of trust.

- Initiate the transition from "getting to know one another" to "learning to trust one another."

PREPARATION AND MATERIALS

None

DIRECTIONS

Ask each student to find a partner who is wearing a similar color of clothing. You are "it" and do not have a partner.

Ask students to snap their fingers and tap their toes in an even rhythm. On the beat, you say "student to student," and the class repeats the phrase after you. Now, on the beat, call out two body parts, like "foot to foot" or "wrist to elbow." Each pair of partners must then touch these parts together.

Continue calling out body parts for a while—then call out "student to student" again. At this point, everyone must find a new partner. You are going to find a partner as well, which means that a new person will be "it." Have the new "it" start by saying "student to student," and then begin calling out body parts as you did.

After a few rounds, tell students they are now going to play the "Twister" version of the game. This means that each time they touch two body parts, they must keep them stuck together until they hear "student to student" again. Make sure students agree to keep this G-rated and to not ask anyone to do something that might be too uncomfortable.

PROCESSING PROMPTS

- Was it fun?

- Would you have enjoyed doing this activity on the first day of school? Why or why not?

- Did you have to take some risks in this activity?

- What risks do we take in our class? How does trust affect our willingness to take risks?

Activity 15
CLASSROOM COMMONALITIES

FOCUS POINTS

- We cannot always tell what people are like just by looking—we need to listen to each other.

- If we take the time to talk, we might find we are more alike than we think.

PREPARATION AND MATERIALS

A large piece of paper and 2–3 markers for each small group

DIRECTIONS

Instruct the class to break into groups of three to five students. Give each small group a piece of paper and some markers. Begin by asking students within the small groups to look at each other and make a list of things they can *see* they have in common (we are all human beings, all have noses, all wear shoes, and so on). Then ask them to make a second list of things they have in common that cannot be seen. It will be necessary for them to ask each other questions to learn what these commonalities are. After 5–10 minutes, ask each group to choose their top three to five favorite commonalities to report to the whole class.

PROCESSING PROMPTS

- What cliques do we have here at school?

- Do you consider cliques good or bad for our class? Our school?

- How might being part of a clique be helpful or limiting to us?

- What does it mean to stereotype?

- How might we stereotype people?

- Have you ever been stereotyped? How did it feel?

- Have you ever stereotyped someone else? How do you think that person felt?

- What efforts can we make to learn what people in our class and school are like on the inside?

EXTENDING ACTIVITIES

- Allow small groups time to write/create a role play that depicts cliques at your school. Students can present their role play live or videotape it. Process the experience with the whole class.

- Instruct students to write a composition in which they take the position that cliques in school are either good or bad.

Chapter 6

Learning to Trust and Depend on Each Other

My father told me not to be afraid. That the doctor would put me to sleep, that I would feel nothing, and I would wake up all better. I could not understand how you could sleep so deep that someone could cut into your body without waking up. There was nothing in my experiential bank to validate it. But my Dad had earned my trust and so I believed. I decided to nix my plan to run away and to go ahead with the operation. TRUST is AWESOME!

—Memory of an 8-year-old boy

Chapter 6

Learning to Trust and Depend on Each Other

The challenges and activities in this chapter are designed to help you build a culture of trust. Trust affects the quality and productivity of all long-term relationships. It is a basic sense of trust that allows a president to lead a country, a parent to guide a child, a teacher's union to work with a board of education, and a teacher to help a classroom community become everything it has the potential to be. In a classroom where students trust each other, there is an unspoken covenant that allows many wonderful, very human interactions to occur. There is an assurance that individuals will treat and be treated fairly. There is an assumption that words and actions will be carried out with good purpose. There is a belief in the collective character of the class. Because of this covenant, students act with confidence, take emotional and academic risks, expect to be supported, and try to support each other. They expect the best of each other and give each other the benefit of the doubt. They relax with each other, and collective pressure is replaced by collective energy.

In today's climate of standards-driven educational reform, a teacher's ability to limit stressors originating inside his or her classroom is of great significance. This ability is important because entities outside the classroom—such as federal and state government, blue ribbon commissions, business leaders, and so on—have dramatically increased pressures on the classroom. The following challenges and activities will support you and your students as you struggle with pressure and expectations from outside the classroom. They will also foster interpersonal relationships that can endure not only the daily grind of classroom life, but the inevitable conflicts inherent in any long-term group endeavor. When you build a classroom community based on trust, you help your students

- Adopt positive and productive assumptions about the group.

- Take positive risks and support positive risk-taking behavior.

- Tolerate the little things—little mistakes, little miscommunications, and little differences.

- Negotiate win-win solutions.

- Learn to depend on each other.

- Trust you to use your experience and knowledge to help them make decisions, decide on goals, and choose behaviors.

Activity 16
ZIP, ZAP, POP

FOCUS POINTS

- Have fun.

- Learn to become comfortable with making mistakes.

- Learn to support others when they make mistakes.

PREPARATION AND MATERIALS

None

DIRECTIONS

Have everyone sit or stand in a circle. Teach the class the following series of motions and sounds:

1. Place your hand (either hand) on your forehead like a salute. Say "Zip."

2. Make the same hand motion as a salute, but at the throat. Say "Zap."

3. Put your hands together as if you are clapping. Say "Pop."

Tell students they can use either hand to do the Zip and Zap motions. Begin the game by doing the Zip motion and saying "Zip." If your fingers are pointing left (a salute with the right hand), the person on your left does the Zap motion. If your fingers are pointing right (a salute with the left hand), the person on your right does the Zap motion. Whichever way the Zap person's fingers point is the person who does the Pop motion. The Pop person can point to anyone in the circle. Then the whole cycle starts again with the person who is pointed to.

As students become more comfortable with the game, speed it up. When someone makes a mistake, the game stops and he or she gives high fives to the people on either side of him or her, and then starts the next round.

PROCESSING PROMPTS

- How did you like being put on the spot?

- Are you ever put on the spot in class? In school?

- Was it helpful to celebrate making a mistake?

- What usually happens when you make a mistake? How does it feel?

- How would this game change if we excluded people for making mistakes?

- How might celebrating mistakes allow us to learn more in school?

- Why is it important to learn from our mistakes?

- When is it not OK to make a mistake?

LEARNING TO TRUST

Activity 17
GRADUATION TRAIL

FOCUS POINTS

- Have fun.

- Explore how learning from mistakes can help the learning process.

- Practice supporting each other when mistakes are made.

PREPARATION AND MATERIALS

Two boundary markers (such as rope, tape, or sticks) set about 20–30 feet apart;
10 items to step on (such as carpet squares, boards, or bathmats cut into
squares)

DIRECTIONS

Before beginning the activity, introduce the idea that mistakes can be learning
tools and discuss the concept of "trial and error" with the class. Then ask
students to stand behind one of the boundary markers. Explain that graduation is
behind the other boundary marker, and their mission is to make sure everyone
graduates. Between the two markers is all the "stuff" of their lives between now
and graduation. Have students briefly brainstorm various things that might be
included in the "stuff" area. (High school students may say things like exams,
clubs, dating, getting a driver's license, athletics, and cliques. Elementary students
may say things like recess, peer pressure, homework, soccer, and spelling tests.)

Tell students that they are not allowed to step in the "stuff." They must use only
the 10 items that they have to help them get through it. (If you want, you can
designate these as friends, family, confidence, and so on.) Give them the 10
items, and explain the following rules:

1. They must get everyone to the other side by touching only the 10 support
   items.

2. They must keep in contact with the items at all times. If one is left by itself, it
   is taken away.

3. If someone should touch the "stuff," then the whole group must go back and start over.

4. It is important to get as many of the support items to the other side as possible, so that they can continue to be used after "graduation."

Ask students to work together to complete the activity. Once finished, have them count how many support items they have. Then ask them to do it again—but this time, they should set a goal for how many support items they think they can retain.

PROCESSING PROMPTS

- What happened when you lost a support item? How did you deal with it personally and as a group?

- How did you learn (or not learn) from your mistakes? How do we learn or not learn from our mistakes in school?

- What does it mean to take a trial-and-error approach? Is it useful?

- How did you use a trial-and-error approach here?

- How could you use a trial-and-error approach in class?

- When is a trial-and-error approach not good?

LEARNING TO TRUST

Activity 18
SIMON SAYS "OOPS!"

FOCUS POINTS

- Have fun.

- Become comfortable with making mistakes.

- Practice supporting others when they make mistakes.

PREPARATION AND MATERIALS

None

DIRECTIONS

Instruct students to stand in a circle. Explain that they will be participating in a very familiar activity and that some people will make mistakes during the activity. The game is Simon Says. In this version, however, no one will be eliminated.

The rules are the same as in the traditional Simon Says game. One person is "Simon," and he or she will ask the others to do different physical motions (for example, "Simon says put your hand on your head" and "Simon says touch your toes"). Students are to do the motion *only* when Simon begins the command with the phrase "Simon says." If the person who is Simon says "Put your hand on your head," the students are to do nothing.

Traditionally, the people who move at the wrong commands are excluded from the game. This time, however, when students make a mistake, they are to put their hand to their mouth and say "Oops!" They are to then move to the other side of the circle while everyone claps and cheers for them. After the students have played the game for a while, try having different people play the role of Simon.

PROCESSING PROMPTS

- How did it feel to make a mistake during this activity?

- How does it usually feel to make a mistake?

- Is it OK to make a mistake? Why or why not?

- What benefits are there to making mistakes?

- What types of mistakes might we make in school?

- How can we support each other (or be supported) when a mistake occurs?

- What does the ability to make mistakes have to do with trusting one another?

EXTENDING ACTIVITIES

- Ask the class to brainstorm possible mistakes a student might make in class. Lead a discussion on how to be supportive when someone makes a mistake.

- Ask the class to brainstorm possible mistakes a teacher might make in class. Lead a discussion on how to be supportive when the teacher makes a mistake.

- Ask students to react (verbally or in writing) to the prompt, "If you're not making mistakes, you're not trying hard enough."

Thanks to Faith Evans for this activity idea.

LEARNING TO TRUST

Activity 19
TENNIS BALL TRANSFER

FOCUS POINTS

- Have fun.

- Become comfortable with making mistakes.

- Practice supporting others when they make mistakes.

PREPARATION AND MATERIALS

3–4 tennis balls; 6–8 empty pop bottles; and 3–4 round $1\frac{1}{2}$-inch metal rings, each with 6–8 parachute cords (4–8 feet long) tied around it; the rings should look like this:

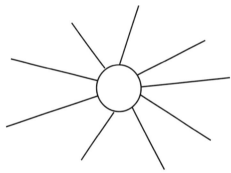

Set up activity spaces for three or four groups of students. For each activity space, place two pop bottles far apart from each other, put a ring with the parachute cords over the neck of one pop bottle, then balance a tennis ball on that pop bottle.

DIRECTIONS

You will need to have enough space for students to move around while holding a parachute cord. Ask students to get into groups according to the clothes they are wearing. For example, have all those wearing jeans get into a group, those wearing sandals, or those wearing sweatshirts. Once you get a group of six to eight students, instruct them to stay together, then continue with the rest until everyone is in a group.

Tell students the object is for each group to work together to transfer the tennis ball from one pop bottle to another. They may not touch the tennis ball, the ring, or the pop bottle. In fact, they can only get within 4 feet of the ring. This means they must manipulate the parachute cords to pick up the tennis ball from one pop bottle, carry it over to the other bottle, and set it down. If the tennis ball is dropped, they must start over. After they accomplish it the first time, try timing them a few times.

PROCESSING PROMPTS

- Was it fun?

- What did you do to avoid dropping the tennis ball and having to start over? What strategies did you use?

- What communication skills did you use? Could these same skills work in class?

- When (if) the tennis ball dropped, how did you handle it? How might you have handled it?

- What did you do to support each other when someone made a mistake?

- What can you do to support each other in class when someone makes a mistake?

- When you dropped the tennis ball, what did you learn from that mistake?

EXTENDING ACTIVITY

Direct students to do the same activity, but blindfold one or two group members. Explain that these students represent students who might be having a hard time learning what the class is studying or who might be having difficulties at home that keep them from coming to school rested. Remind the class that these students would be supported in a classroom community.

Activity 20
CHANNELS

FOCUS POINTS

- Have fun.

- Practice supporting others when they make mistakes.

- Explore the idea of degree when making a mistake.

- Practice helping each other reach a common goal.

PREPARATION AND MATERIALS

Channels made from 1-inch PVC pipe that has been cut into 12- to 16-inch sections and then cut lengthwise (Alternatively, you can take the cardboard centers from paper towel rolls and cut them lengthwise. Channels can also be made of corner molding found in supply stores and cut into 12- to 16-inch sections.*); various objects to travel through the channels (a marble, ball bearing, golf ball, ping pong ball, raw egg, stone, and so on); a boundary marker; a receptacle for the traveling objects (a cup or coffee can)

Place the boundary marker and the receptacle on the ground, preferably outside and at least 20 feet apart.

DIRECTIONS

Begin by talking about different kinds of mistakes. Hold up a marble or stone. Ask what would happen if this object were dropped on the floor. Then hold up the raw egg. Ask the same question. Have a short discussion about mistakes and how there are varying degrees of mistakes. Ask for examples of mistakes that are harmless and for examples of mistakes that could be problematic.

Give each person a channel. Tell them they may not give their channels to anyone else during the activity. Explain that the object of the activity is to get the objects safely from the boundary marker into the receptacle. Give students the following rules for the activity:

---

*Channels can also be purchased from Project Adventure (www.pa.org) under the name "pipelines."

ADVENTURE EDUCATION FOR THE CLASSROOM COMMUNITY

1. Each object must start behind the boundary marker.

2. Neither the boundary marker nor the receptacle may be moved.

3. The object may not hit the ground or touch a person or his or her clothing. If it does any of these things, the object must go back to the beginning and start over.

4. If someone is holding an object in his or her channel, that person may not walk.

PROCESSING PROMPTS

- How did you treat each of the objects? What made the difference?

- What strategies did you use to keep your objects safe?

- How were the consequences different with each item?

- Give some examples of mistakes we make in school. Of these mistakes, which ones would need to be corrected or made right in some way?

- How does it usually feel when you make a mistake in school? In life? What makes you feel better about it? What makes you feel worse?

Activity 21
INTEGRITY BALL

FOCUS POINTS

- Have fun.

- Explore what it means to have integrity and how it relates to trust.

- Practice making choices about what one believes to be right.

PREPARATION AND MATERIALS

A beanbag or ball

DIRECTIONS

Ask students to stand in a circle. Tell them the object of this game is to throw the ball from person to person. Explain that this is an elimination game, but that the only way to be "out" is to eliminate yourself, based on the three rules of the game:

1. You must call the name of the person you are throwing to before the throw.

2. Throws must be good.

3. Catches must be good.

Tell students that during the game, if someone feels he or she has broken one of the rules, then he or she should take him- or herself out. However, no one can tell someone else to leave the game or disagree with a decision someone else has made.

Start the game by calling someone's name and throwing the ball to that person. That person should then call the name of someone else and throw the ball to him or her. Continue this for a few minutes, and then start another round.

PROCESSING PROMPTS

- For those of you who left the game, what criteria did you use to determine that your throw or catch was bad?

- Did anyone disagree with a decision someone else made about leaving, or not leaving, the game?

- This is a game about integrity. What is that?

- How might having integrity help when trying to build trust? Will trust help in building a classroom community? How will it help?

- Have there been times in your life when you have felt that you exercised integrity?

- Have there been times in your life when you wished you had exercised more integrity?

EXTENDING ACTIVITY

Instruct students to write a short essay in response to the following prompt: "Integrity in School Means . . . " Share responses by (1) having students read their essays aloud, (2) posting the essays, (3) making a binder of essays and sending it home with a different student each night to be discussed with a parent, or (4) having students create and share video vignettes depicting their essays.

Adapted from "Fireball" by Chris Cavert, Affordable Portables (1996), p. 23.

Activity 22
EVIDENCE RESCUE

FOCUS POINTS

- Have fun.

- Learn to place trust for one's physical safety in another.

- Demonstrate that others can be trusted to keep a person safe from physical harm.

PREPARATION AND MATERIALS

Enough soft items to throw for half the class; box or wastebasket; optional: blindfold

Place the box or wastebasket in a central location. If this activity is taking place in a gym or on a field, you can place obstacles in the space to make this activity more of a challenge for the students.

DIRECTIONS

Ask students to find partners who were born in a different season than themselves. Explain that their job is to "keep the peace." To do this, they must retrieve the evidence from a conflict and put it in the "evidence room" (box or wastebasket) so that the parties in conflict can work out the problem. Give each set of partners a soft item. Ask each pair to decide which person will be the first to be led and which will be the guide. The person who is being led should either put on a blindfold or close his or her eyes. The guide is to then throw the object (evidence) somewhere in the room/gym/field.

The guide is to direct the blindfolded partner to the object using only voice commands. Once the partner picks up the evidence, the guide is to direct him or her back to the evidence room for safekeeping. Once the evidence is safely stored, the partners switch roles and try it again.

Be sure to discuss how to direct someone safely and point out possible hazards along the way. Emphasize that everyone must take it slowly. Also, emphasize that if an object is thrown near a wall or other barrier, the guides must point out the barrier before asking their partners to bend over to pick up the object!

PROCESSING PROMPTS

- Were you more comfortable guiding or being led? Why? In what role are you more comfortable in school?

- Did you feel your partner was trustworthy?

- What did your partner do to prove that he or she was trustworthy?

- What did you do to keep yourself safe when you were being led?

- What did you do to prove that you were trustworthy?

- What makes someone trustworthy?

- What makes someone a trustworthy classmate?

EXTENDING ACTIVITY

Lead the class in brainstorming a list of ways that trust can affect the classroom.

LEARNING TO TRUST

Activity 23

DEFENDER

FOCUS POINTS

- Have fun.

- Explore the concept of being trustworthy.

- Practice working together and helping others.

PREPARATION AND MATERIALS

A soft ball, such as a Nerf or fleece ball

DIRECTIONS

Instruct the class to stand in a circle. Ask for two volunteers: one to be the defender, and the other to be the defendee. Have the two volunteers stand in the middle of the circle. Explain that the object of the game is for the people forming the circle to try to tag the defendee by hitting him or her with the ball **below the neck.** The defender's task is to protect the defendee in any way possible. If the defendee is hit with the ball below the neck, then he or she is to join the circle, and the person who threw the ball is to become the new defender. The old defender will become the new defendee.

PROCESSING PROMPTS

- How did it feel to be the defender?

- How did it feel to be defended?

- Can you think of times in your life when you took on either of those roles for real?

- Who might you defend if they were in trouble? Why would you choose to defend those people?

- Who might defend you if you were in trouble? Why would they choose to defend you?

- How might the notion of trustworthiness relate to the idea of defending others? Who would you trust, and who would trust you?

- How does one gain someone's trust?

- How could we be defenders for each other in our classroom community?

Activity 24
SHERPA WALK

FOCUS POINTS

- Have fun.

- Practice trusting others for one's physical safety.

- Explore being responsible for the safety of oneself and others.

PREPARATION AND MATERIALS

Long rope (cotton clothesline works well); optional: blindfolds

The entire class will be moving from one place to another, either in the school or outside. It may be necessary to pre-plan the route in order to reduce distractions. If you are using a gym or field, it can be fun to set up obstacles for the class to navigate.

DIRECTIONS

Tell students they are going to move across an area as a group. Explain that everyone is to hold onto the rope that will be provided and that everyone is to be blindfolded or have their eyes closed, except two guides. Have the class vote on which two students will be guides. Give the class the following rules, and then instruct the guides to lead the rest of the class through the course.

1. Anyone who is blindfolded can talk.

2. The guides may make noises, but may not talk.

3. The guides may lightly tap people, but may not hold onto them.

PROCESSING PROMPTS

- How did it feel to be blindfolded with all of those other people?

- For the guides, how did it feel to be guiding everyone else?

- How did you choose the guides? What attributes were you looking for?

- How did the guides do? What did they do to keep you safe?

- Were those of you who were blindfolded involved in keeping yourselves safe as well? How?

- When do you feel like you have a blindfold on in class? When do you feel like you have 20/20 vision?

- Is it OK for different people to be class leaders? How should we choose leaders for different activities?

EXTENDING ACTIVITY

Ask students to write short essays explaining the different types of activities and situations in which they like to lead and in which they like to follow. Share the essays with the class, if you wish.

Activity 25
FACT OR FICTION?

FOCUS POINTS

- Have fun.

- Explore what it means to be trustworthy.

- Introduce the concept of emotional trust.

PREPARATION AND MATERIALS

None

DIRECTIONS

Instruct the class to sit in a circle. Ask students to think about their own lives—what they have done, where they have lived, and their experiences up to this point in time. Tell them to pick two things about their lives that they are willing to share with the class. Then ask them to think of something that has *not* occurred in their lives.

Go around the circle and have each person share these three items (two points of fact and one of fiction). The other students guess which two are the real experiences and which one is made up. If the class is large, try doing this in small groups to increase the participation level.

PROCESSING PROMPTS

- Did you have any trouble thinking of a fact or fiction to share? Why?

- This is an activity about truth and lies. What does telling the truth have to do with trusting others? How could telling the truth help our classroom community relationships?

- How does it feel when you have been lied to? What do you do to resolve the situation when you catch someone in a lie or when you are caught in a lie?

- Why might someone feel the need to lie? What does it accomplish?

- How might you handle a situation in which you have a choice about telling the truth or lying?

- What factors enter into your decision?

- Why might you choose to tell the truth even if it is difficult?

LEARNING TO TRUST

Activity 26
EMOTIONAL GIFTS

FOCUS POINTS

- Have fun.

- Practice giving and receiving compliments.

- Explore the concept of emotional trust.

PREPARATION AND MATERIALS

Ball of yarn

DIRECTIONS

Instruct the class to form a circle. Discuss what a compliment is and how to accept a compliment by saying "thank you." Tell students they are going to be asked to give a compliment to themselves and then to someone else in the class. Give them the following two rules for complimenting:

1. All compliments must be real.

2. They cannot be about physical appearance or clothing (such as "you have pretty eyes" or "you are wearing a nice sweater").

Without unraveling it, use the ball of yarn as a throwable and give it to someone in the circle. Have that person say a compliment about him or herself. He or she is then to pass the ball to his or her right. That person is to say a self-compliment and pass the ball to his or her right. Continue until you have gone all the way around the circle. Then go around two more times, repeating the same compliment each time.

Have the class line up in alphabetical order and re-form the circle so that the original circle is mixed up. No matter where they are, everyone always throws to the same person (who used to be on his or her right). Depending on the alphabetical order one may or may not still be next to the person they throw to. Send the ball of yarn around again, throwing to the same person. This time, however, have the person passing the yarn ball say the compliment to the person he or she is throwing to instead of saying their own compliment. The person receiving the compliment says "thank you."

Each time the yarn ball is thrown, the thrower holds on to a piece of yarn. In this way a web is formed by the yarn. Once it has returned to the start position, the yarn is rolled up, and the process is reversed. Each person offers the original compliment to the person and the receiver says "thank you."

PROCESSING PROMPTS

- Was it fun?

- How did you like giving a compliment to yourself?

- Was it easier to give a compliment or to receive one? Why?

- Was it risky to give and/or receive compliments? Why or why not?

- How might giving and receiving compliments create trust between people?

EXTENDING ACTIVITY

Ask students to think of a time when they received a compliment that really made them feel good or special. Form a circle and allow each individual to share his or her story.

Activity 27
GROWTH CIRCLES

FOCUS POINTS

- Have fun.

- Analyze and compare different types of risk taking.

- Explore ways to encourage others without pressuring them to make choices that are counterproductive.

PREPARATION AND MATERIALS

Flip chart and marker or chalkboard and chalk; rope or tape laid out in three large, concentric circles on the floor, as shown below:

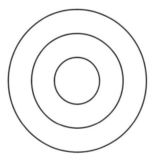

DIRECTIONS

Using the flip chart or chalkboard, introduce the idea of "growth circles" that look like this:

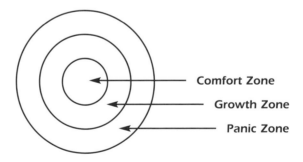

Comfort Zone
Growth Zone
Panic Zone

Explain that the comfort zone is where we feel comfortable, safe, and secure. Ask students to think of a time when they have been in their comfort zone. Tell them that the growth zone is a place where learning occurs. It might be when we have made a mistake or are pushing our limits. Ask students to think of a time when they have been in their growth zone. Tell them that the panic zone is a place where learning *cannot* occur. It is when people feel threatened. Explain that we strive to step into the growth zone and to stay out of the panic zone.

After discussing growth circles, tell students that the circles on the floor correspond to those on the drawing. Explain that you are going to name some common fears. For each fear you name, students are to stand in the growth circle that best describes their reaction. Start with "spiders." After students have taken their places in the circles, ask them to look around to see where others are standing. Then continue with some other fears, such as the following:

1. Heights

2. Going into a dark room without a flashlight

3. Giving a speech to more than 20 people

4. Singing in a choir

5. Singing by yourself

6. Snakes

7. Going into a cave

8. Flying

9. Confronting a friend about a problem

10. Taking a test

11. Taking a driving test

12. Swimming in a pool

13. Swimming in a lake or in the ocean

14. Bungee jumping

Ask for other fears from the class.

PROCESSING PROMPTS

- Were you surprised by where you found yourself at any time? Why? Were you surprised by who was standing next to you?

- What factors do you think might affect people's ability to take risks?

- How might one's background affect how he or she trusts others?

- How can we encourage others to take risks to learn without pushing them into the panic zone?

- What kinds of academic risks do we take in school? What kinds of non-academic risks do we take?

- What is the difference between encouragement and pressure?

EXTENDING ACTIVITY

Ask students to brainstorm things their classmates could do to encourage them to take risks without pressuring them. Form a circle and allow individuals to share their thoughts.

Activity 28
60-SECOND SPEECHES

FOCUS POINTS

- Have fun.

- Learn to take emotional risks.

- Practice supporting others who are taking risks.

PREPARATION AND MATERIALS

Stopwatch

DIRECTIONS

Tell students they will be given 5–10 minutes to prepare a 60-second speech about anything they wish. They may use this preparation time simply to think about their topic or to write down notes. Help students choose a topic relative to the amount of challenge they wish to have. For example, one student may choose to speak about a hobby, while another may choose to give a talk on a controversial issue.

Give each student exactly 60 seconds—no more and no less—to give his or her speech in front of the class. If a student finishes early, the time continues until the 60 seconds are up. If a student is still speaking when the 60 seconds are up, he or she is cut off in mid-sentence.

Because speaking in front of a group causes much anxiety for many people, this activity may be difficult for some students. Encourage them to do whatever is necessary to make this activity something they can do—such as practicing first with a friend, writing down some notes, or using props. It may also be beneficial to discuss in advance how to support others when they are taking risks. Refer back to the "Growth Circles" activity to remind the class that people have different levels of anxiety about different risks. For some, this activity will be easier than for others.

PROCESSING PROMPTS

- How would you rate the level of risk for you in this activity (from a low of 1 to a high of 10)? Why did you rate it that way?

- What did you do to help yourself overcome the challenge and accomplish the task?

- How did the other students support you when you were taking the risk? What helped? What did not help?

- Why might this activity be categorized as an emotional risk?

- What other emotional risks are there in class? In life?

EXTENDING ACTIVITY

Repeat the activity, increasing the length of the speeches.

Activity 29

WE'RE GETTING CLOSER

FOCUS POINTS

- Have fun.

- Explore the idea of risk taking.

- Begin learning about personal space.

PREPARATION AND MATERIALS

None

DIRECTIONS

Discuss the concept of personal space and how it has different meanings for different people. Ask students how they feel about their own personal space and how much space they need to feel comfortable in interpersonal interactions. Explain that this activity is all about personal space and risk taking.

Ask everyone to stand in a circle and bring both hands up in front of the body with the palms facing out. Tell the class that the object of this activity is to get to the other side of the circle. The challenge, however, is that everyone will have their eyes closed. Give students the option of "sitting out" and watching if they feel uncomfortable about either being in others' personal space or having others be in their personal space.

Start this activity very slowly. Tell students to walk forward carefully, with their arms outstretched. When they feel like they are on the other side of the circle, they can open their eyes. Try it again a little faster and then once more at a faster pace.

PROCESSING PROMPTS

- What was your comfort level with this activity (from very comfortable at 1 to very uncomfortable at 10)? Why did you rate it that way?

- Did this activity get riskier for you with each round? Why or why not? Why is the idea of personal space so important to us?

- When someone is in your personal space and it makes you feel uncomfortable, what do you usually do?

- How might you handle a personal space intrusion in a constructive way?

- How do we handle personal space in our classroom? How should we handle it? Are there particular trouble spots regarding personal space?

Activity 30
HIGH RISK, LOW RISK

FOCUS POINTS

- Have fun.

- Practice taking risks and receiving support from the class.

- Practice making choices to step out of one's comfort zone into the growth zone.

PREPARATION AND MATERIALS

Create two decks of cards: one containing high-risk prompts and one containing low-risk prompts. Use the following prompts for the cards:

LOW RISK

1. Name two things you think should be taught in school that are not currently being taught.

2. Describe one thing that other people have said you do well.

3. Describe something you have done that made someone else feel good.

4. Name a book you have read or a movie you have seen in the last month, and try to persuade the others to read it or see it.

5. Hum a sound.

6. Tell a (clean, nondegrading) joke.

7. What would you do if a person accidentally ran into you in the hallway and caused you to drop what you were carrying?

8. Shake hands with each person in the class.

9. Tell the class about your favorite TV show.

10. Tell the class what you hope to be doing in 10 years.

11. Tell the class about something bad that has happened to you this year.

12. Tell the class what you would do if someone gave you $500, with no strings attached.

13. Give a 1-minute speech on "How I think my school should be changed."

14. Wink at one person in the class.

15. Tell the class two things that make you angry.

16. Name at least three things you would like adults to do that they do not do now.

17. Tell the class the most boring thing that has ever happened to you.

18. Tell the class something good that happened to you this week.

19. Tell the class how you think school can affect your life.

20. Teach the class something.

HIGH RISK

1. Say something positive about each person in the class.

2. Walk like one of the members of this group, without putting him or her down.

3. Tell the class at least three of your strengths.

4. Tell the class something about yourself that no one else knows.

5. Do a 1-minute dance.

6. Tell us your views about a controversial topic.

7. Give three people a hug.

8. Give the name of the person you love most and explain why.

9. Make eye contact with one person for 1 minute.

10. Without words, show the class how you feel about these things: homework, your future, and your family.

11. How do you feel about dating?

12. Sing a song.

13. Share how you feel when something really bad or sad happens.

DIRECTIONS

Tell students they can volunteer to take a risk and they can choose whether it is a high risk or a low risk. When a student volunteers, he or she should draw a card from the appropriate deck, read the card to the class, and then do whatever it says. If anyone is unhappy with the first card drawn, he or she has one chance to draw again.

Encourage students to step out of their comfort zone without entering the panic zone by trying things that make them mildly uncomfortable. Explain that they can ask the class for support to help them get through the risk. For example, if the card says, "do a dance," the student may ask for music, or ask the whole class to dance with him or her. If a student feels the risk is too great, see if another student is willing to try the action. If not, allow the student to pick another card. After students are done, ask them to report whether they were in their comfort zone, growth zone, or panic zone during the activity.

PROCESSING PROMPTS

- Why did you choose to be put on the spot?

- Why did you choose a low or high risk?

- What did the class do to help you through the difficult moments?

- How did you feel watching someone else take a risk?

- Were you able to ask the class for help, or did you feel it was necessary to do this on your own?

- Did you learn anything about yourself from this activity?

- What did you learn that might help you take risks in class?

- What did you learn that might help you support other people taking risks in class?

EXTENDING ACTIVITY

Brainstorm high-risk/low-risk activities with the class, make new cards using their list, and play again. Repeat as often as you like, allowing students to set their own degree of difficulty. Be sure to screen out items you feel are inappropriate and to share with the class why you did so.

Activity 31
TRUST WAVE

FOCUS POINTS

- Have fun.

- Practice risk taking.

- Explore the concept of being trustworthy.

PREPARATION AND MATERIALS

Boundary marker (rope, tape, two cones)

DIRECTIONS

Direct students to stand in two lines facing each other. Tell them to put their arms out in front of them, with their hands alternating in a zipper-like configuration, as below.

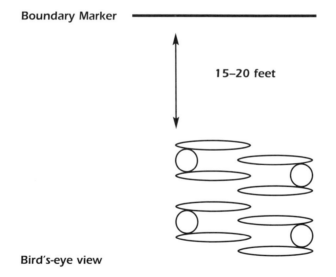

Boundary Marker

15–20 feet

Bird's-eye view

Place a boundary marker about 15–20 feet from the beginning of the corridor. Ask for a volunteer who is willing to try to walk through the corridor. Have the volunteer stand behind the line, and call out to the class, "Ready?" The class is to reply with "Ready!" The volunteer should call back, "Walking!" and the class should respond with "Walk on!" The volunteer is to walk through the corridor. As he or she reaches each hand, that person should lift it up to let him or her through. It should look much like the wave at a ball game.

Make sure that the class is ready each time and that everyone is paying attention, especially after a few people have tried this. It may be necessary to have two corridors going if the class is big or to stop the activity for a while if people begin to get bored standing in the line. If someone is interested in a different challenge, he or she may choose to jog or run through the corridor.

PROCESSING PROMPTS

- Why did you choose the level of risk that you did (walking, jogging, running, or not going through the corridor at all)?

- Was it harder for you to be the walker or to be in the line?

- Why does the walker need to trust the people in the line? Where does the element of trust come into play here?

- Where does the element of trust come into play in our classroom?

- Why is it important for us to trust each other?

LEARNING TO TRUST

Activity 32
WILLOW IN THE WIND

FOCUS POINTS

- Have fun.

- Explore the idea of risk taking.

- Explore the idea of being trustworthy.

PREPARATION AND MATERIALS

None

DIRECTIONS

Have a group of 8–12 students stand in a tight circle, shoulder to shoulder. Instruct them to put one foot back to give them a wide base, and put their arms up in front of them with palms facing outward. Explain that this is called the "spotting position," and it is how they will support and protect someone who chooses to be in the middle of the circle. The people in the circle will provide the "wind" for the "willow."

Ask for a volunteer to be the "willow," who will be passed around by the group. That person should stand in the middle of the circle, with feet together and arms crossed over his or her chest. Tell the willow that he or she is to stand straight and keep his or her body as stiff as possible. Reassure the willow that his or her feet will never leave the ground.

The willow is to call out, "Ready," and the spotters are to call back, "Ready!" The willow then says, "Falling!" and the spotters respond with "Fall on!" The willow then tips back toward the waiting hands. He or she is gently passed back and forth around the circle.

Tell the spotters to be sure that at least three hands are on the willow at all times, so no one person ever has to take the entire weight alone. Also, caution the spotters not to push too hard, because pressure that may not feel like much to them can be quite disconcerting to the willow.

After students have done this activity for a while, consider letting other volunteers be the willow.

PROCESSING PROMPTS

- Did you prefer to be the willow or a spotter? Why?

- What did the spotters do to make the willow feel like he or she could trust them?

- Was there anything the spotters did that made the willow more nervous?

- If you volunteered to be the willow, why did you do so? How much of a risk was it for you?

- How can we support a classmate who is taking a positive risk?

EXTENDING ACTIVITY

Ask if any willows are willing to do the activity blindfolded. If so, allow them to.

Chapter 7

Setting Goals

Far better it is to dare mighty things, to win glorious triumphs, even though checkered by failure, than to take rank with those poor spirits who neither enjoy much nor suffer much, because they live in the gray twilight that knows neither victory nor defeat.

—Theodore Roosevelt, 26th president of the United States

Chapter 7

Setting Goals

Goals give direction to behavior. The challenges and activities in this chapter are designed to help your students understand the importance of consciously setting goals and developing plans for achieving them. They will help your students learn to assess and expand their resources, evaluate their progress, and make necessary changes in both goal achievement and selection. The importance of setting goals cannot be overemphasized:

> Being able to set goals and develop plans for attaining these goals is a necessary life skill. Helping students to see the connection between planning and doing is necessary if we expect them to take control of their lives. Teaching students to evaluate along the way and, more importantly, to be flexible thinkers, capable of adjusting both goals and plans for goal attainment, will increase tolerance for frustration and tenacity for task completion. Repeated experience in setting goals, developing plans, evaluating progress, and making necessary adjustments positions your students to develop an internal locus of control.
>
> —Ambrose Panico, *Discipline and the Classroom Community: Recapturing Control of Our Schools (1999)*

We suggest that students write academic and behavioral goals at the beginning of the year and at the start of each grading period. You may also want individual students to write goals that address special situations. For example, a student who has a problem with attendance might set a goal and write a plan to improve his or her attendance. Whether you choose to use the goal-writing forms we provide, develop your own, or just have your students write their goals on index cards, be sure they commit to their goals in writing. The act of putting pen to paper adds importance and creates a record for your students and you to refer to later.

Once written, goals should be reviewed on a regular basis. Encourage students to view their goals as promises they have made to themselves and use them as an internal compass for self-evaluation. You can reinforce this self-evaluation process in the classroom. Whenever your students' behavior does not support reaching their identified goals, you can ask them to take out their goals and evaluate their current behavior in relationship to the goals they wrote. Many teachers we work with create a copy of their students' goals for their records. The teacher's copy becomes important if a student loses his or her copy or does not want to produce it when asked to self-evaluate.

Remember to help students apply the goal-setting strategies and skills they learn in these sessions to the rest of classroom life. The processing phase of each activity is an especially good time to point out how skills and attitudes learned can be transferred to everyday situations. Never miss an opportunity to encourage students to use their new skills. By helping your students establish goals, develop plans for their attainment, and apply those skills in other areas of life, you

- Ask students to take control of their performance.

- Demonstrate your respect for your students' ability to make good choices and follow through on them.

- Help students give direction to their own behavior, rather than trying to control their behavior for them.

- Help students focus their behavior on the productive pursuit of goals, thus limiting nonproductive, disruptive behavior.

- Provide your students with an internal compass that, when necessary, can be used to compare current behavior to identified goals.

Activity 33

ALL CATCH

FOCUS POINTS

- Have fun.

- Work on setting group and individual goals.

- Explore the idea of setting realistic goals.

PREPARATION AND MATERIALS

A soft, throwable object for everyone in the class

DIRECTIONS

Ask the class to stand in a circle. Give each person a throwable item, which they should then put on the floor. Explain that the object of this activity is to see how many items can be thrown *and caught* at the same time. Ask one person to start by picking up her or his item, counting to three, and throwing it in the air for someone else to catch. *The item cannot be thrown to oneself or to the person immediately to the right or left of the thrower.*

If the item is caught successfully, have another person pick up his or her item. The two throwers should count to three and throw the items simultaneously. If both items are caught, a third person joins in, and all three throwers toss their items at the same time. Whenever an item is missed or dropped, it is taken out of play, and the action resumes with whatever items are left. If, for example, five items are thrown and two are dropped, then the next round starts with the three that are still in play. If the three are caught, then another is added and the rounds continue.

After students understand this activity, ask them to set a goal for themselves. How many items do they think they can get to in a given amount of time? How many rounds do they think it will take? Be sure to give them time to create strategies for reaching their goals. If you are working with a large group or with younger students, have the class break into smaller groups to start this activity. Later on, you can try it in larger groups for a greater challenge.

PROCESSING PROMPTS

- Did it help to establish goals for this activity?

- Were your goals too easy or too difficult to accomplish? How realistic were they?

- What are the benefits of establishing realistic goals?

- What kinds of goals do you set for yourself? Are they realistic?

- What is the difference between an individual goal and a group goal?

EXTENDING ACTIVITY

Ask each student to write one goal for him- or herself on a full sheet of notebook paper. (You may want to specify a particular type of goal, such as a school, family, work, or social goal.) Then instruct everyone to crumple his or her sheet of notebook paper into a ball and do the above activity using the paper balls as throwing items. When you finish the action part of the challenge, have students read whatever ball they have. You may then want the person who wrote the goal to identify him- or herself.

Activity 34

THE RIVER OF LIFE

FOCUS POINTS

- Have fun.

- Practice setting individual goals.

- Explore obstacles to meeting goals.

PREPARATION AND MATERIALS

Using rope or tape, set boundaries on the floor (about 6–8 feet apart) that simulate a river. Fill the river space with stuff, such as wadded-up paper, toys, balls, rulers, tape rolls, extra clothing, or shoes.

Using an old deck of cards, cut each card in half to look like two puzzle pieces. Separate the card halves and put them in a pile. There should be just enough card pieces for every student to have one, and for every half, there should be a corresponding half (for example, half of the queen of hearts for one student, and the corresponding half for another student). You will also need a blank Post-It™ note and pencil for each student. Blindfolds are optional.

DIRECTIONS

Give each person a Post-It note and a pencil. Discuss the idea of personal and academic goals. Talk about how setting a personal goal is about changing or extending a behavior, and give an example that has meaning for you. For example, you might say that you have realized that you (as the teacher) make almost all of the decisions in the class without any discussion. A goal for you, then, might be to hold a 10-minute class meeting every other day to bring issues to the class for discussion.

Explain that an academic goal has more to do with what one wants to accomplish with their work. You might tell the class that grades are coming up, and you still need to go through half of the portfolios. A goal for you, then, might be to get your grades in on time. This means that you will have to dedicate at least 2 hours per night to the portfolios in order to accomplish this goal.

Ask each student to write a personal or academic goal on the Post-It note. Once they have done this, ask them to think about possible obstacles to accomplishing the goal. Explain that an obstacle to your own personal goal might be that you have so many other things to do in class that it will be difficult to find time for a meeting every other day. An obstacle to the academic goal of getting the grades in on time might be that it takes time away from your family.

Have everyone choose half of a playing card at random. Ask them to then find their partners by matching the two pieces to make one card. Once everyone has a partner, give each set of partners a blindfold and bring them to the "river" you made earlier. Tell them that this is the "river of life" and that the object is to navigate the river, achieve their goals, and leave the river on the other side. Explain that the objects in the river are obstacles to achieving their goals. While navigating the river, they are to touch as few obstacles as possible. Their partner is to help them. Each pair will do the following:

1. Decide who is going to try to achieve a goal first. This person is to share his or her goal with the partner and then find a place to put it in the "river of life."

2. After placing the goal in the river, the goal-seeker should then either put on a blindfold or close his or her eyes, and enter the river. The partner will attempt to help the goal-seeker get to the goal by using *verbal directions only*.

3. Whenever the goal-seeker touches an obstacle in the river, he or she must tell his or her partner what one obstacle is for this particular goal.

4. When the goal-seeker reaches the goal, he or she is to pick it up and continue to the other side of the river. Once the goal-seeker makes it out of the river, the partners switch roles.

PROCESSING PROMPTS

- What did your partner do to help you through the river of life?

- What resources are available to help you achieve your particular goal? These can be people, technology, or things. Tell your partner what resources you have available.

- Do you think you set a realistic goal for yourself? Why or why not?

- How realistic are your real-life goals?

EXTENDING ACTIVITY

Let students design a way to monitor when their goals are achieved.

Activity 35
WARP SPEED

FOCUS POINTS

- Have fun.

- Practice setting and meeting realistic group goals.

- Recognize that there can be different ways to achieve the same goal.

PREPARATION AND MATERIALS

A soft, throwable item and a stopwatch

DIRECTIONS

Ask the class to stand in a circle. Using the throwable item, set up a group juggle in which the item is thrown from person to person. Each person should get the item one time, until everyone has had it. Then it is thrown back to the first person. Ask the class to go through the juggle a few more times, always throwing the object to the same people in the same order.

Once the pattern has been established, tell the class that you are going to time the activity. Explain that the rule is that the item must touch everyone in same order as it previously did. However, students do not have to remain in the circle and can position themselves in any way they want. Ask them, "What do you want to do? Do you have a goal?" Generally, students choose to try to get through the pattern faster (although one group's goal was to go as slow as possible, and they took three days to get through the pattern). If the class chooses to go faster, they might try a variety of strategies, such as moving closer, keeping the item stationary and having everyone touch it, or putting their hands together like a slide and dropping the item through the hands. The most common strategy is for everyone to stand side by side in the correct order and simply hand the item down the line.

PROCESSING PROMPTS

- What goal did you set for yourselves? Did you all agree to the goal?

- Did it help to have a common goal? Why or why not?

- How did it feel to accomplish (or not accomplish) your goal?

- How many different solutions did you try to achieve your goal?

- Was your goal realistic?

- Could you have chosen a different goal? What are some examples?

EXTENDING ACTIVITY

Have the class discuss a current group (community) goal and decide if they are approaching the goal with the best possible strategy.

Activity 36

Low Drop Juggle

FOCUS POINTS

- Have fun.

- Explore the idea of how reaching a common goal can result in a win-win solution.

- Demonstrate how people can accomplish more by focusing on what they can control rather than on what they cannot control.

PREPARATION AND MATERIALS

15–20 soft, throwable objects (Nerf balls, wadded-up pieces of paper, rubber chickens, and so on)

DIRECTIONS

Ask the class to stand in a circle. Explain that you are going to pass an object around the circle, and everyone is to throw this item to the person on his or her right. Tell them that they will always throw to this same person throughout the activity. Send an item around the group two or three times to make sure students remember who they are supposed to throw to. Then ask them to line up in alphabetical order by their last name and re-form the circle.

Ask everyone to identify the person he or she is supposed to throw to (remind them that it was the person who was on their right). Then send an item around to make sure everyone remembers. Tell them that the next task is to throw all of the items around the circle, one after the other. Ask students to count the number of times they miss catching an object. Explain that a miss occurs whenever the person who was supposed to catch the object didn't (even if it was a bad throw, or the person next to them caught it). At the end, all the misses will be counted for a group total.

During the activity, if anyone sees an unclaimed item on the floor, he or she can pick it up and throw it to his or her designated person. When an item returns to you (completing the sequence), place it on the floor until you have all the items back. Then go around the circle, add up all of the misses, and announce the number to the class. Tell them they are going to attempt the activity again and try to reduce the number of misses.

Explain that because some things are outside of our control, all of the same items must be used and everyone must stay in the same places. Given that they cannot change those two rules, ask the class what *can* be done to reduce the number of misses. They may offer suggestions such as slowing down, focusing on the person who throws to you, being sure to make good throws, making sure the person is ready, or making eye contact. Try the activity again. Usually, the number of misses will be reduced. People may also become more polite (saying "sorry" for a bad throw, for example) and more aware of what they can do to make the activity work well.

PROCESSING PROMPTS

- What were the differences between the first and second attempt?

- What was your goal for the first attempt? For the second?

- How did having a common goal help us achieve a win-win solution?

- Did it help to focus on what we could control?

- When handling a conflict, what do we generally have control over and what do we not have control over?

- In earning good grades, what do we control?

EXTENDING ACTIVITY

Have the class set a group goal and plan some kind of community celebration for when the goal is reached.

Activity 37
MOON BALL

FOCUS POINTS

- Have fun.

- Begin to establish the importance of setting goals.

- Empower students to set the bar (the standard) for their community.

- Introduce the difference between class (community) and individual goals. Suggest the possibility that the two might be related.

- Examine the importance of communication to class (community) activities.

- Optional: Introduce or review a particular goal-setting/writing technique.

PREPARATION AND MATERIALS

One beach ball per group (Note: The group for this activity may be as large as 30 students. If you have more than 30 students, form two groups.)

DIRECTIONS

Form a circle, hold up a beach ball, and ask if anyone knows what it is. When they answer "It's a beach ball," say "Of course not! It's a moon ball. Why else would the activity be called moon ball?!" Tell students that before starting the activity, you would like them to take a few minutes and think about a goal that they have. Tell them it can be a big or little goal, and it can be in the near or far future. Allow them a few minutes to think; then go around the circle and have each student share his or her goal. Acknowledge students' goals, saying, "They all sound like good goals. Some sound very challenging."

Tell students that in playing moon ball, the goal is to keep the ball in the air. Let them choose whether to measure success by how many times they hit the ball or by how many minutes they keep it in the air. When they have decided how to measure success, ask if anyone has an idea for how to achieve the goal. Listen to the ideas, and let the students decide if they want to use a particular strategy or just jump in without a specific plan of attack. In either case, you can make the activity a little tougher and possibly more meaningful by reminding the class:

"You are a community. As such, you want to make sure everyone is included."
Ask them to make sure that everyone hits the ball at least once. Play the game.

PROCESSING PROMPTS

- Was it fun?

- Did you feel like you were included?

- Did you have a plan or did you just jump in?

- Are there goals we have that do *not* require plans? What are some examples?

- Are there goals we have that *do* require plans? What are some examples?

- Do we have both types of goals in our class? What are some examples?

- Is the goal in moon ball a class (community) or individual goal?

- Do we have both class and individual goals in our classroom? What are some examples? Are they related?

- Optional: If you introduced or reviewed a particular goal-setting/writing technique, process the technique's steps (Did you consider your resources? Did you consider specific activities? Did you evaluate and make necessary adjustments?).

EXTENDING ACTIVITY

You may want to apply the short-term goal-writing processes included in this chapter (Activity 41, page 144) to write a goal or plan for playing moon ball. Simply have a student volunteer facilitate the class in completing the goal-writing form. Then try their plan for playing moon ball, stop, evaluate, and try again.

Activity 38
POG'S JEWELS

FOCUS POINTS

- Have fun.

- Practice dealing with frustration when pursuing a goal.

- Work on identifying tasks that need a plan.

PREPARATION AND MATERIALS

A 30- to 35-foot rope; nine 10-foot ropes; 2 large coffee cans; 2 old bicycle inner tubes (get them free from a bike shop); 10–20 golf balls painted gold and/or silver for the "jewel" effect.

Set up the large rope in a circle and then put one of the 10-foot ropes in a circle in the middle of the large circle, so that it looks like a target. Fill one coffee can with golf balls, then place it in the middle of the small circle.

The rest of the items are tools for the class to use. These should be placed on the outside of the circle.

DIRECTIONS

Tell the class that the object is to rescue the jewels from the abyss using the tools provided (inner tubes, ropes). To do this, the class must find a way to retrieve the can of jewels without stepping inside the circle, using the tools provided (inner tubes, ropes). Explain that when students are bringing the jewels out, the can may not touch the ground.

To perform this activity, students generally tie the ropes to a folded inner tube and stretch it over the can. They then manipulate the ropes in an attempt to bring the jewels out.

PROCESSING PROMPTS

- Was it fun or frustrating or both?

- For what parts of this activity did you feel the need to create a plan? Why?

ADVENTURE EDUCATION FOR THE CLASSROOM COMMUNITY

- Did everyone know what the goal was? Did you discuss what you wanted to accomplish?

- Have you ever not met a goal at all, or only partially? How do you feel when that happens?

- What do you do when you have not completely achieved a goal?

- Was your goal realistic?

- Did anyone have an idea that did not get heard? Why?

- Did everyone feel included? Is it important to our community that everyone feels included?

- What did we learn that we could use in class when we set group (community) goals and make plans for achieving them?

EXTENDING ACTIVITIES

- Ask each student to write two to three sentences describing how he or she felt about this challenge. Tell them not to put their names on the descriptions. Collect them and read them to the class.

- Ask each student to write—on an index card—two real-life goals that require plans. Collect the cards and read them to the class.

Activity 39
GOAL TOSS

FOCUS POINTS

- Generate an interest in goal setting.

- Broaden individual students' thinking regarding possible goals.

- Build a culture that supports goal setting.

- Build a culture that supports individuals in their effort to reach their goals.

PREPARATION AND MATERIALS

One index card per student

DIRECTIONS

Discuss the importance of having goals and how goals give direction to behavior. Share a few goals you have and ask your students to spend a few minutes thinking about a goal they have or might want to set for themselves at school. Give each student an index card and ask that he or she write one school goal on the card. Tell them *not* to write their names on the cards. Form a circle, and instruct students to pretend the index cards are Frisbees™ and toss them to the center of the circle. Have students take turns picking up a card and reading the goal. Allow a few minutes for discussion on each card.

PROCESSING PROMPTS

Note: You may want to do your processing as you go, with a little bit after each card is read, or you may want to do it after all cards are read.

- Was it fun?

- Was it easy or hard to think of goals?

- Did you hear any goals that you might want to use as goals for yourself?

- Do you have more goals now than when you started the exercise?

- How can we support each other in our efforts to reach our goals?

EXTENDING ACTIVITY

Have students do the activity again, but this time ask them to write goals that apply to their lives outside of school.

Activity 40
ALL ABOARD

FOCUS POINTS

- Have fun.

- Learn to identify tasks that need a plan.

- Practice working toward group goals.

PREPARATION AND MATERIALS

A tarp, blanket, or sheet

DIRECTIONS

Lay the tarp (or blanket or sheet) out on the floor. Tell the class that the object is to fit everyone on the tarp for a count of five. Demonstrate the following rules for being on the tarp:

1. Your feet must be completely on the tarp.

2. Standing on your toes is acceptable, but having your toes touch the tarp while the rest of your foot is on the floor does not count.

3. It is OK to stand on one foot, but the other foot must be off the floor.

4. Everyone must have at least one foot on the tarp (no piling people on top of each other).

Give students time to perform the activity. Basically, they should find that there is plenty of room for everyone to simply stand on the tarp.

Ask students to move away from the tarp. Fold it so that it is roughly one-third smaller. Ask them to solve the problem again. Once they have completed the challenge, fold the tarp smaller, and then smaller yet. Once they are struggling a bit, you might fold it slightly smaller one more time for a greater challenge.

Remind students to make sure that they are leaving the tarp in a safe manner. It is easy to move too quickly and end up pushing someone over.

PROCESSING PROMPTS

- What strategies did you use at the beginning?

- What strategies did you use toward the end? Were they different? Why or why not?

- Was it necessary to discuss strategy much at the beginning? At the end? Why or why not?

- What are some things you do in your life that are "no-brainers"—things so easy or routine that you do not even need to think about them?

- What are some things in your life that you must plan for—things that might be new or unknown?

- What kinds of goals have you set for yourself?

EXTENDING ACTIVITY

Ask students to list three "no-brainer" goals and three goals that require plans. Form small groups of four to six students and allow about 30 minutes for discussion. The group is to make a list of "no-brainer" goals and goals that require plans to share with the whole class. To make the list, the small group must agree unanimously on the category in which each goal belongs.

Activity 41
WRITING SHORT-TERM GOALS

FOCUS POINTS

- Help students begin thinking about the importance of having goals.

- Help students identify possible goals.

- Help students select goals.

- Provide a simple procedure for writing plans to achieve short-term goals.

PREPARATION AND MATERIALS

Transparency of the "Goal Form: Short-Term Goals" worksheet (pages 146–147) and a copy of the worksheet for each student; a chalkboard and chalk or flip chart and markers

DIRECTIONS

Introduce the topic of goals by asking the following:

1. Do any of you have a goal or goals?

2. Does anyone set goals regularly?

3. Does anyone have some goals for this school year?

Ask students to help you make a list of possible goals, and write them on the chalkboard or flip chart. Suggest that while most people have goals, few take the time to think them through—and even fewer make a plan for achieving them. Show your students the "Goal Form: Short-Term Goals" transparency, and complete the form for one or two goals as a whole-class, teacher-led activity. It can be fun to start by sharing one of your goals for an example. Once you think students have the idea, give them each a copy of the worksheet and have them complete it on their own. End the activity by asking them to share their goals and discussing them as a class.

PROCESSING PROMPTS

- Was it fun?

- Was it hard? Scary?

- Do you think identifying your goals and writing plans to achieve them will actually help you do so?

- What does it take besides a plan to achieve goals?

- What can get in the way of achieving a goal?

- What academic goals might an individual set?

- What behavioral goals might a person set?

- What social goals might a person set?

- What happens when our behavior does not support our goals? What should happen?

EXTENDING ACTIVITIES

- Make "Goal Ladders" as an art project. The goal should be the top rung, and the rungs leading up to it should be the steps to achieving the goal.

- Design "Color-It Plans" to self-reinforce productive behavior. For example, a student might set a goal of doing his or her homework and then create an appropriate "Color-It Plan." This could be a drawing of a bookcase full of books. Every time the student does his or her homework, he or she would color in a book on the drawing.

- Create collages of goals or of people working on and achieving goals. This can be a fun small-group art project.

- Make a transparency of "Goal-Setting/Plan Writing Hints" (page 148) and lead a class discussion on how to use these hints in goal evaluation. You may want to use the hints to actually evaluate some sample goals.

- Make a transparency of "Goal Attainment Resources to Consider" (page 148) and lead a class discussion on how these resources could aid in goal attainment.

- Make a transparency of "Goal Attainment Resources to Consider" (page 148) and have small groups brainstorm additional resources and share them with the class.

Name: _____

Date: _____

GOAL FORM: SHORT-TERM GOALS

Use this form to write a plan to help you achieve a short-term goal.

Steps

1. State the goal as simply as possible: _____

   _____

   _____

   _____

2. State specific steps or activities for achieving your goal (you may want to include dates or a timeline):

   _____

   _____

   _____

3. Evaluate your results: _____

   _____

   _____

   _____

   _____

   _____

   _____

   _____

   _____

4. If you achieved your goal, **celebrate your success!** If you did not achieve your goal, choose one of the following and act on it.

   A. If you did not make an honest attempt, try again.

   B. If you gave it a good try, but fell short, change or adjust your steps and try again.

   C. If you think you set your goal too high, make the goal a little more realistic and try again (remember you can always raise it next time).

   D. If you found out that you are not really interested in the goal you set, admit it and choose another.

5. If you selected B, C, or D in the question above, write an action plan and act on it (you may want to refer to "Goal-Setting/Plan-Writing Hints").

   _____

   _____

   _____

   _____

   Action Plan Date: _____

GOAL-SETTING/PLAN-WRITING HINTS

1. Before you go any further, ask yourself:

   • Did I stick to the plan I wrote?

   • Did I really try?

   If not, you may want to do so before adjusting your plan or modifying your goal.

2. Ask yourself if your goal is realistic. Consider these questions:

   • Can I do anything to make it more realistic?

   • Could it be realistic at a later time?

   • Do I want to consider adjusting or changing my goal?

GOAL ATTAINMENT RESOURCES TO CONSIDER

Your knowledge	Your parents
Your intelligence	Your friends
Your physical strength	Your teachers
Your energy	Your counselor
Your spirit	Your church
Your commitment	Groups you belong to
Your effort	Other
Your creativity	Other

Reprinted from Ambrose Panico, *Discipline and the Classroom Community: Recapturing Control of Our Schools,* available (with accompanying software) from Stylex Publishing Co., Inc., 529 East Maple Lane, Mequon, WI 53092; Phone (262) 241-8347; Fax (262) 241-8348; Email: info@stylexonline.com; Web: http://www.stylexonline.com

Activity 42

WRITING LONG-TERM GOALS

FOCUS POINTS

- Help students begin to think about long-term goals.

- Help students identify some long-term goals.

- Help students select long-term goals.

- Provide a simple procedure for writing plans to achieve long-term goals.

- Help students predict obstacles to achieving a goal and explore ways to address them.

PREPARATION AND MATERIALS

Transparency of the "Goal Form: Long-Term Goals" worksheet (page 151) and a copy of the worksheet for each student; a chalkboard and chalk or flip chart and markers

DIRECTIONS

Assuming you have already introduced the topic of goals (if you have not done so, see Activity 41, "Writing Short-Term Goals," page 144), you may begin by asking students to identify the difference between short-term and long-term goals. Ask for some examples of long-term goals, and list them on the chalkboard or flip chart. Show your students the "Goal Form: Long-Term Goals" transparency and complete one or two goals as a whole-class, teacher-led activity. It can be fun to share one of your own goals for an example. Once you think your students have the idea, give them each a copy of the worksheet and have them complete it on their own. End the activity by asking them to share their goals and discussing them as a class.

PROCESSING PROMPTS

- Was it fun?

- Was it hard? Scary?

- Why do we need long-term goals?

- How do short-term goals support the attainment of long-term goals?

- What long-term goals might an individual have for school? For education?

- What long-term goals might an individual have for life?

EXTENDING ACTIVITIES

- Ask students to write short essays supporting the need for long-term goals.

- Ask students to work in small groups to write a short story entitled "The Kid Who Had No Goals." Share stories with the class.

Name: _____

Date: _____

GOAL FORM: LONG-TERM GOALS

Use this form to do some long-term planning.

Steps

1. State your long-term goal (set a deadline for achieving the goal):_____

   _____

   _____

2. List some short-term goals that support your long-term goal: _____

   _____

   _____

3. Record some obstacles or roadblocks you might face in reaching your long-term and/or short-term goals: _____

   _____

   _____

4. Record some ways to overcome obstacles and roadblocks: _____

   _____

   _____

Optional

5. If you are serious about achieving your long-term goal, complete a Short-Term Goals Form for each short-term goal you listed. Ask your teacher for the necessary forms.

Chapter 8

Using Communication Skills: The Big Picture

To effectively communicate, we must realize that we are all different in the way we perceive the world and use this understanding as a guide to our communication with others.

—Anthony Robbins, American peak performance coach

Chapter 8

Using Communication Skills: The Big Picture

The teacher who helps his or her students get to know one another, trust one another, and ultimately depend on one another builds a foundation that supports effective communication. Students who know and trust one another have many reasons to communicate with good purpose. They are comfortable with each other, they have a positive history with each other, they are interested in preserving established relationships, and—possibly most important—their teacher has helped them establish a community. Their classroom is not an "I"—"me"—"you" environment; instead, there is a sense of "us." The classroom culture is conducive to effective communication.

It is rarely easy, however, to develop a classroom culture that encourages good communication. We have seen too many well-intentioned teachers become discouraged when their efforts do not result in students communicating effectively. Author Ambrose Panico describes one experience he had as a new teacher:

> I remember being a new behavior disorders teacher, fresh out of college, armed with behavior modification and little else. My first job was at an inner-city Chicago public school. Most of our students hailed from Chicago Public Housing families, and most came to school with a lot of unmet needs. My classroom was what the Chicago Schools referred to as an *early remedial approach* (ERA) classroom. What that meant was that I had eight sixth-, seventh-, and eighth-grade boys identified as behavior disordered who considered themselves the "baddest" guys in the building. Most people agreed with their self-assessment. I learned quickly that, one-on-one, my charges were great kids at best and manageable at worst. It was a different story, however, when we attempted to do anything as a group.
>
> My gut told me that succumbing to my behavior modification training—and attempting to control my boys by reinforcing them for not interacting with each other—would be doing them a great disservice. I could, in fact, be limiting any chance they had to be functional in all but the most repressive and controlled settings. I believed my job was to prepare them for society, not prison. I let this simple assumption guide my decisions.
>
> Being young, naive, and certainly not the sharpest knife in the drawer, I decided to try to help us all learn to know, accept, and maybe even like each

other (just a little bit). Please understand I had not heard about experiential education, nor had I met experiential educators like my friend Laurie Frank. However, my youth, my respect for the boys, and their durability won the day. We succeeded in developing a sense of "us."

My next brainstorm was to start having what I referred to as "classroom meetings." I knew enough not to go for the gold immediately by addressing issues of shared resources or conflict in general. I instead started with easy things, like what book would they choose for me to read to them, what time would they like to have their breaks, what free-time activities would they like, and where would they like to go on a field trip.

What resulted was what Laurie Frank likes to refer to as the "rule of loud." We were all screaming at and over each other. The boys did not have the necessary communication skills, and my frustration level and bruised feelings prevented me from using mine. Repeated well-intentioned attempts by all involved provided the same disheartening results. Probably the most significant pedagogical decision I have ever made was made immediately after I finished feeling sorry for myself. I decided not to give up and go back to my controlling ways. I decided to teach my highly motivated students the communication skills they were so sorely missing. I also made a commitment to myself to model the skills I would ask my boys to learn. Together, we learned a lot.

Too often, we assume our students possess skills they simply do not have. Usually the skills in question are what we refer to as social or communication skills. Therefore, whether we are asking our students to master academic content through a cooperative learning approach or offering the possibility of a classroom meeting to find solutions to group conflict, we have a recipe for failure unless we allocate adequate time for skill instruction.

In classrooms where students are asked to exercise self-discipline, share responsibility for individual and class outcomes, make decisions, and resolve conflicts, teachers must teach and students must master communication skills, decision-making skills, and conflict-resolution processes. Basic communication skills include active listening, taking turns in conversation, and using "I" messages.

- **Active listening** means being able to focus your attention and your physical senses on what the speaker is saying, screening out distractions, and maintaining concentration. It also entails being able to clarify what the speaker says and provide the speaker with ongoing feedback that indicates you are listening.

- **Taking turns in conversation** means being able to allow the speaker to complete his or her thought before offering yours. This skill becomes more complex as the number of people involved in the conversation increases.

- **Using "I" messages** can be difficult for students to grasp, but teaching the concept is definitely worth the time and effort. There is a big difference between "you" messages, such as "You make me snap when you call me names" and "I" messages, such as "I don't like it when you call me names." The use of "I" messages will

  1. Help promote ownership of feelings and personal responsibility for behavior.

  2. Facilitate your students' ability to connect feelings to behavior.

  3. Help your students see that they have choices and that they are responsible for the consequences of their choices.

  4. Limit your students' tendency to blame other people and to be judgmental.

  5. Provide a behavioral benchmark or reference point, should a student attempt to blame or become judgmental. (You can, at any time, ask a student to rephrase a blaming or judgmental statement as an "I" message.)

Once students have mastered these basic communication skills, they are ready to learn and apply a decision-making process. Learning to apply such a process positions students to successfully make classroom decisions and address the issues and problems inherent in any long-term group endeavor. If you proactively teach a sound decision-making process and facilitate the application of the process to daily classroom life, you offer your students a real opportunity to become responsible decision makers and to prepare for citizenship in a democratic society. As effective decision makers, your students can accept a role of shared responsibility with you, their teacher. The decision-making process we share is simple, but effective, and we have had success with it.

DECISION-MAKING/PROBLEM-SOLVING PROCESS

STEPS

1. **Identify and define the decision to be made or the problem to be solved.**

2. **Brainstorm your options.**

3. **Select the best option.** (If in selecting an option, you reached a decision and/or solved the problem, then no further action is required. Otherwise, go on to Step 4.)

4. **Develop a plan and act on it.**

5. **Evaluate the results** of your decision and/or actions.

After gaining confidence in their new roles as decision makers and problem solvers, your students are ready to learn to resolve conflicts. Conflicts that may arise in your classroom and your school might include disputes between individual classmates, disputes between groups of students, disputes over limited resources, and disputes resulting from rumors or gossip. Whatever the cause of the conflict, productive long-term relationships will be built on and sustained by the participants' desire and ability to find win-win solutions.

A win-win solution is one that both parties accept. The ability to brainstorm possibilities is an important part of developing win-win solutions. Brainstorming is the process of generating multiple ideas, solutions, or plans without engaging in evaluation. While brainstorming would appear to be a very simple and easy skill to teach and learn, our experience has proven otherwise. People in general, and young people especially, seem to find it difficult to refrain from evaluating each idea, solution, or plan as it is generated. As the topic or conflict becomes more important or emotionally loaded, it becomes increasingly hard for individuals to avoid offering evaluation until all options have been generated. These are exactly the situations in which the ability to brainstorm successfully is often paramount to success.

The ability to see things from another person's perspective is a very important skill and one that supports the creation of win-win solutions. Understanding an individual's perspective is more than being able to identify with his or her feelings or right to have an opinion. It entails being able to see *why* that individual might feel as he or she does. The ability to understand that two people may process the same experience in totally different ways and arrive at very different, but equally valid, conclusions positions your students to avoid letting individual and cultural differences act as roadblocks to potential win-win solutions.

The ability to identify areas of common interest is also an integral part of arriving at win-win solutions to conflict situations. For example, the parties in a conflict might agree on the following areas of common interest:

1. They both value and want to preserve their friendship.

2. They both value and want to preserve their status as responsible students.

3. They both wish to avoid sanctions, such as calls to parents, parent conferences, detentions, or suspensions.

4. They both wish to preserve privileges, such as free time, ability to choose assignments or activities, and high levels of individual responsibility.

The ability to brainstorm, understand individual perspectives, and identify areas of common interest is the foundation upon which your students will build their conflict resolutions. The steps below outline the basic conflict-resolution process that can lead to a win-win solution.

WIN-WIN CONFLICT-RESOLUTION PROCESS

STEPS

1. **Identify and define the conflict.** Give each student the opportunity to tell his or her side of the story. You may need to remind them that they have been taught how to take turns in conversation and that they need to use that skill now. You might also remind students of some of the individual-perspective activities they have participated in, and ask them to use the skills they learned in those activities to try to see the other person's viewpoint.

2. **Identify areas of common interest.** Ask each student, "What do you want? What do you need to have? What is the worst thing that could happen if you don't solve this? What do you want to protect or maintain?"

3. **Brainstorm as many options as you can.** Ask students, "What are you willing to do to make this right? How could this be solved if you weren't so angry?"

4. **Select a solution.** Ask both students if the solution is at least OK with them. Help them consider the effects of the solution they selected. Is it fair to both students? Are both students' interests considered?

5. **Finalize the solution/agreement.** This can be done verbally, with a handshake, or by a written agreement. You can use the written agreement form on page 161 or develop your own.

The following two chapters are devoted to activities designed to help build your students' ability to make decisions, solve problems, and resolve conflicts. We have categorized the activities according to the discrete skill or process they primarily apply to. However, we acknowledge that many challenges and activities support more than one skill or process. Therefore, we advise you to use them as you think they will best benefit your students.

CONFLICT-RESOLUTION SOLUTION AGREEMENT

Disputants' Names: _____

_____

_____

_____

Brief Description of the Conflict: _____

_____

_____

_____

Brief Summary of the Solution (including what each disputant agrees to do/not to do):

_____

_____

_____

_____

_____

_____

_____

Disputant Signatures: _____

_____

_____

Witness Signature: _____

Date: _____

Chapter 9

Active Listening, Taking Turns, and Using "I" Messages

Seek first to understand; then to be understood.

—Stephen R. Covey, *The Seven Habits of Highly Effective People* (1989)

Chapter 9

Active Listening, Taking Turns, and Using "I" Messages

We suggest you begin by giving your students an opportunity to consider how important communication skills are to both individual and community success. The first activity presented in this chapter, "Communication Skills Introduction," is intended for this purpose. It defines each of the skills addressed in the chapter. After you read through the "Communication Skills Introduction" activity, we encourage you to preview the remainder of the chapter's activities, selecting some activities for each of the three skills presented: active listening, taking turns, and using "I" messages.

Activity 43

COMMUNICATION SKILLS INTRODUCTION

FOCUS POINTS

- Familiarize students with the three basic communication skills.

- Emphasize the need for communication skills in a functional and fun classroom community.

- In classrooms where the classroom community meeting is used: Encourage students to consider the importance of the communication skills to the meeting process.

PREPARATION AND MATERIALS

A copy of the "1-2-3: Communication Skills for Classroom Communities" handout (page 168) for each student; optional: transparency of the handout

DIRECTIONS

Distribute the student handout and review it. Present each skill and check for student understanding.

Ask students to save their copies of "1-2-3: Communication Skills for Classroom Communities" for future reference.

PROCESSING PROMPTS

- Do you think we have the skills?

- Do we use the skills?

- Can we list at least two classroom situations in which each skill would be useful?

EXTENDING ACTIVITIES

- Divide the class into small groups. Assign one of the three skills to each group, and ask them to make a list of five or six applications for the skill in your classroom community.

- In the same small groups, have students make similar lists for other communities they belong to, such as family community, church community, clubs, or teams.

1-2-3: Communication Skills for Classroom Communities

1. **Active listening** means being able to focus your attention and your physical senses on what the speaker is saying. It includes the ability to screen out distractions and maintain concentration. It also includes being able to clarify what the speaker says and provide the speaker with ongoing feedback that indicates you are listening.

2. **Taking turns in conversation** means being able to allow the speaker to complete his or her thought before offering yours. This skill becomes more complex as the number of people involved in the conversation increases.

3. **Using "I" messages** can be a difficult skill to master. However, it is definitely worth the time and effort. There is a big difference between "you" messages, such as "You make me snap when you call me names," and "I" messages, such as "I don't like it when you call me names." Using "I" messages will

   - Help promote ownership of feelings and personal responsibility for behavior.

   - Facilitate the ability to connect feelings to behavior.

   - Help people see that they have choices, and that they are responsible for the results of their choices.

   - Limit people's tendency to blame other people.

   - Help people not to be judgmental.

Activity 44
ONE-TO-ONE INTERVIEW

Skill Supported: Active Listening

FOCUS POINTS

- Have fun.

- Practice active listening skills.

PREPARATION AND MATERIALS

Optional: paper and pencil

DIRECTIONS

Have each student find a partner who has a different number of siblings than him- or herself (count step- and half-brothers and sisters). Tell them that they will each have a minute to get the life story of their partner. If they wish to take notes, they may. After they each have a chance to listen to their partner, give them two or three minutes to ask questions of their partner. When everyone is ready, each person is to introduce his or her partner to the class.

PROCESSING PROMPTS

- What strategies did you use to remember the information?

- How did your partner show that he or she was listening to you?

- What did you do to show that you were listening to your partner?

- Did you take advantage of the question time at the end to clarify information with your partner? If so, how did it help?

- Why do you think it is important to be an active listener?

- How can being an active listener help you be a better student? Better friend?

EXTENDING ACTIVITY

Repeat the activity, but narrow the scope of the interview. Suggested interview topics include the following:

1. Find out about the funniest thing your partner ever did.

2. Find out about the biggest mistake your partner ever made.

3. Find out about your partner's greatest success.

4. Find out about your partner's favorite place to go on vacation or favorite day trip.

Activity 45

BLIND POLYGON

Skill Supported: Active Listening

FOCUS POINTS

- Have fun.

- Practice active listening skills.

PREPARATION AND MATERIALS

One 25-foot rope segment for every five or six participants (a cotton clothesline works well); blindfolds

DIRECTIONS

Divide the class into small groups of five or six. Give each small group a rope, and ask them to tie the ends together so that the rope is in a circle. Have everyone in each small group hold onto their circle of rope, so they are evenly distributed around it.

Tell them that you are going to ask them to make geometric shapes out of the rope, but that they may not use their vision to help them. This means they must either close their eyes or wear a blindfold. When making the shape, everyone must have at least one hand on the rope at all times.

Ask students to close their eyes and make a circle with the rope. Tell them they are allowed to communicate verbally with each other. When they think they have it, they can look. Then ask them to make a rectangle—then perhaps a triangle, a square, a trapezoid, or a five-point star. Have them choose shapes of their own.

If the small groups are going well, ask two or three groups to join their ropes together and all work together for a bigger challenge. Have younger students hold hands instead of using a rope.

PROCESSING PROMPTS

- How easy or difficult was it to communicate with the others in your group? Why?

- What did you do to communicate when your sight was taken away?

- Explain the verbal and nonverbal communication you used.

- What active listening skills did you use to communicate during this activity?

Activity 46
ESTO ES UN LAPIZ ROJO

Skill Supported: Active Listening

FOCUS POINTS

- Have fun.

- Practice active listening.

- Increase "feelings literacy" by practicing different emotions.

PREPARATION AND MATERIALS

3–7 objects that can be passed from one person to another (red pencils are best)

DIRECTIONS

Ask everyone to stand in a circle. Teach them the phrase, "This is a red pencil." Try it in other languages, such as Spanish: "Esto es un lapiz rojo." Tell them they can use any language that they know, as long as they say the same phrase.

Now bring out the objects and ask that everyone agree to pretend that they are all red pencils. Tell them that the "red pencils" will be passed around the circle in this manner:

Person #1 will turn to Person #2 and say, "Esto es un lapiz rojo!" Person #2 will reply to Person #1, "This is a red pencil?"

Person #1 will say, "Si, esto es un lapiz rojo!" and hand the pencil to Person #2.

Person #2 will then turn to Person #3, and start the process over. Each time a person starts the process, he or she is to say the phrase with a different type of emotion. The person receiving the pencil must mirror that emotion when responding. For example, Person #1 may laugh heartily, "(Ha, ha, ha) Esto es (ha, ha) un lapiz rojo (ho, ho)." Person #2 must then respond with, "This (hee, hee) is a red pencil (ha, ha, ha, ha)?" And so on. When Person #2 turns to Person #3, he or she may say the phrase with surprise, fear, or sadness.

Once one object is going around the circle, start other ones in different places. You can also teach the activity and then have the large class split into smaller groups.

PROCESSING PROMPTS

- When observing the person handing you the object, what were you focusing on to figure out the feeling he or she was trying to convey?

- Did you find it easier to give the object or receive it?

- When someone is trying to tell you something, what are some of the ways you can get information from them?

- What can you focus on besides his or her words?

- Show some different kinds of body language. What messages are you trying to convey?

- Could understanding body language be helpful in working through conflict situations in our classroom?

- Is it important for us to be able to solve conflict peacefully in our classroom?

EXTENDING ACTIVITIES

- Ask students to pair up and try to convey a message without using words.

- Have small groups use newspapers and magazines to make collages that depict different emotional states. It may be fun to assign a particular emotion to each group.

Thanks to Abelino Perez for this activity idea.

Activity 47
BLIND MESSAGES

Skill Supported: Active Listening

FOCUS POINTS

- Have fun.

- Explore active listening by using only verbal cues.

PREPARATION AND MATERIALS

Paper and pencil for each participant (You can also use other media, such as pipe cleaners or clay.)

DIRECTIONS

Ask students to line up in order of their birthdays. Fold the line in half, and tell them that whoever is across from them is their partner. Have each pair of partners decide who is going to deliver and who is going to receive the message, then instruct them to sit back-to-back.

The deliverer should draw a simple picture on his or her paper, using only geometric shapes (triangle, square, rhombus, and so on). He or she should then verbally describe this picture to the receiver, who is to replicate it as closely as possible on his or her sheet of paper. The first time, have the partners attempt this without allowing any questions and answers. Then allow the receiver to ask any question he or she wants of the deliverer. When done, have the partners compare pictures and then switch roles.

PROCESSING PROMPTS

- Which attempt gave the better results? Why do you think this happened?

- What kinds of clarifying questions did you ask when you were receiving the message? What did the deliverer do that helped you understand what you needed to draw?

- What made the task more difficult?

- What would have made the task easier for you?

- When do we need to ask questions in class?

- What might stop someone from asking a question in class?

EXTENDING ACTIVITY

Give a student volunteer directions to a rather involved homework assignment, and then have the student deliver the instructions to the class. Have individual students write down their understanding of the assignment and share their responses with the class. Then have the student deliver the instructions again, but this time let the class ask clarifying questions. Again, have students write down their understanding of the assignment and share their responses with the class. Usually it becomes obvious that clarification through questioning prevents mistakes and saves extra work.

Activity 48
THINK, PAIR, SHARE

Skills Supported: Active Listening and Taking Turns in Conversation

FOCUS POINTS

- Have fun.

- Practice active listening.

- Practice taking turns.

PREPARATION AND MATERIALS

None

DIRECTIONS

Have students pair up or put them in pairs. Tell them they are going to have an opportunity to use active listening to discuss a topic with another person. You may want to allow the partners to choose their own topics, or you may want to assign the same topic for everyone. Possible topics might include a subject the class is discussing, a controversial issue, a topic of mutual concern, or a chance to reflect upon feelings or another activity.

Explain that there is a strict structure for this activity, and provide the following guidelines:

1. Everyone gets 1 minute to think.

2. Each partner gets 1 minute to talk.

3. The listener is to show he or she is listening by making *eye* contact, nodding, or making sounds to signify understanding.

4. The listener may *only* listen; he or she may not talk at all.

5. After 1 minute, the partners are to switch roles, and the listener gets his or her chance to talk for 1 minute.

6. After each partner has had 1 minute to talk without interruption, the pairs get 3 minutes or so to openly discuss the topic. During this time, both people can listen and talk.

Sometimes it is beneficial to share with the larger class "nuggets" that the partners talked about.

PROCESSING PROMPTS

- Did you find it uncomfortable to just talk without being interrupted? Did you find it uncomfortable to just listen without being allowed to interject comments? Why or why not?

- What did you do to show you were listening actively?

- There are times when all of us are less-than-perfect listeners. What are some symptoms of someone not listening well? When do you see these symptoms in our class?

- What shows that someone is listening well?

- How is it helpful to listen to others well? How is it helpful to be listened to well? When is it really important that we listen well in class?

Activity 49

PAPER CONNECTIONS

Skill Supported: Active Listening

FOCUS POINTS

- Have fun.

- Practice active listening skills.

- Practice giving and receiving directions.

PREPARATION AND MATERIALS

A sheet of $8\frac{1}{2}$ x 11 scrap paper for each student

DIRECTIONS

Give everyone a piece of scrap paper and tell them you are going to give them some very specific directions. Ask them to close their eyes. Without commenting or answering questions, give them the following instructions:

1. Fold the piece of paper in half.

2. Tear off the bottom left corner.

3. Fold the paper in half again.

4. Tear a piece out of the middle.

5. Fold the paper one more time.

6. Tear a piece out of the top right corner.

Ask students to open their eyes and compare their product with those around them. Although some may be similar, each person will have a different and unique product.

PROCESSING PROMPTS

- What caused so many of the papers to be different?

- What could we have done to clarify the directions?

- How might active listening have helped you understand the directions better?

- When trying to work together, what can we do to make sure that we communicate clearly and that everyone has a common understanding of what is expected?

EXTENDING ACTIVITY

Repeat the activity, this time allowing students to ask questions to clarify their understanding of the directions.

Activity 50
ACTIVE LISTENING ROLE PLAY

Skill Supported: Active Listening

FOCUS POINTS

- Help students master the skill of active listening.

- Reemphasize the advantages of being an active listener.

- Identify classroom applications for the skill of active listening.

PREPARATION AND MATERIALS

One "Active Listening Skill Sheet" (page 183) for every three students; optional: transparency of the "Active Listening Skill Sheet"

DIRECTIONS

Review the skill of active listening: present the four skill steps and make sure students understand the behavior associated with each step. Ask students, "Why is it important to our success as individuals and a class that we practice active listening?" Explain that active listeners

1. Get all the information the first time and get it correctly.

2. Make few mistakes because of miscommunication.

3. Very seldom have to do extra work caused by misinformation.

4. Usually do better in school.

5. Usually do better in social settings.

6. Make new friends easier.

7. Tend to be very productive in group problem-solving settings like classroom community meetings.

Have students form groups of three for the role-play activity, and hand out copies of the "Active Listening Skill Sheet." Point out that the handout has three different situations: (1) playground, (2) classroom, and (3) field trip. For each situation, one student is to use the active listening skill; one student is to play the role of the friend, teacher, or group leader; and one student is to observe the role play and make sure that all the skill steps are included. The observer may want to take notes. Ask triads to make sure that each individual plays a different role in each of the three different situations. In this way, the group will cover all three situations. Before students start their role plays, you may want to demonstrate the procedure with a volunteer.

Have triads process the role plays after each situation. Once all triads have conducted and processed all three role plays, it is time for overall processing, using the prompts below. This may be conducted in the triads or as a whole-class activity.

PROCESSING PROMPTS

- Was it fun?

- Was it easy? Hard?

- Did it feel and look phony? Why? Do you think it can become natural? How?

- How could active listening help us in our classroom communication?

- Did you ever have a situation where not using active listening caused you extra work? Got you in trouble? Hurt someone's feelings?

EXTENDING ACTIVITIES

- Ask students to write and role-play their own active listening situations.

- Ask students to rewrite the skill of active listening, including specific skill steps that make sense to them. Use the "Skill Builder" form provided on page 184.

ACTIVE LISTENING SKILL SHEET

Skill Steps	**Cue**

1. Look at the person who is talking. Make eye contact.

2. Stay still. This will help you concentrate and lets the other person know you are listening.

3. Hear what is being said. Think about it. Nod your head.

4. Summarize and repeat what was said; ask a question to clarify what was said; and acknowledge your agreement by saying yes.

Situation 1: On the playground, a friend tells you the rules to a new game.

Situation 2: In the classroom, your teacher gives directions for an art project.

Situation 3: On a field trip, your group leader tells you where to meet after lunch.

Reprinted from Ambrose Panico, *Discipline and the Classroom Community: Recapturing Control of Our Schools,* available (with accompanying software) from Stylex Publishing Co., Inc., 529 East Maple Lane, Mequon, WI 53092; Phone (262) 241-8347; Fax (262) 241-8348; Email: info@stylexonline.com; Web: http://www.stylexonline.com

SKILL BUILDER

Use this exercise to figure out the building blocks (specific steps) to the skill you have chosen.

Skill: _____

Step #1 _____

_____

_____

Step #2 _____

_____

_____

Step #3 _____

_____

_____

Step #4 _____

_____

_____

Step #5 _____

_____

_____

Reprinted from Ambrose Panico, *Discipline and the Classroom Community: Recapturing Control of Our Schools,* available (with accompanying software) from Stylex Publishing Co., Inc., 529 East Maple Lane, Mequon, WI 53092; Phone (262) 241-8347; Fax (262) 241-8348; Email: info@stylexonline.com; Web: http://www.stylexonline.com

Activity 51
PAY ATTENTION—NO! PAY ATTENTION

Skill Supported: Active Listening

FOCUS POINTS

- Help students understand the frustration a speaker experiences when people do not pay attention.

- Reinforce the skill of active listening.

PREPARATION AND MATERIALS

One copy of the "I Hear You Talkin' But You Can't Come In" handout (page 187) for every five participants

DIRECTIONS

Have students work in groups of five. Provide each small group with one "I Hear You Talkin' But You Can't Come In" handout. Have students take a few minutes to think about something they would really like to share with the group. They may want to talk about an activity they are involved in, a team they play on, a funny family story, a new movie they want to recommend, a joke, or anything else they like.

Tell them everyone will have a turn, and ask them to choose someone to go first. Explain that while the speaker speaks, the rest of the group is to play the four communication-blocker roles listed on the "I Hear You Talkin' But You Can't Come In" handout. Ask the groups to decide who will take which role.

Begin round one. Give the speaker 2–3 minutes to try to share his or her information, and then stop. Continue with the exercise until everyone has had the opportunity to be the speaker and to experience each of the communication-blocker roles.

Give students 10–15 minutes to discuss the results either in their small groups or as a class.

PROCESSING PROMPTS

- Was it fun?

- Was it frustrating?

- Can you see why I (teacher) get frustrated when people don't pay attention?

- Are there times in class when you get frustrated because people don't pay attention? When? What happens?

- Would active listening help in any of these situations?

EXTENDING ACTIVITIES

- Ask a volunteer to stand in front of the class and try to communicate something important while the class plays various communication-blocker roles. Process.

- Perform the same activity, but have the speaker play the role of a teacher attempting to assign homework or give directions to a very important test. Process.

- Ask students to identify communication blockers of their own.

I HEAR YOU TALKIN' BUT YOU CAN'T COME IN

Communication Blockers

Blocker Roles

#1 Do not make eye contact with the speaker (look down, look away).

#2 Fiddle with an object (for example, some papers, a book, or a comb).

#3 Yawn and rub your eyes, or even put your head in your hands or on the table.

#4 Drum your fingers or tap a pencil (pay attention to what you are doing).

Activity 52
THE "I" JUGGLE

Skill Supported: Using "I" Messages

FOCUS POINTS

- Have fun.

- Practice using "I" messages.

PREPARATION AND MATERIALS

A soft, throwable object (such as a Nerf ball, fleece ball, wadded-up piece of paper, or stuffed animal)

DIRECTIONS

Have the class stand in a circle. Explain that they are to pass an item around the circle by throwing it to the person on their right. Tell them to be sure to remember who they are throwing to because they will be throwing to that same person throughout the activity. Send the item around the circle two or three times. Then ask students to line up in order of their birthdays (from January to December), and re-form the circle. Ask everyone to identify the person they are supposed to throw to. Then send the item around to make sure everyone remembers.

Give the class a topic or unfinished sentence that allows them to make "I" messages. You can ask for an opinion, a belief, or a preference. Here are some examples:

1. What is your favorite holiday? Answer by saying "I like _____ because _____."

2. What is your opinion about open campus for high school students? Answer by saying "I think _____."

3. Describe a time when you feel calm (nervous, frightened, angry, etc.). Answer by saying "I feel calm when _____."

4. What do you believe should happen when a student skips school? Answer by saying "I believe _____."

5. How do you usually feel when you get up in the morning? Answer by saying "I feel _____."

After giving students a question, send the object around in the group pattern. This time, each person should answer the question with an "I" statement before throwing the object to the next person.

PROCESSING PROMPTS

- When we use the term "I," are we speaking in first person, second person, or third person? What is the difference?

- What do "I" messages help each of us do?

- What other kinds of messages are there? Try turning one of the messages we gave during this activity into that type of message. How is it different? Is it a "you" message?

- Using "I" messages is especially helpful during a conflict. Why do you think that is? How can using "I" messages help us solve classroom conflicts?

Activity 53
PLEASE, YES

Skills Supported: Using "I" Messages and Taking Turns in Conversation

FOCUS POINTS

- Have fun.

- Practice stating personal needs.

- Learn how to ask for help.

- Practice the "I" message of asking for help.

PREPARATION AND MATERIALS

None

DIRECTIONS

Have the class stand in a circle. Lead a discussion on times when students have asked for help. Talk about how these requests for help are a special type of "I" message that involves stating needs. Tell students that this activity will give everyone a chance to ask for help and give help to others. Give the following guidelines for the activity:

1. Stand in the middle of the circle, make eye contact with a student, and say "Please?" The student will then say yes.

2. At this point, you will both move from your spots, and you will take the student's place.

3. The student, who will be in the middle of the circle with nowhere to go, will make eye contact with someone else, and say "Please?"

4. That person is to say yes, and the process continues.

5. If, during the activity, someone says no, the person asking must then make eye contact with another person and say "Please?"

Continue this pattern, while periodically picking up the pace.

PROCESSING PROMPTS

- How did it feel to ask someone else for something?

- Did you find yourself saying yes unquestioningly, or did you think about saying no?

- How did it feel when someone responded with yes? When someone responded with no?

- In class, do you find it easy to ask for help? Why or why not?

- In your life, do you find it easy to ask for help? Why or why not?

- Who are some people in your life that you feel comfortable asking for help?

- Who might be some other people who are available to help?

- What are some examples of times that someone might seek help?

EXTENDING ACTIVITY

Instruct students to work in groups of approximately four to six to make a list of times in class where they would like to be able to ask for help. Each group should take turns reporting to the whole class. Have the class then suggest people they could call on for help in the situations they have identified.

Thanks to Alyssa Kenney for this activity idea.

LISTENING, TAKING TURNS, "I" MESSAGES

Activity 54
COMMUNITY STORY CIRCLE

Skills Supported: Taking Turns in Conversation and Active Listening

FOCUS POINTS

- Help students understand the importance of taking turns in conversation.

- Provide an opportunity to apply the skills of taking turns and active listening in a fun and relaxed setting.

- Emphasize how important these skills are to various types of classroom communications.

PREPARATION AND MATERIALS

None

DIRECTIONS

Ask students to sit in a circle. Explain that you are going to create a group story. Choose a topic ("the class picnic," "the best teacher in the world," "growing-up in . . . ," and so on)

The first student should start the story by saying a sentence (such as "At our class picnic, we ate the biggest hot dogs in the world.") The second student is to continue the story with another sentence ("After we ate our hot dogs, we ran a race.") The third student continues the story with his or her sentence, and so on.

PROCESSING PROMPTS

- Was it fun?

- Was it hard to wait for your turn?

- Is it ever hard to wait for your turn in class? When? Do you do anything specific to make it easier?

- What happens when people do not wait for their turn?

- How did being an active listener help you follow the story? How would it help you follow classroom communications? What are some of our most important classroom communications?

- What happens when people are not active listeners in class?

- Optional for classes that plan to hold classroom community meetings: How important is it to take turns in community meetings?

EXTENDING ACTIVITIES

- A variation on this activity is to have one student start a sentence and the next one finish it. For example, the first student might begin, "I ran to the water fountain and . . . " The second student might then finish, ". . . drank until the water ran out my ears." And so on.

- It can be fun to tape-record your stories and then play them back.

Activity 55
NEIGHBORS

Skill Supported: Taking Turns in Conversation

FOCUS POINTS

- Have fun.

- Practice taking turns and meeting individual needs.

- Learn to include everyone.

PREPARATION AND MATERIALS

Spot markers for each person (half sheets of scrap paper work well for this)

DIRECTIONS

Have the class form a circle, with each person standing on a spot marker. You stand in the middle. Tell students the object is to find out information about each other. Explain that the person in the middle (you at this point) can ask any yes-or-no question he or she wants, with only one condition: *the question the person is asking must be one that he or she would answer yes.* For example, it would be acceptable for Student X to ask "Do you have a sister?" *only* if Student X has a sister. Student Y could ask "Do you like math?" only if he himself liked math.

When the person in the center asks a question, everyone who can answer yes to that question is to move from his or her spot and find an empty one. The catch is that the person in the middle also has to find a spot in the circle, which means there will be one person left without a spot. That person is to go to the middle of the circle and ask the next question.

With elementary age students, many *want* to be in the middle, which causes a bit of a dilemma. If a half dozen students are pretending not to see an empty spot, the game soon slows to a snail's pace and becomes boring for those who wish to keep moving. If this occurs, stop the action and ask how those who want to be in the middle can meet their need, while those who want to keep the game moving can also meet their need. Choose a strategy and try it out. When working with older students, being in the middle is often perceived as less desirable, and people generally hurry to the spot markers.

PROCESSING PROMPTS

- Why was it necessary to take turns in this activity?

- What types of questions made the most people move?

- What types of questions made the fewest people move?

- Did you feel put on the spot by being in the middle? Do you ever feel put on the spot in class? Do I ever put you on the spot?

- How did everyone meet their needs in this game?

- What can we do to try to meet the needs of everyone in this class?

Activity 56
A WHAT?

Skill Supported: Taking Turns in Conversation

FOCUS POINTS

- Have fun.

- Practice taking turns.

- Experience what happens when everyone talks at once.

PREPARATION AND MATERIALS

Two items that can be passed from person to person

DIRECTIONS

Have everyone sit in a circle, and sit with them. Explain that you are going to turn to the person on your right and say "This is an aardvark." That person is to reply "A what?" You will then say "An aardvark" and hand one object to him. He (#2) then turns to the person on his right (#3) and says, "This is an aardvark." She replies with "A what?" and he turns back to you and says "A what?" You reply with "an aardvark." He turns back to #3 and repeats, "an aardvark." Person #3 turns to #4 and says, "This is an aardvark." Person #4 says "A what?" to #3, who passes it to #2, who then passes it to you. You reply with the standard "an aardvark," which is passed back up the line. As you can see, each time the message travels back to the beginning (you), the new message slingshots back to the end of the line.

Once the aardvark message travels for a while, send another object to your left, with the message: "This is a gorilla." Eventually, the "aardvark" and the "gorilla" will meet on the other side of the circle, and chaos will ensue. Students will likely find it almost impossible to focus well enough to get the two objects all the way around.

PROCESSING PROMPTS

- What happened when the two messages met?

- Why do you think it was harder to communicate then?

- What strategies did you use to try to make the communication work?

- What happens in real life when many people try to communicate at the same time? What happens in class?

- What strategies can we use in class to make our communications more clear?

Activity 57

CLAYMATION

Skill Supported: Taking Turns

FOCUS POINTS

- Have fun.

- Practice taking turns.

- Learn to include everyone.

PREPARATION AND MATERIALS

A lump of clay for each group of four to five students; several cards, each with the name of a different object written on it—each object should fall into one of three categories: things around the house, monuments, and animals

DIRECTIONS

Divide students into groups of four to five, and have them sit together in those groups. Give each group a lump of clay. Explain that in this activity, they will take turns being the "claymaker" who creates an object. The other students' task will be to try to identify what the claymaker is creating. Give the groups an opportunity to decide on an order.

Have the first claymaker from each group choose a card at random. The claymakers are then to go back to their groups and begin sculpting the object that is on their card. When the group guesses what it is, the next claymaker should return the card and get another.

PROCESSING PROMPTS

- How did your group decide the order in which you would do this activity? Was it fair?

- Did you keep the order or change it during the activity? Why?

- Did you feel the role of claymaker was more important than the role of guesser? Why or why not?

- Working together means taking on different roles and taking turns. What things should we consider when deciding about taking turns?

- How and when do we take turns in class? Is it sometimes difficult to wait your turn?

Activity 58

IMPULSE

Skill Supported: Taking Turns in Conversation

FOCUS POINTS

- Have fun.

- Practice taking turns communicating a nonverbal message.

PREPARATION AND MATERIALS

None

DIRECTIONS

Ask the class to sit or stand in a circle. Tell students the objective of this activity is to pass a nonverbal signal, or impulse, from person to person around the circle, much like "the wave" at a basketball game. Start with a handclap. Clap once by yourself, then turn to the person on your left, who will attempt to clap at the same time. That person will then turn to the next person, who will try to clap at the same time. This continues until it returns to the beginning. Then try doing it both directions at once.

Try sending another signal around by holding hands and gently squeezing the hand of the person next to you. He or she squeezes the hand of the next person, and so on around the circle. Try both directions. Then try adding a word to the hand squeeze: perhaps adding "hello" in one direction and "goodbye" in the other.

Finally, instruct everyone to move their tables or desks together in a circle and put both hands flat on the table. Try passing an impulse in which you gently slap your right and then your left hand on the table, the person to your left does the same, and it continues around the circle until it returns to the beginning. Then have everyone cross their arms over the arms of the people on either side of them. Try sending the impulse around in order of the hands.

PROCESSING PROMPTS

- Which of these impulses was the easiest? Most difficult? Why?

- Was it hard handling more than one message at a time? How did you deal with it?

- Did you ever find yourself going out of turn? When and why do you think this happened?

- What do you think would happen to the message if we just took a turn whenever we wanted? Let's try it.

- What strategies can we use to make sure everyone gets a turn to speak in class discussions?

Activity 59
KING/QUEEN FROG

Skill Supported: Taking Turns

FOCUS POINTS

- Have fun.

- Practice taking turns.

PREPARATION AND MATERIALS

None

DIRECTIONS

Have the class sit in a circle so everyone can see everyone else. Teach students a motion that signifies King/Queen Frog. This motion consists of holding one palm up and bounding the other palm off of it, thus making a slapping noise. Ask everyone to practice it. Now ask each student to make up a motion that signifies some animal. For example, one person might put both hands on his head with the fingers up, signifying a deer. Another person might flap her arms, pantomiming a chicken.

Give everyone a turn to show his or her motion, then go around one more time to help people remember a few of them. Explain that you will start the game by doing the King/Queen Frog motion and then passing to someone else by doing his or her motion. That person is to do his or her own motion, and then someone else's. For example, you might do the King/Queen Frog motion and then flap your arms to pass to the "chicken." The chicken might flap his or her arms and then make the signal for the deer. The deer would then take over and pass to another person.

This activity continues until someone makes a mistake, like forgetting to do his or her own motion, doing a motion incorrectly, or being too slow to make a motion. The person who made the mistake should then take your spot as the King/Queen Frog, and everyone should move over one spot until that person's spot is filled. This means that some of the students will not move. The challenge here is that the motion stays with the spot and not the person. The new

King/Queen Frog starts the game, and it continues again until someone makes a mistake.

PROCESSING PROMPTS

- How much concentration did it take to do this activity? How could you tell that people were concentrating?

- Are there times when you do not get a turn to speak during a group discussion because people just are not paying attention? How does that make you feel?

- How can we make sure that people get a turn to speak?

EXTENDING ACTIVITY

Have a class discussion to help students realize that in class (in life), different situations have different conventions. As an example, you might point out that students may be required to raise their hands and be acknowledged during full-class instruction, but may speak at will during small-group work. Be sure to talk about the different skills required by different situations.

Activity 60

WATCH IT

Skill Supported: Taking Turns

FOCUS POINTS

- Have fun.

- Practice taking turns.

- Work on communicating about taking turns.

PREPARATION AND MATERIALS

A few soft, throwable objects

DIRECTIONS

Have the class stand in a circle. Take out an object and tell students that this activity is designed to help them communicate about taking turns. Explain that each person will take turns throwing or ducking the object. It will be difficult for them to know when to duck, however, unless the person throwing communicates that he or she wishes to throw the object.

Tell students they will be tossing the object around the circle. When someone has the object, he or she is to throw it to the *second person* away on the right or left. Before throwing, the person must communicate to the person next to him or her by saying "watch it." That person, then, is to duck so that the object can be thrown. Once the object is going around smoothly, add more. Give them to different people in the circle, and have them go in both directions.

PROCESSING PROMPTS

- How easy or difficult was it to communicate when there was so much going on? How did you make sure the person next to you knew when to duck?

- When taking turns at anything, it is necessary to sometimes be the active participant and sometimes be the passive participant. How do we make these decisions?

ADVENTURE EDUCATION FOR THE CLASSROOM COMMUNITY

- When there is an opportunity to speak or do something in a group, do you tend to get in there to take your turn, or do you wait to be invited? Is one way better than the other?

- Do you think it would help our class if the people who usually jump in considered waiting for people who wait to be invited? How about if the people who usually wait to be invited jumped in once in awhile? How would it help? Why?

- How do we make sure everyone gets a turn taking on both the active and passive role?

Activity 61

FEELINGS FIND

Skill Supported: Using "I" Messages

FOCUS POINTS

- Help students associate feelings and "feeling words" with specific situations.

- Help students discuss their feelings with their classmates.

- Encourage students to use "I" messages to express (own) their feelings.

PREPARATION AND MATERIALS

Index cards with feeling words printed on them (Use the "Suggested Feeling Words" list provided on the next page, create your own, or ask your students to do so.) You may want to print the prompt, "I feel ___Feeling Word___," on your index cards if you think your students need it.

DIRECTIONS

Explain to students that this activity is designed to help them match feelings to situations. Tell them it is also a time to practice using "I" messages. You may want to have them refer to their "1-2-3: Communication Skills for Classroom Communities" (page 168) handout and briefly review the "I" messages section. Explain that you have a stack of cards and that each card has a different feeling word on it. Tell them you will call on a student, and that student will (1) draw a card, (2) say "I feel [word on card] when . . . ," and then add a situation in which he or she feels that feeling. For example, if the feeling word was "accepted," the student might say "I feel accepted when people let me join in a game." Do the activity, making sure that each student gets at least one chance to read a feeling word.

PROCESSING PROMPTS

- Was it fun?

- Was it easy? Hard?

- How might associating feelings with specific situations help a person (1) choose situations, (2) predict outcomes, and (3) control their feelings?

- Are there situations in school that you really like? Don't like? Need to be aware of?

- Why did I ask you to use "I" messages?

- How can using "I" messages help us communicate concisely in class? How can they help us communicate fairly?

- How important is it to use "I" messages in situations where we can predict that people's feelings will run high? Why?

EXTENDING ACTIVITY

Do the activity above, but this time allow other members of the class to respond to each feeling word after the individual student has responded. Doing this can help students see that not everyone views the same situation the same way.

SUGGESTED FEELING WORDS

Happy	Thrilled	Angry	Upset
Excited	Cheery	Furious	Lost
Foolish	Worried	Delighted	Giddy
Forgotten	Rotten	Afraid	Up
Silly	Betrayed	Hurt	Successful
Content	Rejected	Helpless	Enraged
Sad	Jumpy	Proud	Mediocre
Glad	High	Useless	Lonely
Scared	Trapped	Positive	Loved
Powerless	Secure	Intimidated	Fortunate
Frustrated	Safe	Mad	Protected
Nervous	Crazy	Respected	Needed
Jealous	Disappointed	Admired	Disturbed
Hated	Connected	Good	Accepted

Activity 62
FEELINGS BANK

Skill Supported: Using "I" Messages

FOCUS POINTS

- Help students develop a feeling word vocabulary.

- Practice labeling feelings.

- Help students accept their feelings.

PREPARATION AND MATERIALS

Chalkboard and chalk or flip chart and marker; a copy of the "Fabulous Feelings Vocabulary List" (page 210) for each student

DIRECTIONS

Explain that everyone has feelings and that having feelings is one of the things that makes us human. If you are working with older students, you may want to introduce the idea of man being the feeling animal or the sentient animal (possessing self-awareness). Brainstorm a list of feeling words with the class and record it on the chalkboard or flip chart. When the class runs out of suggestions, distribute a "Fabulous Feelings Vocabulary List" to each student. (If you are working with younger students, you may need to pass out the list almost immediately.) Ask students to compare the list on the board or flip chart with the one you passed out. Ask them to add any words from the board or flip chart that do not already appear on the list you passed out. Instruct students to put their names and the day's date on the list and keep it somewhere safe for future reference.

PROCESSING PROMPTS

- Was it fun?

- Was it easy or hard to think of feeling words? Why?

- Are feelings good or bad?

- Are feelings always OK? How about the behaviors we *choose* to express our feelings—are they always OK?

- What feelings do you experience in our class?

- How do you handle your feelings in class?

- What could we do to handle our feelings in class more productively?

EXTENDING ACTIVITIES

- Have the class write short stories that show how the main character handles his or her feelings.

- Read the class an account of a current event with the goal of identifying the participant's feelings. Discuss in small groups or as a class.

- View a segment of a video with the goal of identifying the actors' feelings. It can be productive to divide the class into small groups and assign each member of the group a specific actor. It is wise to have your students take viewing notes. Discussion can occur in the viewing groups or in the whole class.

- Make collages that illustrate a particular feeling. It can be fun to have the class work in small groups, with each group choosing or being assigned a specific feeling. When the collages are complete, the groups can present them to the whole class. Be sure to display the collages, along with the names of the students who created them.

LISTENING, TAKING TURNS, "I" MESSAGES

Name: _____

Date: _____

FABULOUS FEELINGS VOCABULARY LIST

Happy	Thrilled	Angry	Upset
Excited	Cheery	Furious	Lost
Foolish	Worried	Delighted	Giddy
Forgotten	Rotten	Afraid	Up
Silly	Betrayed	Hurt	Successful
Content	Rejected	Helpless	Enraged
Sad	Jumpy	Proud	Mediocre
Glad	High	Useless	Lonely
Scared	Trapped	Positive	Loved
Powerless	Secure	Intimidated	Fortunate
Frustrated	Safe	Mad	Protected
Nervous	Crazy	Rejected	Needed
Jealous	Disappointed	Admired	Disturbed
Hated	Connected	Good	Accepted

_____   _____   _____   _____

_____   _____   _____   _____

_____   _____   _____   _____

Activity 63
HELP ME TAG

Skill Supported: Using "I" Messages

FOCUS POINTS

- Have fun.

- Practice using the "I" messages of asking for and giving help.

- Practice stating needs.

PREPARATION AND MATERIALS

2–3 rubber chickens or other throwable objects; 3 bandannas; boundary markers

DIRECTIONS

You will need space to run around because this is a tag game. Set out boundary markers and show everyone where they are. Ask for two or three people to be "it," and then have them each get a bandanna and tie it around their arm. Pass out the chickens at random.

Explain that the students who are "it" are to tag as many of the other students as they can. When someone is tagged, he or she must squat down for the remainder of the game.

If someone is holding a chicken, however, he or she is safe and cannot be tagged. If someone feels he or she is in danger of being tagged, that person can ask for the chicken, saying "I need the chicken!" Only then can someone throw the chicken to that person. A person cannot get the chicken without first asking for it.

When there are only those people who are "it" and those holding chickens left, play another round. A variation of this is for those who have been tagged to ask for the chicken. When they get it, they are back in the game.

PROCESSING PROMPTS

- When did you find yourself asking for the chicken? Did you wait until the last second or try to get the chicken when there was still plenty of time?

- Are there times when people give their help to you even when you do not want it? Give an example.

- How might giving help without being asked for it be seen as disrespectful?

- How can we give each other help in this class in a respectful way?

- How can asking for help when we really do not need it make it hard for a teacher to give help to students who really do need it?

EXTENDING ACTIVITY

- Have the class develop a short list of things a student could do before asking for the teacher's help. This can be done in small groups or as a whole-class experience. Suggestions might include trying to work it out themselves, asking their learning partners, or looking in another resource.

Activity 64

PLAYING THE IFS

Skill Supported: Using "I" Messages

FOCUS POINTS

- Help students express (own) their feelings.

- Help students understand the connection between what they feel and what they do.

- Help students realize that while feelings are always OK, behaviors must be adaptive and fair.

- Help students see that they have choices and that they are responsible for their actions.

- Reinforce the use of "I" messages.

PREPARATION AND MATERIALS

Series of index cards listing different situations and prompts for a feeling and an action statement

Example

If I bumped into a classmate by mistake and she pushed me . . .

I would feel _____.

I would do _____.

Example

If a classmate told me my new coat was ugly . . .

I would feel _____.

I would do _____.

Example

If I asked to join in a kickball game on the playground and was refused . . .

I would feel _____.

I would do _____.

DIRECTIONS

Tell students that while feelings are always OK, behaviors must be adaptive and fair to be OK. Explain that the term "adaptive" means the behavior has a reasonable chance of being successful, and the term "fair" means the behavior does not hurt anyone or violate anyone's rights. Tell them you have a stack of cards with different situations listed on them. Explain that they are going to take turns drawing a card and telling the class how they would respond in the situation given on the card. Remind them of the importance of using "I" messages.

Have each student read the situation on his or her card and then respond with "I would feel . . ." and "I would do . . ." statements. If a student responds with a behavior that is not adaptive and fair, ask the student to rethink his or her response or ask the class for help. This is a perfect opportunity to point out that as responsible people, we always have choices and are responsible for our behavior. Remind them that the step between feeling and doing is choosing.

PROCESSING PROMPTS

- Was it fun?

- Was it easy? Was it hard?

- Why did I say feelings are always OK, but behavior must be adaptive and fair?

- What did I mean when I said the step between feeling and doing is choosing?

- Are there situations in class, at school, or on the playground where we need to make more or better choices?

- Is there only one adaptive and fair choice for a particular situation? Is it OK for people to respond differently to the same situation? Is it OK for people to feel differently about the same situation?

- Why did we use "I" messages?

- How will using "I" messages help us communicate? How might it help the other person hear what you are trying to communicate?

EXTENDING ACTIVITIES

- As a variation on the above exercise, you can have several students respond to the same card. This points out individual differences and perspectives.

- Have students write short stories that can be interpreted differently depending on one's perspective. It may be easier and just as useful to interpret fairy tales from a unique perspective. For example, a student could do "Little Red Riding Hood" from the wolf's perspective or "The Three Bears" from the bears' perspective. The wolf could be an environmentalist and Red Riding Hood could be an irresponsible, interloping flower picker. The bears could be seen as responsible homeowners and Goldilocks as a burglar.

Chapter 10

Problem Solving and Conflict Resolution

Would you persuade, speak of interest, not reason.

—Benjamin Franklin, American writer, scientist, and statesman

Chapter 10

Problem Solving and Conflict Resolution

In this chapter, activities designed to introduce students to the processes of decision making/problem solving and conflict resolution are presented first. You are encouraged to expose students to one of the processes through the introduction activity followed by several preselected supporting activities. If you plan to teach both the decision-making/problem-solving and conflict-resolution processes, we suggest teaching the decision-making/problem-solving process first. The conflict-resolution process can then be presented as a particular form of problem solving (such as problem solving applied to disputes between individuals and groups). It can then be followed by several supporting activities.

Activity 65

DECISION-MAKING/PROBLEM-SOLVING PROCESS INTRODUCTION

Skill Supported: Decision Making/Problem Solving

FOCUS POINTS

- Reinforce the principle that students are shareholders in every classroom situation and that they are expected to function as decision makers and problem solvers.

- Introduce a decision-making/problem-solving process.

- Prepare students to use a formal decision-making/problem-solving process in real-life classroom community issues.

PREPARATION AND MATERIALS

A copy of the "Our Decision-Making/Problem-Solving Process" handout (page 223) for each student; a copy of the "Possible Decisions and Problems" handout (pages 224–225) for each small group of 6–8 students; optional: a transparency of each handout

DIRECTIONS

Remind the group that in a classroom community, students are empowered to make decisions and solve problems. Explain that while there are many good decision-making and problem-solving models, it is important that everyone learn the model you will be sharing because it is the model you will be using in class decisions and problems. Show the class the "Our Decision-Making/Problem-Solving Process" transparency and distribute their copies to them. Review the process steps. Show the class how to apply the process, using one or two sample decisions or problems.

Be sure to emphasize the brainstorming step, reminding students not to stop and evaluate during this step. Explain that brainstorming is the process of generating multiple ideas, solutions, or plans without engaging in evaluation. Ask questions to check for understanding. When you think students have a basic understanding of the process, distribute the "Possible Decisions and Problems" sheet, one per small group. Assign a decision from the sheet, and ask students to use the process they just learned to reach a decision. When finished, have the groups report to the class and process the results. You may choose to do a second decision application or go directly to a problem application. For a problem application, assign one of the problems on the sheet and ask the groups to develop a solution using the process. Have them report to the class and process the results. Ask your students to keep their "Our Decision-Making/Problem-Solving Process" handout for future reference.

PROCESSING PROMPTS

Decision Application

- Were you able to reach a decision?

- What was the process like?

- Were you able to brainstorm without evaluating?

- Do you think we will be able to use this process for our real-life classroom community decisions?

- What kind of classroom community decisions would you like to make?

Problem Application

- Were you able to solve the problem?

- What was the process like?

- Were you able to brainstorm without evaluating?

- Do you think we will be able to use the process for our real-life classroom community problems?

- What kind of problems do we encounter? Will we encounter?

- What was easier—making a decision or solving a problem?

EXTENDING ACTIVITIES

- Ask students to brainstorm a list of decisions they would like to make or at least influence. Post the list and let it serve as a source of topics for some great initial classroom community meetings.

- Ask students to brainstorm a list of typical discipline problems they experience in class, in school, and on school grounds. Post the list and let it serve as a source for topics for some interesting intermediate classroom community meetings.

- Ask an artistic student to create a poster that lists the class's decision-making/problem-solving process steps. The poster can serve as a prompt for students trying to apply the process to real-life situations.

OUR DECISION-MAKING/PROBLEM-SOLVING PROCESS

Step 1: Identify and define the decision to be made or the problem to be solved.

Step 2: Brainstorm your options. Brainstorming is the process of generating multiple ideas, solutions, or plans without engaging in evaluation.

Step 3: Select your best option. If in selecting an option, you reached a decision and/or solved the problem, no further action is required. Congratulations! If not, proceed to Step 4.

Step 4: Develop a plan and act on it.

Step 5: Evaluate the results of your action and/or decision.

POSSIBLE DECISIONS AND PROBLEMS

Decision 1: We need a pet.

Your classroom community decided that it would like to have a classroom pet.

Now you need to decide what kind of pet the class should have. Things to consider include the following:

1. A pet is a living thing and requires care.

2. You are not in school on the weekends, and you have a long summer vacation.

3. Some classmates might be allergic to or scared of certain pets.

4. Unless you have a means of acquiring a pet for free, you will need to consider the cost of the pet and where you will get the money to buy it and take care of it.

5. There may be school rules that apply to pets.

6. In what ways will the classroom community enjoy a particular pet?

7. Anything else you want to consider.

Go for it!

Decision 2: Homework—do we really need it?

Your teacher has explained that the question of whether there would be homework was non-negotiable: there will be homework. However, he or she has explained the educational reasons for homework and indicated that he or she intends to assign five hours of homework a week. Your teacher ended the discussion by telling you that he or she would like your input into how the five hours is scheduled. Your task is to decide on a weekly homework schedule. Things to consider include the following:

1. Distribution of the workload.

2. The weekend.

3. Individual student activity schedules.

4. Predictability of having a fixed schedule.

5. Flexibility issues.

6. Anything else you want to add.

Be creative!

Problem 1: Gyms are not meant for sitting.

Your class has had to sit out its gym period four times in the last two weeks. The gym teacher has a rule that if things get out of hand, the activity stops, and you sit the rest of the period. The gym teacher knows you want to enjoy your time in the gym, and he or she has agreed to listen to any solution you might propose. Your task is to develop a proposal for the gym teacher that will solve the problem. Things to consider include the following:

1. The gym teacher's concerns have included people misusing the equipment, rough-housing, and not listening to corrections immediately.

2. You want to stay on your feet, not sit on your seat.

3. What things could you do to change or control your behavior?

4. What things do you think the gym teacher could do differently?

Keep your goal in mind and see what you can propose.

Problem 2: We don't have time to eat!

Your classroom is at the opposite end of the building from the cafeteria. Because you are not allowed to run in the halls, it takes 4 minutes to get from your classroom to the cafeteria. There are only two serving lines in the cafeteria, and it takes a long time to get your food. Your lunch period is 20 minutes long, so you usually have only about 10 minutes to sit and eat your lunch. People are choking on peanut butter sandwiches and developing indigestion usually seen only in old folks: something must be done! Your task is to help your principal solve this very real problem. Decide on a plan for doing so. Things to consider include the following:

1. How can you get to the cafeteria in less time?

2. How can you arrive at the cafeteria earlier?

3. How can you get your food faster?

4. How rigid is the 20-minute period?

5. Can your teacher make any changes in the classroom schedule to help?

6. Will you need input and feedback from your teacher or the principal? When?

Draft an initial proposal. If you need input or feedback from anyone, include it in your proposal.

Lunch is important—get going!

Activity 66

CONFLICT-RESOLUTION PROCESS
INTRODUCTION

Skill Supported: Conflict Resolution (Win-Win Solutions)

FOCUS POINTS

- Reinforce the principle that students are responsible for resolving conflicts they are directly involved in and for assisting in the resolution of conflicts involving classmates.

- Prepare students to use a formal conflict-resolution process on real-life classroom community conflicts.

- Teach the conflict-resolution process.

- Introduce students to several ways and settings in which the conflict-resolution process may be used.

PREPARATION AND MATERIALS

One copy of the "Our Conflict-Resolution Process" handout (page 229) for each student; one copy of the "Possible Conflicts" handout (pages 230–231 for elementary students, 232–233 for high school students) for each group of three students; optional: a transparency of both handouts

DIRECTIONS

Remind the class that in a classroom community, students are empowered to solve conflicts. Tell them that while you believe it is your responsibility to teach them how to solve conflicts, it is their responsibility to do so. Explain that while there are many good conflict-resolution models, it is important that everyone learn the model you are going to share because it is the model you will be using in classroom situations.

Explain that while understanding the individual perspective of another person is not a step in the model, it is an important skill that actually helps people want to solve conflicts. You may want to share the discussion of understanding individual perspectives in the "Teacher Resource Sheet: Background Information" on page

234. You may also want to use the resource sheet to help explain the conflict-resolution process steps of identifying areas of mutual interests and developing win-win solutions. (Note: The resource sheet may also be used as a student handout.)

Show the class the "Our Conflict-Resolution Process" transparency and pass out their copies of the handout. Review the process steps. Explain how to apply the process, using one or two examples of conflict situations. Ask questions to check for understanding. When you think students have a basic understanding of the process, have the students form groups of three. Distribute one copy of the "Possible Conflicts" handout to each group. Review the role of the mediator, using the "Mediation Musts: The Mediator's Role" handout on page 235.

Assign the groups a conflict from the sheet, and have them use the conflict-resolution process to create win-win solutions. Instruct students to take turns at being the conflict disputants and the mediator. Have them process the results of each round in their groups. Do at least three rounds, so everyone has the chance to experience being both a disputant and a mediator. Finally, have the groups report to the class, and process the results as a class.

Ask students to keep their copies of the "Our Conflict-Resolution Process" handout for future reference. At the conclusion of this activity, tell the class that this process will be used to mediate disputes between students privately and in community meetings. Explain that at some point, students will begin to act as mediators.

PROCESSING PROMPTS

- Did you solve your conflicts? If not, why?

- What was the process like?

- Did knowing how to brainstorm, take turns in conversation, understand individual perspectives, and identify areas of common interests help?

- Do you think we will be able to solve our real-life classroom community conflicts?

- Could we use the conflict-resolution process for teachers to do private mediation for students? For another student to do private mediation for students?

- Could the process work for a teacher to do mediation for students during a community meeting? For another student to do mediation for students during a community meeting?

- Are there other times it could be used?

EXTENDING ACTIVITIES

- Hold a class discussion to predict probable conflicts. Provide the list generated to groups of four to six students and allow them some time to discuss ways of avoiding these conflicts. Have the groups share their ideas with the class.

- On index cards, list conflicts that usually occur in your classroom, listing one conflict on each card. Have students take turns drawing a card and responding to the conflict. They might respond with ways it could have been prevented or with a possible win-win solution. If the student is unsure, simply ask the class to help.

OUR CONFLICT-RESOLUTION PROCESS

1. ***Identify and define the conflict.***

Each student takes a turn telling his or her side of the story.

- Why don't you go first?
- You'll get your chance when he's finished.
- Don't interrupt. He let you tell your side.

2. ***Identify areas of common interest.***

A common interest is something both students would like, such as preserving a friendship or avoiding a detention.

- What do you want?
- What do you need?
- What will happen if you don't solve this?

3. ***Brainstorm as many options as you can.***

- *Don't* evaluate!
- What are you willing to do?
- How can this be solved?

4. **Select a win-win solution.**

Be specific about who, what, where, when, how, and how much.

- Evaluate options and select one.
- Is it fair to both students?
- Can both parties say "I'm OK with it?"

5. **Finalize the solution and/or agreement.**

- Verbally
- Handshake
- Written agreement

POSSIBLE CONFLICTS: ELEMENTARY SCHOOL

Conflict #1: I Got Game

Background: Amy and Sandy are in the same room—the best room. Their teacher gives them and their classmates a lot of input into their classroom procedures. At the beginning of the year, the students held some classroom community meetings to decide how they could free up a little class time to spend on things they like to do that fall outside the regular instructional program. Everyone agreed that if they all stayed focused and worked hard, they would be more effective, get their work done, and have a little extra time. They also agreed on activities they could do during free time. One of these activities was to play board games.

Specific situation: For a few days, Amy has had her eye on a new board game that her teacher brought into the classroom. She has not been able to play it because it is new, and everyone wants to try it. She would like to play the game with someone who does not make fun of other people because she's not sure of the rules and she's not the best reader either. Today, when Amy starts to play the game, Sandy says she gets to play, too. She says she has to play because she is writing about the game for a report on her favorite free-time activity—and the report is due by the end of the day tomorrow. Last week, Sandy made fun of Amy during a game of Clue.

Conflict #2: I'm Puzzled

Background: James and Peter love to do jigsaw puzzles and spend most of their free time doing them. They sometimes work puzzles on their own, but really enjoy doing them together. They have been working on a 500-piece puzzle together for the past three days.

Specific situation: James and Peter are working together on their 500-piece puzzle. James takes a piece out of Peter's hand, says "It goes right here," and puts the piece in place. Peter gets mad and pushes the table. The puzzle slides off the table, hits the floor, and gets wrecked. The boys begin blaming each other. One thing leads to another, and by the time the teacher gets there, they are calling each other names and pushing each other.

Conflict #3: My Stomach Hurts

Background: The serving line in the cafeteria is really long, and it takes a long time to get lunch. Jay is upset because every day, Albert cuts in line. Jay follows the "no cuts" rule and thinks Albert needs to do the same. He has mentioned the situation to one of the supervisors, but nothing has changed. Jay thinks Albert is a bully, and if the supervisor won't handle things, he just might. Albert has stomach problems and must eat slowly. If he doesn't get his lunch right away, he has to eat fast and he gets really sick. Every day, he has a friend save him a place in line so he can get his food quickly and have enough time to eat. He is getting annoyed with Jay, who keeps telling everyone that Albert cuts in line and must think he's special. Albert thinks Jay should just mind his own business.

Specific situation: Jay is waiting in line, hoping the supervisor finally did her job so that he doesn't have to deal with Albert cutting in front of him. Sure enough, though, here comes Albert . . . and there goes Albert cutting in front of Jay again. Jay challenges Albert. The boys start to argue, and the supervisor intervenes.

POSSIBLE CONFLICTS: HIGH SCHOOL

Conflict #1: The Book Battle

Background: William and Sarah are two of the best art students in school. They both want to study art in college and both are trying to qualify for a special scholarship. They are in the same advanced-placement art class and have the same end-of-the-term project, due a week from the day the conflict occurs.

Specific situation: William and Sarah see each other in the school library, say hello, and go their separate ways. They end up at the same place at the same time, the reference desk, asking for the same book. The reference librarian says she has the book and asks who to check it out to. They both say "me," and an argument starts. Sarah says she *needs* the book to complete her project, and William says the same thing. The librarian says that if they don't quiet down, they will have to leave and neither of them will get the book. The librarian then agrees to hold the book for 30 minutes while Sarah and William figure things out.

Conflict #2: He's My Man—Or Is He?

Background: Mary and Tara have been good friends for six years. They are both good students, interested in getting good grades.

Specific situation: Mary has been going out with Joe for 4 months. She really likes Joe and thinks he likes her just as much. The Spring Dance is coming up, and Mary assumes she is going with Joe. In fact, they have already talked about the dance and about where they would go afterward. Out of nowhere, Joe calls Tara up and asks her to the dance. Tara accepts, assuming that Mary has broken up with Joe. At school the next day, Mary hears some people talking about the dance. She can't believe it when they say that her Joe is going with her friend Tara. Mary is furious. She waits for Tara at lunch and accuses her of stealing her boyfriend. The girls start yelling and end up in the dean's office.

Conflict #3: Social Studies Stuff

Background: Mr. Sarantennello is the best social studies teacher in school. He really makes things interesting. One of his best assignments is a research project that students do in teams of two. On this project, Rafael and Dawn are working as a team. Every time they go to the library, Dawn spends all of her time going through books looking for new ideas and additional material. Rafael has been working on the actual writing, and he wants to finish the outline. He is concerned that they will not finish on time and he also feels that he is doing all the work. Dawn thinks that she has been finding good information and that the project will be really good because of the research she is doing. She has no doubt they will finish on time—maybe *just* on time, but still on time. Rafael always has his work in early.

Specific situation: Rafael takes a book out of Dawn's hands, closes it, and says, "You are going to help me finish this outline." Dawn picks the book back up, opens it, and says, "Sure, just as soon as I'm through checking this book out. It could really help our project." Rafael replies, "How can you say *our* project when you haven't picked up a pencil?" Dawn gets upset and explains, "I'm creative: I don't work like you do."

TEACHER RESOURCE SHEET: BACKGROUND INFORMATION

- Understanding Individual Perspectives

- Identifying Areas of Mutual Interest

- Developing Win-Win Solutions

The ability to see things from another person's perspective is a very important skill and one that facilitates arriving at win-win solutions. Understanding another's perspective is more than being able to identify with his or her feelings or right to have an opinion. It involves being able to see *why* that individual might feel as he or she does. The ability to understand that two people may process the same experience in totally different ways and arrive at very different, but equally valid, conclusions is the first step to peaceful conflict resolution.

The ability to identify areas of common interest is also an integral part of arriving at win-win solutions to conflict situations. For example, the parties in a conflict might agree on the following areas of common interest:

1. They both value and want to preserve their friendship.

2. They both value and want to preserve their status as responsible students.

3. They both wish to avoid sanctions, such as calls to parents, parent conferences, detentions, or suspensions.

4. They both wish to preserve privileges, such as free time, ability to choose assignments or activities, and high levels of individual responsibility.

The ability to brainstorm, understand individual perspectives, and identify areas of common interest will help us in our endeavor to solve conflict peacefully through the development of win-win solutions.

MEDIATION MUSTS: THE MEDIATOR'S ROLE

Introductions: Put everyone at ease. Say hello, and use your name and the names of your classmates involved in the conflict.

Explanations: Explain your role. Tell your classmates that you are there to help them find a win-win solution. Explain that whatever solution is reached, they will both have to say, "It's OK!" Be sure to state that you are not a judge and your role is not to find somebody guilty and somebody innocent.

Ground Rules: Remind your classmates that you will expect them to be honest, to really try to find a solution, and to avoid trying to simply fix blame on the other person. Ask them to make sure only one person talks at a time, and tell them that name-calling and put-downs are not allowed.

Procedures: Decide who should speak first, and then have your classmates take turns telling their sides of the story. You can help by asking questions like "What happened?" "What happened next?" and "How did you feel about it?" After each person speaks, summarize what you heard. After both speak, you can share what you think the problem is (optional).

Common Interests: Listen for and point out common interests, such as both people wanting to maintain their friendship, both people wanting to avoid a suspension, and so on.

Brainstorm: Help your classmates look for possible solutions. Be sure to stop any attempts they make at evaluation. If there are a lot of options, write them down.

Select a Solution: Be specific. The solution should include who, what, where, when, how, and how much. Remember: both people must feel good about the solution or it's not a win-win solution. Both parties should at least be able to say "I'm OK with that."

Finalize the Solution/Agreement: Participants may choose to finalize by verbally restating the solution, shaking hands on it, or writing it out and signing it.

Activity 67

PATHFINDER

Skill Supported: Decision Making/Problem Solving

FOCUS POINTS

- Have fun.

- Practice giving and receiving help when asked.

- Practice shared problem solving

PREPARATION AND MATERIALS

A pathfinder grid (10-foot x 10-foot grid drawn on a tarp, taped on the floor); a copy of the solution below

Pathfinder Solution

Beginning

	•	•			•				•
		•		•					•
		•						•	
			•	•					
	•	•							
	•		•						
			•						
	•	•	•						
			•						
				•					

End

DIRECTIONS

Tell students that using the grid on the floor, they are to find the path to graduation. Tell them that although there is only one path that leads to the graduation ceremony, they will have multiple chances to figure it out. Explain that there are many pitfalls along the way, such as dead ends and places that they cannot go. Tell students you have the solution to the challenge, and their job is to find the path together, using the following rules:

1. They must go in single file.

2. Only one person can be on any given row at a time (horizontal), but there can be more than one person in a column (vertical).

3. They may move forward only one row at a time (rows cannot be skipped).

4. They may move only forward or laterally (to the sides, forward at a diagonal, or forward). They may not move backward or diagonally backward.

5. If someone steps on a solid part of the path, you will give a thumbs-up sign. This means they can continue.

6. If someone steps on a part of the path that is not solid, you will give a thumbs-down sign and that person must go to the back of the line.

7. Only one person can be moving at a time.

8. If someone wants advice, he or she must ask for it. No one may give any hints or thoughts on the next move (even by pointing) unless someone asks for help.

9. No outside props may be used to mark the path (only people).

Give students time to find the path.

PROCESSING PROMPTS

- Was it difficult for you to refrain from offering advice unless it was asked for?

- Did some people ask for help more than others?

- If you asked for help, what caused you to do that?

- How did you work together to get everyone to graduate? What worked?

- Were there communication problems? When?

- Did you experience frustration? How did you handle it? When do you experience frustration in class? How do you handle it?

Activity 68
BRAINSTORMING OUR BRAINS

Skills Supported: Decision Making/Problem Solving and Brainstorming

FOCUS POINTS

- Help students expand their thinking and problem-solving skills.

- Help students control their tendency to immediately evaluate ideas.

- Prepare students for success in creating win-win solutions.

PREPARATION AND MATERIALS

Several objects to be used as catalysts for brainstorming, such as a brick, bucket, towel, spoon, or book; one copy of the "Man, We Are Really Creative!" worksheet (page 241) for each group of 8–10 students

DIRECTIONS

Instruct students to work in groups of 8–10, and give each group a copy of the "Man, We Are Really Creative!" worksheet on page 241. Tell them they are going to practice brainstorming. Explain that brainstorming is the process of generating as many ideas, solutions, options, or plans as possible without engaging in evaluation. Tell students you will be giving each group a different item and challenging them to list all of the possible uses for that item. For example: a brick can be used to build a house or it can be used as a doorstop, as a paperweight, and so on.

Remind students that they are to generate ideas without evaluating as they go. Let them know that after you call time, each group will have the opportunity to present their list to the class. The rest of the class will then add uses the group missed. (Note: This will introduce an element of competition. We have known it to create an upbeat, fun atmosphere; however, if you think it counterproductive for your class, omit it.) Allow around 15 minutes for groups to complete their lists. Allow about 30 minutes to process small-group work with the class. It is a good idea to display the lists.

PROCESSING PROMPTS

- Was it fun?

- Was it easy? Was it hard?

- How hard was it to not evaluate each use as it was suggested?

- Were you surprised at how many uses you came up with?

- Do you think brainstorming will help solve problems and negotiate conflicts in our classroom? In our school? How?

EXTENDING ACTIVITIES

- If you really want to introduce an element of lighthearted competition, give points to your small groups for every use they come up with that was not on the initial group's list. Keep track of points and make it a game.

- Have students take their lists and turn them into an art project or computer publishing project. Display their work.

- Front-load activities such as "Pog's Jewels" (Activity 38, page 138) with brainstorming. Present the brainstorming process and ask students to apply it before they act.

MAN, WE ARE REALLY CREATIVE!

Item:_____

Most Common Use:_____

Creative Uses:

_____   _____

_____   _____

_____   _____

_____   _____

_____   _____

_____   _____

_____   _____

_____   _____

_____   _____

_____   _____

Use the other side of this paper if you are that *creative!*

Group Members' Names:

_____

_____

_____

_____

_____

_____

Activity 69

There's Nothing Common About Common Interests

Skill Supported: Identifying Areas of Common Interest

FOCUS POINTS

- Help students see the difference between positions (what disputants in a conflict believe) and interests (what disputants in a conflict really need or want).

- Help students understand how getting past initial positions can help open minds to identify common interests.

- Help students see that identifying areas of common interest promotes creating win/win solutions.

PREPARATION AND MATERIALS

One copy of the "On The Move From . . . " handout (pages 244–246) for each small group and a transparency of the handout

DIRECTIONS

Explain that being able to identify areas of common interest is a big help in resolving conflicts between individuals and groups. (You may want to remind students that this is actually a step in your conflict-resolution process.) Tell students that people in conflict usually hold an initial position, such as "You need to apologize to me first because it was your fault." Explain that each person in a conflict also has an individual interest—a need or desire that he or she wants met. For example, a person's interest might be "I was hurt by your comments, and I want you to make me feel better." In successful conflict resolution, both people can be helped to identify an area of common interest, such as "We both are hurt and want to feel better, and we want to fix up our friendship."

Present the transparency "On The Move From. . . ." Work through the first situation, and then ask questions to check for understanding. Break the class into small groups, and instruct students to complete the rest of the worksheet in their groups. Allow about 30 minutes for this activity, and then have the groups report to the class and discuss the answers.

PROCESSING PROMPTS

- Was it easy? Was it hard? Why?

- Is it sometimes hard to see the difference between initial positions, individual interests, and areas of common interest? Are there specific questions we might ask people in conflict to help them see the differences and make the move?

- Can you see how important being able to identify areas of common interest is to creating win-win solutions?

- Will being able to identify areas of common interest help us solve our classroom community conflicts? How?

EXTENDING ACTIVITY

Direct students to work in small groups to develop questions and prompts that a conflict mediator might use to help disputants identify areas of common interest.

ON THE MOVE FROM . . .

STATED POSITIONS TO INDIVIDUAL INTERESTS TO AREAS OF COMMON INTEREST

Situation #1: Two friends are in conflict over a coat one loaned to the other.

Stated Positions

Coat Owner: You borrowed my coat, and now it has a stain on it.

Initial Interest: _____

Coat Borrower: I did not spill anything on your coat.

Initial Interest: _____

Common Interest: _____

_____

_____

Situation #2: Two teammates on a baseball team are arguing over who is the better player.

Stated Positions

Teammate A: I'm the best shortstop on the team because I have great hands.

Initial Interest: _____

Teammate B: I'm the best shortstop on the team because I have a great arm.

Initial Interest: _____

Common Interest: _____

_____

_____

Situation #3: A boyfriend and girlfriend are in conflict over a tattoo.

Stated Positions

Boyfriend: I would look great with a tattoo. I'm going to get one.

Initial Interest: _____

Girlfriend: I hate guys with tattoos. If you get one, our relationship is over.

Initial Interest: _____

Common Interest: _____

_____

_____

Situation #4: Two friends have had an argument.

Stated Positions

Friend A: You were wrong and you need to apologize first.

Initial Interest: _____

Friend B: You were wrong and you need to apologize first.

Initial Interest: _____

Common Interest: _____

_____

_____

Situation #5: Two classmates are arguing about who should be punished for a fight.

Stated Positions

Classmate A: You pushed me—you should be suspended.

Initial Interest: _____

Classmate B: You called me names and embarrassed me—you should be suspended.

Initial Interest: _____

Common Interest: _____

_____

_____

Situation #6: Two best friends are in conflict over loyalty.

Stated Positions

Friend A: You are my best friend and you need to spend time with me.

Initial Interest: _____

Friend B: You are my best friend, but I like the new kid, too.

Initial Interest: _____

Common Interest: _____

_____

_____

Activity 70

WHAT I THINK—WHAT I SAY

Skill Supported: Understanding Individual Perspectives

FOCUS POINTS

- Have fun.

- Help students understand how what they believe affects what they say and how they treat individuals.

- Demonstrate how preconceived ideas and predetermined roles stifle open, effective communication.

- Help students understand how preconceived ideas and predetermined roles can hurt feelings and destroy individual relationships and classroom communities.

PREPARATION AND MATERIALS

3 x 5 index cards to make labels; masking or athletic tape

Using a thick marker, make six cards with six different labels. You may use the ones suggested below or create your own labels that better fit your class and their issues. (Note: Print only the label on the index card. The preconceived ideas are provided for use in the processing phase of the activity.)

Label		Possible Preconceived Idea
Talk over me.	⟶	Not important enough to listen to
Laugh at me.	⟶	Not a very cool person
Lecture me.	⟶	A very immature person
"Yeah, but" me.	⟶	Never has a realistic idea
Ignore me.	⟶	Not very popular
Ask if I'm serious.	⟶	Not smart enough to take seriously
Kid me.	⟶	Good for a laugh

DIRECTIONS

Ask six students to volunteer for a class demonstration. Have your volunteers sit in a circle at the front of the room. Explain that you will be assigning the volunteer group a simple task, such as planning a field trip, planning a holiday celebration, or selecting a class pet. Explain that to make things fun and interesting, you will be taping a label on each volunteer's forehead. The volunteers will not know what their own labels say; however, the rest of the group will communicate with them according to what their labels indicate. For example, a student's label may say "Ignore me." The group will do just that. Tape on the labels, assign the group a task, give them a time limit (5 to 10 minutes), and let the fun, frustration, and learning begin.

PROCESSING PROMPTS

For the volunteers:

- Was it fun?

- Was it frustrating?

- Would you like to guess what your label said?

- Even though you knew it was just a game, did any of you get your feelings hurt? Even a little bit?

- Were you successful at completing your task?

For the class:

- How do the labels we have for people get in the way of our communication?

- What preconceived idea(s) could be behind each label?

- How do preconceived ideas stop communication?

- Do labels and preconceived ideas get in the way of our classroom community communication? When? How?

- Do labels and preconceived ideas get in the way of our solving conflicts between classroom community members? When? How?

EXTENDING ACTIVITIES

- Have students write brief essays about the effects of preconceived ideas on (1) relationships, (2) communities, and (3) communication.

- Have students write brief essays on a specific current event where disputants hold preconceived ideas/stereotypes about each other. Ask students to explain how the disputants' preconceived ideas/stereotypes affect their ability to reach a compromise or a win-win solution.

- If you intend to run classroom community meetings, now is a good time to discuss how labels and preconceived ideas will affect the process.

Activity 71

EMPATHY

Skill Supported: Understanding Individual Perspectives

FOCUS POINTS

- Have fun.

- Try looking at the world through others' perspectives.

PREPARATION AND MATERIALS

3 x 5 index cards, each with one of the following nouns written on it; several copies of the "Question Sheet" (page 252)

Nouns

Frog	Weak person
Rock	Person wearing glasses
Dirt	Person with lots of money
Tomato	Person with very little money
Pine tree	Person on welfare
Eagle	Person who owns a corporation
Puppy	Person with braces
Bathtub	Person who can hear only with hearing aids
Automobile	Person in wheelchair who is paraplegic
Short person	Euro-American person
Tall person	African American person
Thin person	Asian American person
Heavy person	Native American person
Strong person	Hispanic person

DIRECTIONS

Divide the class into small groups of two to three students. Tell them they are going to try to view the world from different perspectives. Give each group a noun card and a question sheet. Explain that they are to answer the questions on the sheet from the perspectives of the noun on the card. For example, if their noun is a rock, they will answer the questions the way they think a rock might answer. After filling out the sheet, allow each group to present their perspective to the larger class.

This activity can be quite sensitive, especially when talking about people. Begin with nouns that are either inanimate, animals, or plants. This will give the students practice with nonthreatening items. Later in the year, when students are more comfortable with each other, try the same activity and use the people nouns.

PROCESSING PROMPTS

- Did you find it easy or difficult to take a different perspective?

- Why do you think people tend to make fun of people who are different from themselves?

- How might we stereotype people who are different from ourselves?

- Give some examples of stereotypes.

- How could trying to take others' perspectives help resolve a conflict?

EXTENDING ACTIVITY

Have a student come to the front of the room and select a noun card. Let the class then ask that student questions, which he or she answers from the perspective of the person or thing listed on the noun card. The class should try to guess who or what the student is.

QUESTION SHEET

- What might you do in your spare time?

- What makes your life harder or easier?

- Where is a comfortable place for you? Who are you comfortable hanging out with?

- What do people say when they make fun of you?

- How does that make you feel?

- What do people say or do that makes you . . .

  happy?

  sad?

  angry?

  proud?

  confident?

Activity 72
DIFFERENT GLASSES—DIFFERENT VIEWS

Skill Supported: Understanding Individual Perspectives

FOCUS POINTS

- Help students see that different people can view the same event very differently.

- Prepare students to be willing to view a situation or issue from the other person's perspective.

- Begin to build a platform from which students can find win-win solutions instead of just fixing blame.

PREPARATION AND MATERIALS

Select events to be discussed. You can use the ideas presented below, or make up your own.

Event: A big snowstorm

Roles: 1. Young child

2. City snow-removal worker

3. Adult who works 30 miles from home

4. Owner of a hardware store

Event: A big rainstorm

Roles: 1. Farmer who has crops that will die if they don't get rain

2. Homeowner whose house floods easily

3. Weather reporter who predicted sunny and dry weather for the next five days

4. Golf course owner

Event: The value of ACME stock goes down 40 points.

Roles: 1. Woman who just sold 100 shares of ACME stock.

2. Woman who just bought 100 shares of ACME stock.

3. Broker who handled the transactions.

Event: You receive $10 for a birthday present from your parents.

Roles: 1. Your parents are financially well off, and you are used to receiving expensive gifts.

2. Your parents need to be careful with their money. Your usual gift is a birthday cake.

Event: You receive a B on your math test.

Roles: 1. Math is your best subject. You always get As.

2. Math is your worst subject. You work hard to earn Cs.

Event: You are on a school field trip to Washington, DC. When you arrive at the hotel, you discover there has been a mix-up in the number of rooms available. Instead of two students to a room, it will be four students to a room with roll-away beds.

Roles: 1. An only child who has always had a room of your own.

2. A child who has 12 brothers and sisters and who has always had to share a room with at least four siblings.

DIRECTIONS

Lead the class in a discussion of how each event might be perceived by different people. Stress the fact that our individual perspectives play a large role in how we react to things.

PROCESSING PROMPTS

- Was it fun?

- Was it confusing?

- How can different people see the same event so differently?

- Do individuals in our class ever see things differently?

- Can we use our understanding of individual perspectives to help us solve conflicts? How?

EXTENDING ACTIVITY

Divide the class into small groups and assign each group a particular role for an event to be discussed. Ask the groups to evaluate the event from the perspective of the role you assigned them. Instruct the small groups to report to the whole class, attempting to convince the class that their point of view is the correct one.

PROBLEM SOLVING AND CONFLICT RESOLUTION

Activity 73
YOU WANT TO BE A WHAT?

Skill Supported: Understanding Individual Perspectives

FOCUS POINTS

- Have fun.

- Introduce the concept of individual perspectives.

- Prepare students to be able and willing to view an issue or dispute from the other student's perspective.

- Begin to build a platform from which individual differences are celebrated.

- Begin to build a platform from which students learn to find win-win solutions instead of just fixing blame.

PREPARATION AND MATERIALS

Four posterboards (see illustration); four markers (It is helpful to laminate your posterboards and use dry erase markers, so that the posterboards can be easily cleaned and used again.)

POSTERBOARD ILLUSTRATION

We want to be a turtle. We do not want to be a . . .		
Tiger	**Hawk**	**Chameleon**

Make four boards, rotating each animal into the "We want to be a . . . " category.

DIRECTIONS

Explain that you are going to give students the chance to choose an animal they most admire—one they feel has really good qualities. Tell them they can choose between a turtle, chameleon, tiger, or hawk. Ask for four volunteers to be the head turtle, chameleon, tiger, and hawk. Direct these head animals to go to the four corners of the room, and let students go to the corners representing the animals of their choice. Give each group the posterboard that corresponds with its chosen animal. Ask each group to list on their poster all the reasons they would want to be the animal they have chosen, and also all of the reasons they would never want to be the other three animals. After they do so, have three members from each group report to the whole class—two students holding the posterboard and one reading the answers. The results are usually hilarious.

PROCESSING PROMPTS

- Was it fun?

- Which group is right?

- How can one group be right if the others are not wrong?

- Why do people see things so differently?

- How can we use what we learned in this activity to have a better class and to solve conflicts?

- Do you think it will strengthen or weaken our class to have some hawks, turtles, tigers, and chameleons? How?

PROBLEM SOLVING AND CONFLICT RESOLUTION

Activity 74
WRITE YOUR NAME HERE

Skill Supported: Understanding Individual Perspectives

FOCUS POINTS

- Have fun.

- Try doing a routine task from different perspectives.

- Explore how people have different perspectives.

PREPARATION AND MATERIALS

Paper and pencil for each student

DIRECTIONS

Tell students you are going to ask them to perform a task they do every day—but from a variety of new perspectives. First ask them to divide their paper into four sections. In the first section, ask them to write their first and last name just as they usually would. In the next section, have them put the paper on their own forehead and write their name, using their forehead as a "desk." For the third section, ask them to again write their name, but with their nondominant hand. The final section is reserved for a drawing. Have students turn to a partner sitting next to them, and draw a picture of that person—but they must do it with their eyes closed.

PROCESSING PROMPTS

- Which of these sections was most difficult for you? Which easiest? Why?

- Have you ever had an argument with someone because you disagreed on what you saw or heard? Give an example.

- Did you find it threatening to draw a picture of someone? Did it help to have your eyes closed? Why or why not?

- How does the fact that people have different perspectives affect communication?

- What can we do to honor people's perspectives in this class?

EXTENDING ACTIVITIES

- Ask students to try other tasks from different perspectives. For example, use only their nondominant hand for an hour or try reading upside down.

- Have students talk about issues from different perspectives or collect articles on the same topic that are written from different perspectives.

Thanks to Craig Dobkin for this activity idea.

PROBLEM SOLVING AND CONFLICT RESOLUTION

Activity 75
PUT YOURSELF HERE

Skill Supported: Understanding Individual Perspectives

FOCUS POINTS

- Have fun.

- Introduce the concept of making choices based on one's experiences.

- Demonstrate how people have different perspectives.

PREPARATION AND MATERIALS

A list of questions with multiple choices, such as the following:

Multiple-Choice Questions

1. It is most important for me (a) to be optimistic, (b) to have strong family ties, or (c) to be unencumbered by possessions.

2. I believe it is important (a) to have good self-discipline, (b) to be part of a family, or (c) to know I am capable.

3. My personality is most like (a) salsa, (b) kiwi fruit, (c) cheddar cheese, or (d) pop tarts.

4. I consider myself to be (a) spontaneous, (b) organized, or (c) gregarious.

5. School is (a) a place of belonging, (b) a drag, or (c) none of the above.

6. Right now, I wish I was (a) riding a bike, (b) reading a book, (c) fishing, or (d) playing soccer.

7. Of these colors, my favorite is (a) green, (b) orange, (c) purple, (d) blue, or (e) yellow.

8. When I'm angry, I (a) get quiet, (b) get loud, (c) ignore it, or (d) confront it.

9. I hope that someday, there will be no (a) violence, (b) hunger, or (c) pollution.

DIRECTIONS

Tell the class they are going to place themselves in a group according to a list of choices. For each question asked, they must pick only one of the choices, even though they may see themselves in all of them.

Read the first question and list of choices. Designate group gathering places for each of the choices and have students go to the gathering places according to how they answer the question. Give them time to talk to each other about why they made that particular choice. Then have each group share their discussion with the whole class. After the class has processed the various choices, read another statement and have students again choose their groups. Continue in this manner.

PROCESSING PROMPTS

- When you talked in the small groups, did you find that most people had made their choice for the same reasons as you or for different reasons? Did this surprise you?

- What did you learn about yourself and/or others from this activity?

- Why do you think we end up seeing the same things from different perspectives?

Activity 76

HAVE YOU EVER?

Skill Supported: Understanding Individual Perspectives

FOCUS POINTS

- Have fun.

- Discover differences and similarities in experience within the class.

- Explore how different experiences influence a person's perspectives.

PREPARATION AND MATERIALS

None

DIRECTIONS

Instruct students to sit in a circle, and tell them you are going to ask them a series of questions. If they can answer yes to each question, then they are to stand and be recognized. If you want to make the activity more dynamic, you can have them go to the middle and high-five with the others who stood.

Ask the following list of questions—or, if you prefer, generate your own.

Have you ever . . .

- Broken a bone?

- Had a pet?

- Whistled through your teeth?

- Tried the art of origami?

- Made a sand castle?

- Skipped a stone in the water?

- Been to a professional sporting event?

- Eaten lutefisk?

- Not bought something because you didn't have enough money?

- Laughed so hard you fell down?

- Eaten lox on a bagel?

- Eaten chitlins?

- Been in a synagogue?

- Broken something and tried to hide it?

- Eaten at a friend's house and not liked what was served?

- Gone to bed hungry?

- Been on TV?

- Known anyone who can speak more than two languages?

- Given blood?

- Pushed on a door when it said "pull" (or vice versa)?

- Eaten grits?

- Been told that you have an accent?

- Been excluded because of your age or the way you look?

- Been included because of your age or the way you look?

- Gotten a gift that you didn't like but said "thank you" anyway?

- Gotten a parking ticket?

- Been out of your time zone?

- Been out of your state?

- Been out of your country?

- Tripped in front of a large group of people?

- Done something you weren't supposed to do and were caught?

- Plugged your ears to hear the shower running on your head?

- Gotten an autograph from a famous person? Who?

- Baked a cake or pie from scratch?

- Eaten kimchi?

- Been in a Catholic church?

- Given yourself a haircut?

- Failed a course?

- Been in a mosque?

PROCESSING PROMPTS

- Were you surprised by the number of people who joined you for certain questions you answered yes to?

- How might a person's experiences affect his or her perspective on things?

- Why might it be helpful to have a wide variety of perspectives?

- How can varying perspectives cause communication problems?

- How can we better understand other people's perspectives? What strategies can we use?

EXTENDING ACTIVITY

Ask students to write their own "have you ever?" questions and repeat the activity.

Adapted from original concept by Karl Rohnke.

Activity 77

CAPTAIN VIDEO

Skill Supported: Understanding Individual Perspectives

FOCUS POINTS

- Have fun.

- Help students understand that people view the world from different perspectives.

PREPARATION AND MATERIALS

None

DIRECTIONS

Have everyone sit in a circle, but facing out from the center. Explain that a visual message will be passed around the circle, but they may not see it until it is their turn. (You may want to have them close their eyes until it is their turn.)

Tell them that when they are tapped on the shoulder, they are to turn around, see the message, tap the person next to them and then pass the message on. Once they see the message, they can watch (and laugh, if appropriate), but they may not say anything.

Start by tapping the person next to you and do a simple three- or four-part mime. For example, you might put your hands on your head, make a surprise face, jump twice, and slap your knees. That person is then to tap the next person and copy the mime as well as he or she can.

The message is passed around the circle until it gets to the last person. At this point, the two of you should face each other, count to three, then both do the message. The message, of course, will have changed. As it goes around, those watching should be able to see the changes unfold before their eyes.

PROCESSING PROMPTS

- How did the message change from beginning to end?

- What do you think caused the changes to occur?

- As an observer, how was your perspective different from the person who was giving or receiving the message?

EXTENDING ACTIVITY

Choose a busy picture that includes people and have each student write a story about what he or she thinks is happening in the picture.

Activity 78

A Very Big Knot

Skill Supported: Finding Win-Win Solutions

FOCUS POINTS

- Have fun.

- Practice finding a solution that includes everyone.

PREPARATION AND MATERIALS

None

DIRECTIONS

Have students stand in a circle, cross their arms over their own body, and hold the hands of the people next to them. In this way, each person's right hand should be holding the left hand of the person to the left while his or her left hand holds the right hand of the person to the right. Explain that the object of this activity is to end up facing in toward the middle of the circle with their arms uncrossed—but *they cannot release hands* to get in that position. Explain that when they are finished, the people to their left and right will be reversed. Give students time to work out a solution.

If they cannot come up with a solution, you may want to help them. The solution is as follows:

First, everyone turns around. Then, one side of the group must move in and step over or under the hands of the other side of the group. In this way, the circle turns itself inside out, and everyone ends up facing the inside.

PROCESSING PROMPTS

- Did you have any doubts that this could be done?

- Did you wish there were not so many people to deal with during the activity? How might it have been easier with fewer people?

- This was a win-win solution. What might a win-lose or lose-lose solution look like?

- What kinds of strategies can we use to arrive at win-win solutions?

- Is anyone facing a challenge in school that seems too tough or too big to get done? Could the community help?

- What kinds of qualities do we need in order to work toward win-win solutions (for example, patience, cooperativeness, and so on)?

Activity 79

COMING TOGETHER

Skill Supported: Finding Win-Win Solutions

FOCUS POINTS

- Have fun.

- Look for win-win solutions.

- Look for creative ways to reach goals and solve problems.

PREPARATION AND MATERIALS

One piece of rope per student (each piece should be a different length between 4–8 feet)

DIRECTIONS

Ask everyone to choose a piece of rope and find a place on the floor. Have each person create a shape on the floor with his or her rope and stand inside the shape. Tell them there will be multiple rounds to this activity, and each round will start when you say "go." Whenever you say "go," everyone must move to a different shape. (Students can walk between the shapes; it is not necessary to jump from one to another.) Explain that there are only two rules:

1. At the end of every round, everyone must have his or her feet totally encompassed within a shape.

2. During each round, you will remove one or more of the shapes. When this happens, the people inside them must move to a different shape (there is no room for argument here; if the shape is removed, they must let it go).

Before starting each round, make sure everyone's feet are totally encompassed by the rope. This means no part of the foot can be hanging over the edge.

The first problem the class must deal with is a willingness to share shapes. After awhile, the dwindling space also becomes a problem, with everyone trying to crowd into the remaining shapes. Eventually, someone usually hits on the solution—because the feet are the only part of the body that must be inside the shape, it is possible to sit down on the ground outside the shape and place one's feet on the inside.

The final round takes place when everyone is in two shapes. Make sure you have left a shape that is big enough for everyone's feet but small enough to make it challenging. Take away the smallest of the two remaining shapes and ask the students to fit all of their feet in the last shape. This is a wonderful photo opportunity.

PROCESSING PROMPTS

- Describe the win-win solutions you created.

- What were the alternatives? How would this have looked as a lose-lose or win-lose solution?

- What are the ramifications (effects) of win-lose or lose-lose solutions?

EXTENDING ACTIVITY

Instruct students to get into pairs. Tell them they are going to be arm wrestling, so it might be good to pair up with someone around the same size. Explain that you will give "free time" to anyone who touches the back of their partner's hand to the table—one minute of "free time" for each touch of the hand. They will have 30 seconds to see how many touches they can get. The solution is to work together instead of resisting each other.

Activity 80

PASS THE CAN

Skills Supported: Decision Making/Problem Solving and Conflict Resolution

FOCUS POINTS

- Have fun.

- Try a variety of solutions.

- Practice collaborative problem solving.

PREPARATION AND MATERIALS

A large coffee can

DIRECTIONS

Have students sit in a circle. Bring out the large can and tell them that the object of this activity is to pass the can around the circle without anyone using their hands. If the can touches the floor, it must start back at the beginning. Once the can has made it around the circle, tell the class to pass it around more times, but that it must be passed in a different way each time.

After the can has gone around several times, try the activity with a smaller can.

PROCESSING PROMPTS

- Did we come up with more ways to pass the can than you thought we could? Why do you think this was?

- How did we come up with so many different ideas? What allowed us to be so creative as a group?

- Did you feel that your ideas were being heard? Why or why not?

- In class, when is it really important for us to generate a lot of different ideas? When is it really important that people feel they are being heard?

Activity 81

PLAYING SOLUTION SQUARES

Skill Supported: Finding Win-Win Solutions

FOCUS POINTS

- Help students understand the concept of win-win solutions.

- Help students see that the best solutions are win-win solutions, especially for people who go to school together, spend a lot of time together, and have an ongoing association with each other.

- Reinforce the need to be willing and able to generate options.

PREPARATION AND MATERIALS

Transparencies of whatever "Solution Squares" forms (pages 274–275) you will be using; one copy of either "Solution Squares: Music Motivation" or "Solution Squares: Nation to Nation" for each small group

DIRECTIONS

Tell students they will be using brainstorming to identify options to conflict situations (introduce or review the brainstorming process if necessary). Explain that they are looking for win-win solutions.

Have students work in groups of four to six, and provide each group with either the "Solution Squares: Music Motivation" or "Solution Squares: Nation to Nation" form. Instruct the groups to first brainstorm all options (it is a good idea to list them on a separate piece of paper). Once they have a list of options, they should go back and place each option in the appropriate square on the form. Allow some time for discussion at the small-group level, and then process the activity with the whole class.

PROCESSING PROMPTS

- Was this an easy or difficult exercise? Why?

- Why are win-win solutions the best solutions?

- Why are win-win solutions so important for individuals and groups who have an ongoing association or relationship?

EXTENDING ACTIVITIES

- Have students suggest conflicts they want to address and then use the appropriate Solution Squares form ("Possible Outcomes—Classroom Community" on page 276 or "Possible Outcomes—The Community at Large" on page 277) to find win-win solutions.

- Study a real conflict, such as the race conflict in America or the conflict between the haves and have-nots anywhere. Ask students to use the "Solution Squares: Possible Outcomes—The Community at Large" form (page 277) to look for win-win solutions.

SOLUTION SQUARES: MUSIC MOTIVATION

During free time, John wants to listen to some rap music he brought to school. Tom wants to listen to alternative rock during free time. Brainstorm all of the possible outcomes and put them in the appropriate squares.

WIN-WIN	WIN-LOSE
Both John and Tom are OK with the solution.	John is OK with the solution, but Tom isn't.

LOSE-WIN	LOSE-LOSE
Tom is OK with the solution, but John isn't.	Neither John nor Tom is OK with the solution.

SOLUTION SQUARES: NATION TO NATION

Two nations with a long history of conflict are about to go to war with each other. They share a common border and are fairly equal in their ability to make and sustain war. Brainstorm the possible outcomes and put them in the appropriate squares.

WIN-WIN	WIN-LOSE
Both nations are OK with the solution.	Nation A is OK with the solution, but Nation B isn't.

LOSE-WIN	LOSE-LOSE
Nation B is OK with the solution, but Nation A isn't.	Neither nation is OK with the solution.

SOLUTION SQUARES: POSSIBLE OUTCOMES—CLASSROOM COMMUNITY

WIN-WIN	WIN-LOSE
Both students or groups are OK with the solution.	Student or Group A is OK with the solution, but Student or Group B isn't.

LOSE-WIN	LOSE-LOSE
Student or Group B is OK with the solution, but Student or Group A isn't.	Neither student or group is OK with the solution.

SOLUTION SQUARES: POSSIBLE OUTCOMES—THE COMMUNITY AT LARGE

WIN-WIN Both parties are OK with the solution.	**WIN-LOSE** Party A is OK with the solution, but Party B isn't.
LOSE-WIN Party B is OK with the solution, but Party A isn't.	**LOSE-LOSE** Neither party is OK with the solution.

Activity 82
ZERO IN ON YOUR ZONE OF CONTROL

Skill Supported: Conflict Resolution

FOCUS POINTS

- Help students understand that they control their own behavior.

- Help students understand that they always have choices.

- Suggest that really proactive people look inside to change what they can control. They are tougher on themselves and easier on those around them.

PREPARATION AND MATERIALS

Copies of the "Zero In On Your Zone of Control: Background Information," "Zero In On Your Zone of Control" graphic, and "Zero In On Your Zone of Control: Self-Evaluation" for each student (pages 280–282); optional: transparencies of all three handouts

DIRECTIONS

Instruct the class to work in small groups of six to eight students. Distribute all three handouts and present the background information. Using the graphic handout, have the groups write three things that fit in their Zone of Control, three that fit in their Zone of Influence, and three that fit in their Zone of Concern. Allow approximately 20 minutes for this activity. Ask the small groups to report to the class.

PROCESSING PROMPTS

- Was it easy? Was it hard? Why?

- Why would it be wise to spend more time working on things that fall in our Zone of Control?

- How could two people in conflict benefit by working in their respective Zones of Control? Would they be more or less likely to arrive at a win-win solution?

EXTENDING ACTIVITY

Assign the "Zero In On Your Zone of Control: Self-Evaluation" exercise for homework. Process the completed homework with the class. Allow individuals the opportunity to post their homework if they would like to do so. The posting amounts to a public commitment to change their behavior.

ZERO IN ON YOUR ZONE OF CONTROL:
BACKGROUND INFORMATION

Take Control

Proactive people maximize the time they spend working on and thinking about things by targeting the things that fall within their Zone of Control. They work on things they can actually fix, improve, or change! They look inward and focus on themselves. They are tougher on themselves and easier on those around them. They hold themselves responsible for their outcomes, accept their defeats, and enjoy their successes. Because they do these things, they can change the future.

Be Controlled

Reactive people spend little time working on and thinking about things that fall within their Zone of Control. Instead, they waste a lot of time worrying about things that fall in their Zone of Influence and Zone of Concern. They burn up time on things they do not have complete control over. They look outward and focus on other people and situational conditions. They are tough on the people around them and easy on themselves. They hold other people and situational conditions responsible for their outcomes. They do not accept responsibility for their defeats and often they cannot truly enjoy their successes. Because they do these things, they cannot change the future—instead, they repeat the past.

Principles of Control

Proactive people accept the principles of control; *reactive people* whine about them. The principles are as follows: You have direct and complete control over things that fall within your Zone of Control. You control your own behavior. You influence and have limited control over things that fall within your Zone of Influence. You influence the behavior of other people, such as your friends, teachers, and parents. You have concern about but no control over things that fall within your Zone of Concern. You have no control over past events or situational conditions.

ZERO IN ON YOUR ZONE OF CONTROL

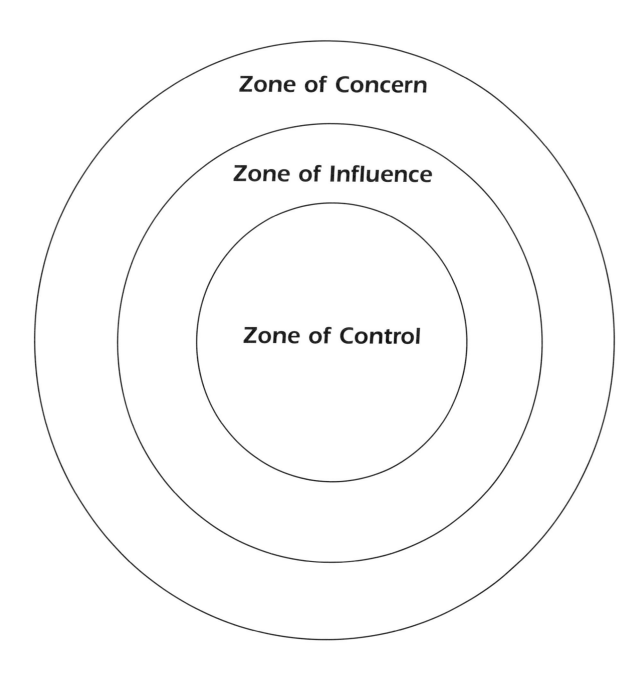

ZERO IN ON YOUR ZONE OF CONTROL:
SELF-EVALUATION

List three things from your group's Zone of Control:

1. _____ 2. _____ 3. _____

List three additional things you place in your Zone of Control:

1. _____ 2. _____ 3. _____

Complete a pie chart estimating how much time you spend working on things in each of the three zones.

Example

Write a promise to yourself indicating how you will spend more time working in your Zone of Control—working on your behavior:

_____

_____

_____

Activity 83
TAKE CONTROL OR BE CONTROLLED

Skill Supported: Conflict Resolution

FOCUS POINTS

- Help students see that their attitude, and ultimately their behavior, is a product of their beliefs.

- Help students consider how their language (spoken and self-talk) indicates the degree to which they believe they control their outcomes.

- Ask students to consider taking a proactive instead of a reactive approach to problem solving and to developing win-win solutions.

PREPARATION AND MATERIALS

A copy of the "Take Control or Be Controlled: Background Information" handout (page 285) for each student; a copy of the "Take Control or Be Controlled: Language Worksheet" (page 286) for each small group

DIRECTIONS

Direct the class to break into small groups of about four to six students. Review the information on the "Take Control or Be Controlled: Background Information" handout. Lead a brief discussion on the examples of proactive and reactive language, using the following prompts:

1. In each example, how does the speaker view him- or herself? Is he or she taking control or being controlled?

2. What do the things the speaker says (spoken language) indicate?

3. How about the things the speaker thinks (self-talk)? What does his or her self-talk indicate?

Instruct the groups to review the "Take Control or Be Controlled: Language Worksheet" and work together to change the reactive language to proactive language. Allow 15 to 20 minutes for this activity. Have the groups share their work with the class.

PROCESSING PROMPTS

- Was it easy? Hard?

- Were you surprised by the language you normally use?

- Can you see how our language (spoken and self-talk) can affect our behavior?

- How can being proactive increase our chances of solving problems? Conflicts?

- If we had a whole class of people who took control, what would it be like?

EXTENDING ACTIVITIES

- Ask students to brainstorm a list of reactive student language and post it in the classroom.

- Ask students to brainstorm a list of proactive student language and post it in the classroom.

TAKE CONTROL OR BE CONTROLLED:
BACKGROUND INFORMATION

Our attitude, and ultimately our behavior, is a product of our beliefs. A belief is an assumption we accept as being true—such as "all men are created equal" or "hard work equals success."

Examining our language (spoken and self-talk) provides a window to our beliefs. The language we use is a good indicator of the degree to which we view ourselves as proactive people . . . people capable of taking control . . . people who refuse to be controlled.

People who give up control use reactive language.	People who take control use proactive language.
I can't do anything—it's out of my hands.	Let's brainstorm some ideas.
The adults won't allow that.	I can convince them if I do some research and present my case well.
If only the coach liked me more.	I'm going to get to practice early, work extra hard, and stand out.

TAKE CONTROL OR BE CONTROLLED:
LANGUAGE WORKSHEET

Change the reactive language in the left-hand column to proactive language. Write your proactive responses in the right-hand column.

Reactive Student Language ("I get controlled.")	Proactive Student Language ("I take control.")
If only they would cut back on the busy work, then I could focus on the important stuff and get good grades.	
If the teachers made stuff interesting, I'd concentrate and get good grades.	
They really make me angry when they keep adding rules.	
I can't do anything about my temper. People just set me off.	

Activity 84

GRIN AND GRID IT

Skill Supported: Conflict Resolution

FOCUS POINTS

- Have fun.

- Help students identify the qualities and behaviors of a responsible classroom community member.

- Help students use self-evaluation to see if they are responsible classroom community members.

- Encourage the development of an internal locus of control.

- Explore how students are responsible for their own behavior and how they can influence the behavior of others.

PREPARATION AND MATERIALS

A copy of the "Grin and Grid It" worksheet (page 293) for each student; one copy of the "Qualities/Behaviors: Definitions and Examples" handout (page 290) and one copy of the "Responsible Classroom Community Members" worksheet (pages 291–292) for each small group

DIRECTIONS

Form the class into small groups of four to six students each. Explain that in this activity, they are going to see if as a group they can identify the qualities and behaviors of a responsible (good) classroom community member. Distribute the "Qualities/Behaviors: Definitions and Examples" handout for the groups to reference.

Distribute the "Responsible Classroom Community Members" worksheet, and allow the groups approximately 15 minutes to discuss and complete the form. The form is completed by listing a quality (such as kindness) on the horizontal line, and then listing three behaviors that operationalize (represent) the quality (such as shares, includes people, talks things out) on the three branches. When the small groups have completed the worksheet, have them report to the whole class and compile one comprehensive class list. You may want to have an individual in each group amend that group's list as you go. Another option is for you to do so and then provide each group with a copy of the composite list or post the composite list (print must be large enough for everyone to read).

Ask each student to complete a "Grin and Grid It" worksheet by listing the qualities the class identified and then graphing themselves. Instruct them to rate themselves on a scale of 1 to 10, with 1 being "No, this quality is not present at all" and 10 being "Yes, this quality is always present." Allow approximately 10 minutes for the individual rating/graphing activity. Then you can either have discussion occur in small groups or with the whole class. It can be fun to have an initial discussion in small groups and then either have an individual from each small group report to the whole class or have a general class discussion.

PROCESSING PROMPTS

- Was it fun?

- Was it scary?

- Are some qualities/behaviors more important to individual success than others? To class success?

- What happens when your qualities/behaviors do not match those of a responsible classroom community member?

- Does having a quality always mean exhibiting the behaviors? Is it possible to have the quality, but not exhibit the behaviors?

- Was anyone surprised when you graphed yourself?

- How important is it that we mentally graph ourselves once in awhile?

- Could we or should we use our graphs as a behavioral benchmark, and actually re-graph ourselves every so often?

- What happens when our behaviors do not match the way that we think of ourselves? What should happen?

EXTENDING ACTIVITIES

- The teacher may choose to complete a "Grin and Grid It" graph, rating the class on the qualities it identified, and share the results with the class.

- The teacher may choose to ask students to complete a "Grin and Grid It" graph, rating the teacher on the qualities the class identified, and process the results.

- The teacher may choose to have the class identify qualities of a good teacher. The teacher can then either rate him- or herself or ask the class to do so. In either case, process the results.

- Create a list of responsible classroom community member qualities that is suitable for displaying. This activity can take the form of an art or computer publishing project.

QUALITIES/BEHAVIORS: DEFINITIONS AND EXAMPLES

Qualities

Definition: Essential characteristic, property, or attribute. Character or nature of a person.

Examples: Kind/Kindness

Trust/Trustworthy

Fair/Fairness

Honest/Honesty

Hard working

Humor/Humorous

Behaviors

Definition: A manner of acting. An action or reaction. Something a person does.

Examples: Shares with others

Follows through on promises

Plays by the rules

Tells the truth

Completes all assignments

Tells jokes/laughs at themselves

RESPONSIBLE CLASSROOM COMMUNITY MEMBERS

Qualities   **Behaviors**

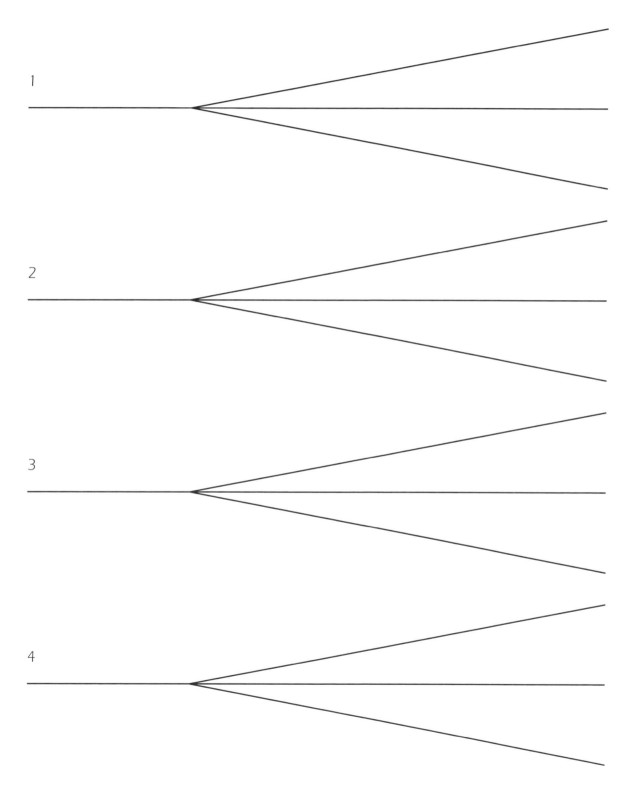

1

2

3

4

RESPONSIBLE CLASSROOM COMMUNITY MEMBERS—PAGE 2

Qualities   **Behaviors**

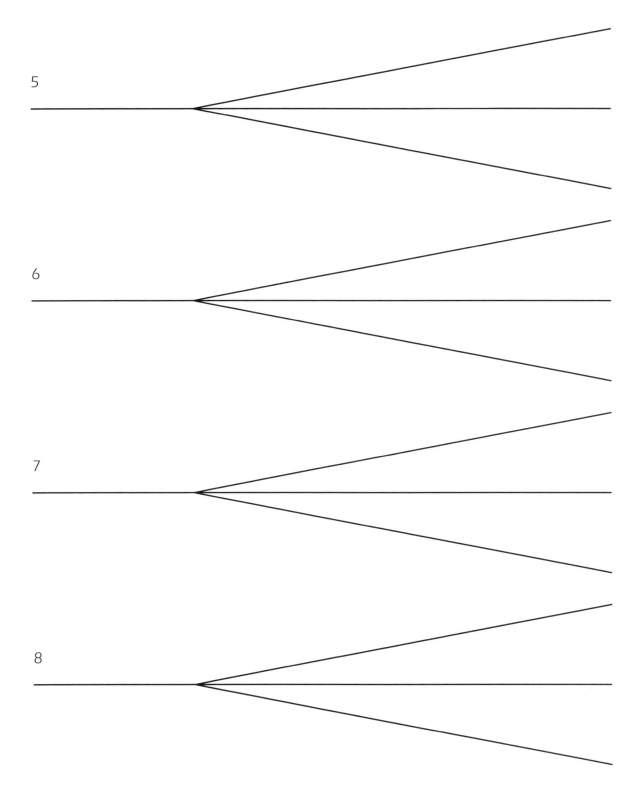

5

6

7

8

ADVENTURE EDUCATION FOR THE CLASSROOM COMMUNITY

Name:_____

Date:_____

GRIN AND GRID IT

	1	2	3	4	5	6	7	8	9	10
_____	•	•	•	•	•	•	•	•	•	•
_____	•	•	•	•	•	•	•	•	•	•
_____	•	•	•	•	•	•	•	•	•	•
_____	•	•	•	•	•	•	•	•	•	•
_____	•	•	•	•	•	•	•	•	•	•
_____	•	•	•	•	•	•	•	•	•	•
_____	•	•	•	•	•	•	•	•	•	•
_____	•	•	•	•	•	•	•	•	•	•
_____	•	•	•	•	•	•	•	•	•	•
_____	•	•	•	•	•	•	•	•	•	•
_____	•	•	•	•	•	•	•	•	•	•
_____	•	•	•	•	•	•	•	•	•	•
_____	•	•	•	•	•	•	•	•	•	•
_____	•	•	•	•	•	•	•	•	•	•

Activity 85
SHOE TIE

Skills Supported: Decision Making/Problem Solving and Conflict Resolution

FOCUS POINTS

- Have fun.

- Practice collaborative problem solving.

- Work on finding win-win solutions.

PREPARATION AND MATERIALS

None

DIRECTIONS

Ask students to get into pairs where at least one of the partners is wearing tied shoes. Tell everyone with tied shoes to untie them. Then tell students that the shoes must be retied, but with each person using only one hand. Each pair must then figure out how to tie the shoes as a team.

PROCESSING PROMPTS

- What strategies did you use to get the shoes tied?

- How did you communicate? What things did you say to make it work?

- What did you both bring to the problem to help solve it? Could you have done this alone?

- How was this a win-win situation?

- When is it a must that we work together in class?

EXTENDING ACTIVITIES

- Divide students into small groups to discuss why working together is working "smarter not harder."

- Have students work in small groups to generate lists of classroom activities where working together is a must and where working together would be a help.

PROBLEM
SOLVING AND
CONFLICT RESOLUTION

Activity 86

TIED FOOD

Skills Supported: Decision Making/Problem Solving and Conflict Resolution

FOCUS POINTS

- Have fun.

- Explore the idea of how reaching a common goal can help us reach win-win solutions.

- Examine how people bring individual skills to problem solving.

- Explore frustration and how to handle it.

PREPARATION AND MATERIALS

A simple lunch that needs to be prepared, such as sandwiches; a bandanna (or piece of cloth) for each person

DIRECTIONS

Instruct students to get into pairs. They should then stand next to each other and use their bandannas or cloths to loosely tie their ankles together (one person's right with the other person's left). With the other cloth, they should loosely tie their wrists together (one person's right with the other person's left). They are then to make and have lunch.

An alternative way to conduct this activity, which is more challenging for many people, is to have one person in the pair use a bandanna as a blindfold and the other person hold a bandanna behind his or her back with both hands. In this way, one of the pair is sighted but without the use of hands, while the other person has the use of hands without sight. Together, they must figure out how to help each other make and eat lunch.

PROCESSING PROMPTS

- What skills did each person bring to the task? How did these skills come together to accomplish the task? In other words, how did you arrive at a win-win solution?

- Had you not worked together, how might this have turned out differently?

- What were some of your strategies for making this work?

- What are some skills you bring to problem solving?

- How can we be sure to draw on *everyone's* strengths/skills when we have a task to accomplish? Why would this even be important to do?

- Did anyone become frustrated? What did you do? Was it helpful?

- How do we handle frustration in class?

EXTENDING ACTIVITY

Invite your principal in for lunch and surprise him or her by serving "Tied Food."

Part III

Going Further

Putting It All Together: Community Meetings and Activities That Make Them Productive

Provide a vehicle for honest, open communication to occur, and it will—the vehicle is the classroom community meeting.

—Ambrose Panico

Chapter 11

Putting It All Together: Community Meetings and Activities That Make Them Productive

The classroom community meeting is, at its core, an opportunity for teacher and students to sit down and talk about what is important to them. One week it may be important to discuss how individuals and the community can prepare for upcoming achievement tests. The next week's agenda might include planning for a holiday celebration or a big field trip. It might also include developing a plan to avoid problems that have been occurring during physical education. Another week, a scheduled planning item might be postponed to allow time for the community to help two students address an ongoing conflict.

The classroom community meeting provides students with a wonderful opportunity to apply the skills and processes they have learned to real-life situations. If you have taken the time to teach them how to be active listeners, they should be able to hear each other. If they have practiced taking turns in conversation, they will probably allow a speaker to finish his or her thought before offering theirs. If they are in the habit of making constructive "I" messages, honest communication should be possible. The best part of having taught these skills is that if communication does break down, you have something to fall back on, to remind students of, and, if necessary, to re-teach.

If you have gone a step further and exposed your students to the decision-making/problem-solving process, you can use classroom community meetings to give them a chance to play a significant role in conducting community (classroom) affairs. Your students will have practiced making decisions and solving problems in a variety of exercises, and they will be prepared for the challenge.

If you have taught your students the conflict-resolution process, they are ready for the greatest challenge of all: applying their conflict-resolution skills during classroom community meetings. A well-functioning community can use the classroom community meeting as a vehicle to help individuals and groups mediate conflict and find win-win solutions. You will have done much to ensure your students' success in this endeavor. They will know each other, be comfortable with each other, and have good, sound communication skills. They will have proven themselves successful at making decisions and solving problems. Most of all, they will be part of a community that supports communicating with good purpose. Still, whenever emotions run high, human interactions become more difficult—so proceed with caution.

MEETING SCHEDULE

We suggest that you have one regularly scheduled, 30- to 50-minute meeting each week. If you have some scheduling flexibility, you can allow the content and flow of the meeting to influence its length. The regular weekly meeting may be used to conduct community business, make important decisions, or solve conflicts. Many teachers find that an added benefit of scheduling regular meetings is that there are fewer day-to-day classroom disruptions. As students begin to rely on the process, their demands for immediate attention to issues become less urgent. Simply saying "I hear you and I'm putting it on Friday's agenda" is usually enough to restore order to the classroom. It is also a benefit to the student, because he or she learns to delay gratification.

It is, of course, vital that these students' concerns and issues actually be addressed at the weekly meeting. To ensure that this happens, you should keep a standing agenda and provide students with a means of putting their items on it. A suggestion box can provide anonymity; a clipboard is OK; and certainly just having your students tell you what they need to talk about is also fine. No matter which method you use, it is very important for students to understand that the meeting is as much or more theirs as it is yours. Initially, you may find that you have to generate most of the agenda items. However, once the process is in place for a while, your students' items will probably crowd yours out.

In addition to the regularly scheduled weekly meeting, many teachers also hold daily meetings. These meetings usually last between 5 and 10 minutes and are used as a way to check in in the morning or check out in the afternoon. They give students a chance to exchange greetings, make others aware of special situations or problems they are facing, review an earlier event or experience, thank someone for a favor, or anything else. Really, the meetings are just another chance to communicate and remind students that they are more than a group of individuals—they are a community.

There are also what we refer to as "as-needed" meetings. Anytime you feel that the learning process has broken down or is in danger of doing so, you have the option of calling for an as-needed meeting. For example, you might call a meeting because there has been a fight on the playground, and you know that nothing much will be accomplished until you process it. You might decide to call a meeting because the general level of classroom disruption is becoming annoying, and you want the students to evaluate their own behavior instead of having you externally control them. You might request that two of your students who are embroiled in an ongoing conflict let you call a special meeting to see if the community can help mediate the situation. As-needed meetings can also be called when there is unfinished business from the regular meeting agenda and you need to clear the communication logjam.

MEETING FORMATS

We believe there is much to be gained by keeping things simple. There is also much to be gained by keeping the end result in mind and focusing on the big picture. Try to remember why you decided to hold community meetings in the first place. You were ready to give up some control and allow your students to accept some responsibility. You wanted to give them an opportunity to apply all of the communication skills and processes you taught them. If you are holding community meetings, and the students are showing up and trying to communicate with good intentions, the big picture is being developed. You may occasionally find that a snapshot or two is out of focus when communication sometimes breaks down, and you have an unproductive meeting. But don't panic and don't let your students throw away their cameras! Let them take enough snapshots over a period of time, and your band of freelance photographers will learn their trade.

The following basic meeting formats should be viewed as mere guidelines. Although we suggest that initially you follow them fairly closely, once your students become comfortable participating in community meetings, they will want the process to become less formal, less structured, and more natural. We think this is a positive thing, and we encourage you to follow their lead. If communication becomes ragged, you can always impose a little more structure for a while.

REGULARLY SCHEDULED WEEKLY MEETING

1. **Open the meeting.** This can take the form of a general greeting, or you can begin the meeting more formally by conducting an introductory exercise, such as having each student give someone a compliment or share one thing he or she will do to make this meeting a success. The idea is to get conversation started in a positive direction.

2. **Review the agenda.** It is very helpful to put agenda items in order, with the highest priority items first. This means that if you run out of time and do not get to some items, those items will have a lower priority.

3. **Discuss items one at a time.** General discussion is fine. However, if an item is very important or if your group needs structure, you may want to go

step-by-step through the decision-making/problem-solving process taught in chapter 10. If you do so, it is helpful to post the process where everyone can see the process steps. If you have a conflict to resolve, we suggest you use the conflict-resolution process also taught in chapter 10. When emotions are involved, structure can help keep students on track and focused on the end result. You can serve as mediator with the group's support and assistance, or, as students become more comfortable with the process, a student can serve as mediator with support and assistance from you and the group.

4. **Review decisions, plans, and/or solutions** and take down items for the next scheduled meeting agenda. Some communities also like to keep meeting notes. This can add continuity to the process, but you should be careful not to let it interfere with communication.

5. **Close the meeting.** Simply saying "thanks" and "See you next week" works fine. Some communities, however, like to close with a simple exercise, such as having each student share one thing the group did really well during the meeting.

"As Needed" Meeting

1. **Open the meeting.** Explain the need or reason for the meeting.

2. **Introduce the issue, problem, or conflict** that is the reason for the meeting.

3. **Discuss the issue, problem, or conflict.** General discussion is fine, or you may choose to use the decision-making/problem-solving process or conflict-resolution process taught in chapter 8.

4. **Close the meeting.** Reiterate why it was important to take time to meet and highlight what was accomplished.

A more complete presentation of the decision-making/problem-solving process and the conflict resolution process can be found in chapter 10.

MEETING SETUP

The best seating configuration for meetings is a circle. The circle says "community" and allows everyone to make eye contact with everyone else. While forming a circle in a traditional classroom can present a problem, it is a problem worth solving. We suggest, then, that you take the time and trouble to form a circle for your regular weekly meetings and for any as-needed meeting expected to run

20 minutes or more. You may want to address the issue of circle-forming in an initial classroom community meeting ("How do we get into a circle quickly, quietly, and safely?"). For morning check-in and afternoon checkout meetings, you may want to have students simply form a standing circle around the perimeter of the room. This is fast and easy, everyone can see everyone, and because it is a very short meeting, you do not need to worry about sitting down.

REASONS TO MEET

The majority of your meetings should deal with community affairs, making positive decisions, and creating plans for action. Remember, the community meeting is not the only place to practice the conflict-resolution process or to solve conflicts. Reasons to meet might include the following:

- Developing a list of possible classroom community meeting topics.

- Making a list of things that would make the classroom more of a community (such as artwork/pictures, plants, or a stereo).

- Deciding whether to have a community pet(s) and if so, what kind of pet?

- Planning a special field trip.

- Planning a holiday celebration.

- Developing a list of activities students would enjoy doing during their free time.

- Developing a "reinforcement menu"—a list of things or activities students find rewarding.

- Selecting and planning individual or group goals.

- Selecting and planning a community service or service learning project.

- Developing a homework schedule and guidelines.

- Developing alternative assignments for the standard curriculum.

- Developing alternative methods for demonstrating content mastery.

- Discussing a particularly difficult learning task (difficult for the class or for individuals) and developing strategies to overcome the difficulty.

- Selecting and planning a culminating event or project for an instructional unit.

- Developing procedures for transitioning from one subject to the next.

- Developing procedures for distributing and collecting books, materials, or supplies.

- Developing procedures for traveling through the building.

- Deciding what qualities make someone a good friend or a responsible classroom community member.

- Deciding what qualities a good teacher has.

- Deciding ways the community can help individuals working on special goals achieve those goals.

- Developing a plan to support a community member who is having an individual difficulty, experiencing a family crisis, and so on

- Making a plan to address difficulties the class is having in the gym, on the playground, at lunch, in the halls, on the bus, and so on

- Resolving community issues, such as ongoing general classroom disturbances, a lack of responsibility in regard to homework/schoolwork, lack of respect in the way students talk to each other, lack of support for each other, and so on

- Resolving conflicts between community members by finding win-win solutions.

- Developing a plan to reunite any factions that may have developed around specific issues/problems, so that the community is preserved.

This is by no means an all-inclusive list, but it does provide a place to start. While we have attempted to present items in a hierarchy of increasing difficulty, the difficulty level of any item is relative and influenced by many factors. Your intuition is your best barometer.

IMPLEMENTATION SUGGESTIONS

Like anything new, classroom community meetings can be a little awkward at first. Most students get excited about having such direct input into their classroom environment, but they may not be totally comfortable with the process. It is not our intent to script for you how to initially implement the classroom community meeting concept. We hope your meetings will be just that—your meetings, unique to you, your students, and your situation. However, to help smooth the edges and get your meetings off to a strong start, we offer the following implementation suggestions for your consideration:

- Your initial meetings should have high-interest, positive topics, such as planning a field trip, deciding on a class pet, deciding how to use free time, and so on. After the first few meetings, you can progress to somewhat tougher topics, such as homework scheduling, the qualities needed in a friend, or how to avoid problems on the playground. Finally, you can attempt to deal with and solve conflicts. Remember, individual conflicts are usually much easier to resolve than group conflicts.

- At first, you should generate the agenda items to control difficulty and ensure success. Gradually, turn the lion's share of the agenda over to your students.

- You should model the role of mediator several times before allowing a student to attempt it.

Activity 87

OBJECT TRANSFER

FOCUS POINTS

- Have fun.

- Practice creating solutions to problems.

- Practice making group decisions.

PREPARATION AND MATERIALS

Two large coffee cans; 15–20 ping-pong balls or golf balls; a 3-foot length of bungee cord or old bicycle inner tube; eight pieces of clothesline, cut in 6- to 8-foot segments; a 25-foot rope for a boundary; a Hula Hoop

Create a circular boundary with the long rope and place the Hula Hoop in the center. Place the two coffee cans inside the Hula Hoop. One of the cans should be empty, and the other should hold all of the ping-pong balls. Place the rest of the materials randomly around the outside of the large circle of rope.

DIRECTIONS

Tell the class that there has been a terrible accident and that some toxic waste is in danger of escaping into the environment. No one knows what effect the toxic waste will have on the ecosystem and on the health of humans, fauna, or flora. To save the environment from this potential disaster, the waste must be transferred to a more stable container. Of course, no one can go near the toxic waste, so this must be done from a distance.

Tell everyone they must stay on the outside of the boundary rope, and the cans must stay inside the Hula Hoop. Using the tools that are strewn about outside the boundary rope, they are to devise a way to transfer the waste (ping-pong balls) to the empty container. Give them time to work on the challenge.

Although not the only way to solve this problem, students will generally tie the bungee cord into a circle and tie some of the ropes to it. They will then maneuver it over the can with the ping-pong balls, stretching it over the top so that it fits snugly. After that, they pick up the can and figure out a way to tip it over so that the ping-pong balls spill into the other can.

PROCESSING PROMPTS

- What was the first thing you did after the directions were given? Did you go and pick up the props, or stand back and think about the problem, or . . . ?

- Do you feel like you were involved in solving this problem? What role did you take? What did you do to help get this done?

- How do you think this worked? What makes you think that?

- What material resources did you have? What human resources?

EXTENDING ACTIVITIES

- Teach or reteach the brainstorming process and have students generate possible solutions and develop plans of action to attempt to solve the problem.

- Split the class into two groups. Have one group jump in and try to solve the problem. Instruct the other group to apply the brainstorming process to the problem first and *then* try to solve the problem. Note: You must separate the groups physically, so that they truly work independently and follow the instructions. At the end of the activity, bring the groups together and discuss both the process and the outcome. Suggest that some problems are "no-brainers" that do not require a lot of thought and planning, but that there are other problems in which careful thought and planning really pay off. Ask students, "Which kind of problem was this?" Discuss classroom and life problems that fall in each category.

Activity 88
SECRET LEADER

FOCUS POINTS

- Have fun.

- Explore the idea of modeling as a part of leadership.

- Help students understand that everyone has the capacity to lead.

PREPARATION AND MATERIALS

None

DIRECTIONS

Have students sit in a circle so that everyone can see each other. Ask everyone to secretly choose someone to follow. Explain that each student's task is to covertly do whatever his or her secret leader is doing. Remind students not to stare at their secret leader, but to be sneaky about it. Tell everyone to close their eyes and count out loud to 25. When everyone opens their eyes, they are to begin following their secret leader. Watch as motions ripple through the group. Sometimes everyone ends up doing the same thing. Other times, there are a few distinct groupings.

PROCESSING PROMPTS

- What did you notice about the movement within the group?

- What is the concept of modeling? What does it mean to be a model for someone else?

- What does it mean to be a leader? What does leadership mean to you?

- Have we just showed here that everyone can be a leader? Can you think of a time when you took on a leadership role?

- When do you like to lead in class? When do you like to follow?

Activity 89

SETTING THE TABLE

FOCUS POINTS

- Have fun.

- Demonstrate that everyone has skills that can be helpful when working in a group.

- Practice working together to solve a problem.

PREPARATION AND MATERIALS

A large tarp, sheet, or shower curtain

DIRECTIONS

Lay the tarp out on the floor and ask everyone to gather around it. Tell them that the tarp represents a table and that they are going to bring things to this table. Ask students to think of a particular skill or quality they have that is helpful when doing group work. In other words, what do they "bring to the table" when working in a group? Go around the group and have each person say his or her attribute or quality and then step onto the tarp.

After everyone is on the tarp, tell them that all of their individual attributes and qualities help make the class strong and that even when there are problems, they can use their skills to work through them. Explain that the challenge for this activity is that the tablecloth (tarp) is going to be pulled out from under them, but they must all remain standing. Their task is to figure out how to make this happen.

Ask the class to choose two people to be the pullers; ask these two people to step off the tarp. Their job is to pull the tarp in the way they are directed by the students still standing on the tarp. The students on the tarp can move anywhere on the tarp, and then decide how the pullers are to do their job. After the tarp is pulled, the students must be standing in the same place (in other words, they cannot jump off of the tarp).

Generally, students choose to rearrange themselves toward the back of the tarp, agree on a count, jump, and have the pullers yank the tarp out quickly.

PROCESSING PROMPTS

- What qualities and skills did you use to figure out how to solve this problem? Were they similar to the ones you announced before stepping on the tarp?

- Why is it necessary to have a variety of skills when working together as a group?

- How do you know when to step up and be heard and when to step back and be quiet during group work? Is it necessary to be able to do both?

- Did anyone accept a leadership role during this activity? Did leadership change hands during the activity?

- How do things like interest, motivation, specific skills, and specific mental or physical abilities help determine who should accept a leadership role in a specific situation? Would it or should it always be the same person? What do you think I mean when I say leadership in our classroom community should be fluid?

EXTENDING ACTIVITY

Use a roll of butcher's paper to create a "table" that is large enough for each student to place a small paper plate on it. Instruct students to work in small groups to discuss the special things each individual brings to group work. Give each student a plate and a marker (other art materials are optional), and have them write their name and what they bring to the "group work table" on the plate. If you provided other art materials, students may also decorate their plates. Post the table on the wall and direct students to take turns sharing with the class their group-work contribution and taping or gluing their plate to the table. You can repeat this activity often, using a different "table," such as problem solving, conflict resolution, community service, and so on.

This activity was created by Jim Dunn and Candace Peterson.

Activity 90
BLIND COUNTING

FOCUS POINTS

- Have fun.

- Practice taking turns.

- Work on solving a problem without verbal communication.

PREPARATION AND MATERIALS

None

DIRECTIONS

Tell the class that their challenge for this activity is to count to 10. Explain that although this sounds simple enough, they must do it as a group and without the benefit of communicating a strategy verbally. They will start the count with someone calling out "one." Someone else, then, will call out "two," another person "three," and so forth. The trick is that only one person may call out a number at a time. If two or more people speak at the same time, the class must start over from "one."

As the class starts over again and again, you will see strategies begin to emerge. Some people call out numbers quickly, while others wait to see if anyone is jumping in. Some people also choose not to call out any number, so that fewer people are involved and the chance of success is better.

PROCESSING PROMPTS

- What strategy did you use as you became more experienced at this task? Did it work for you?

- Did you find it easy or difficult to not be able to communicate verbally? How might this activity have been different if we had been able to strategize together?

- Why were some of you willing to not call out any numbers to make this work better? Was that a useful strategy? Is it ever a useful strategy in class?

- When might it be appropriate to sit back and let others try something instead of being the one to do it?

Activity 91
HAND CLAP

FOCUS POINTS

- Have fun.

- Explore the concept of modeling as part of leadership.

PREPARATION AND MATERIALS

None

DIRECTIONS

Hold your arms out in front of you, with one arm above the other and your palms facing each other. Ask everyone to do the same. Tell them you want them to clap their hands together when you say "go." Count to three, clap, and *then* say "go." Be sure to clap before you say go: "One, two, three (clap), go!"

You will probably find that 95% or more of the students will clap their hands when you do and not when you say go. This is a wonderful way to illustrate the power of modeling, that modeling is part of leadership, and that we are all models.

PROCESSING PROMPTS

- Why do you think so many people clapped when I did and not when I said "go?"

- What is modeling? How could it be considered a type of leadership?

- Who is a model for you?

- Are you a model for anyone? For whom?

- What type of behavior would you want others to learn from you? What type of behavior would you want others to model for you?

- What do you think is meant by the old saying, "Actions speak louder than words?"

- How do our actions in class speak louder than our words?

EXTENDING ACTIVITY

Have students write and share brief essays responding to the prompt, "I can't hear what you're saying—your behavior is too loud," or "Good leaders lead by example."

Thanks to Craig Dobkin for this activity idea.

Activity 92
BY THE NUMBERS

FOCUS POINTS

- Have fun.

- Practice decision making and problem solving.

- Practice using a trial-and-error approach to problem solving.

PREPARATION AND MATERIALS

10 paper plates for each small group of nine students (Number nine of the plates with numbers 1–9, and leave the 10th plate blank. Note: If you have a group of seven students, provide eight plates—seven numbered and one blank.)

DIRECTIONS

Clear enough area in the room, or find a larger area so each group can have ample space in which to work. Give each small group a stack of the paper plates. They should be mixed up so that they are out of numerical order. Tell students not to look at the numbers.

Instruct each group to lay their plates face down on the floor in a grid pattern that looks like the push buttons on a telephone. Tell each student to choose a plate on which to stand. This should leave one plate empty. Have each student choose to represent a certain number between one and nine (or one and seven, if there are seven people in the group). Make sure that each student chooses a *different* number, so that every number is represented. Explain that the object of the activity is for each person to end up standing on the number he or she represents, using the following rules:

1. Students may turn over a place marker to look at a number only if no one is standing on it. Once it is seen, it must be turned face down again.

2. Students may move only into an empty spot. Two people are not allowed to stand on the same plate.

3. Students can move only vertically or horizontally. No one may move diagonally.

Give the groups time to complete the challenge. This activity is much like tile puzzles, where there is one empty spot, and the tiles can move only a certain direction. Sometimes students may find it necessary to move someone off of his or her own number in order to get someone else to the right spot.

PROCESSING PROMPTS

- Did you all agree on how to solve this puzzle? How did you work out differences of opinion on how this should be done?

- What strategies did you choose to use? What worked for you?

- Did you experience any frustration? If so, how did you deal with it?

Chapter 12

Making the Core Curriculum Relevant: Community Service and Service Learning as Experiential Education

Self-esteem cannot be given; it must be earned. To help someone else is to help yourself and to build your self-esteem.

—Academy for Learning (formerly PACE High School) Principles and Practices for Building Reclaiming Environments

Chapter 12

Making the Core Curriculum Relevant: Community Service and Service Learning as Experiential Education

While it is beyond the scope of this book to serve as a community service or service learning primer, we have chosen to include this chapter for five reasons:

1. We believe community service and service learning is actually experiential education taught in the community.

2. We feel that connecting our students to their communities at large is the logical extension of connecting them to their school community.

3. We believe that students' experience as responsible classroom community members has positioned them to work responsibly in the community at large.

4. We know that many of our readers are already engaged in providing some form of community service and/or service learning.

5. We want to encourage those who are not already involved in this potent methodology to get involved.

WHAT IS COMMUNITY SERVICE, WHAT IS SERVICE LEARNING, AND WHAT IS THE DIFFERENCE?

Community service is pure and simple volunteerism. We are all familiar with individuals and groups involved in community service activities, such as food drives, clothing drives, literacy and tutorial programs, or mentoring programs. Because we are so familiar with community service, service learning can initially be a difficult concept to grasp.

The National and Community Service Act of 1990 defines service learning for us:

Students learn and develop through active participation in thoughtfully organized service experiences that meet actual community needs and that are coordinated in collaboration with the school and community. Service learning is integrated into the students' academic curriculum or provides structured time for a student to think, talk, or write about what the student did and saw during the actual service activity. It provides students with opportunities to use real-life situations in their own communities. It also enhances what is taught in school by extending beyond the classroom and into the community and helps to foster the development of a sense of caring for others.

Please be aware that community service does not become service learning just because it is attached to a school. A food drive run by a school, for example, would not be service learning; it would be school-sponsored community service. Such community service activities are valuable in that they provide students with opportunities to develop empathy, a foundation for social conscience, an ethic of service, and often improved self-esteem.

Service learning takes community service one step further by adding well-thought-out learning activities and goals to the simple act of helping others. As explained by Toule and Toule (1992), "Service learning is the blending of both service and learning goals in such a way that both occur and are enriched by each other" (p. 3). It is not difficult to transform a simple community service project into a service learning unit. For example, you could turn the school-sponsored food drive discussed earlier into a service learning unit by including any or all of the following:

- A math lesson

- A nutrition lesson

- A language arts lesson

- Application of higher-order thinking skills (for example, problem-solving the collection and distribution of the food)

- A citizenship lesson (for example, developing awareness of community needs)

- Preparation for the world of work (for example, learning human service skills and developing teamwork skills and attitudes)

- An opportunity for structured reflection

While there are many different models for implementing a service learning project, most follow a plan that includes these basic steps:

1. Select a societal need.

2. Recruit a community partner.

3. Align the service learning objectives with the academic objectives.

4. Implement and manage the project.

5. Facilitate student reflections throughout the project's implementation and at completion.

Service learning is engaged learning at its best, and can enrich the educational experience for all of our students. It offers countless opportunities for students to grow intellectually and socially while developing civic responsibility and gaining exposure to the world of work. It also offers an opportunity for young people to find meaning and worth in a society that often asks them to wait too long to be counted as a significant person with something to offer. According to Bonnie Benard (1992, p. 11), this delay in giving youth a sense of purpose and value contributes to their general disenfranchisement from society:

> Over the past 100 years, dramatic changes have occurred in American society in both the work force and family structure. Young people today do not have the same opportunities and they are generally denied the experiences that could prepare them for responsible adulthood. Lack of a meaningful role in society and the existing view of adolescents as problems contribute to the sense of alienation so prevalent among today's youth.

This disenfranchisement and alienation can lead youth to meet their affiliation and belonging needs in antisocial ways: "Unfortunately many young people seek validation through gang membership and other high-risk behaviors they mistakenly identify with to meet their very human need to belong, to be competent, to be independent and to have fun" (Panico, 1999). Our young people need to become contributing members of society as early as possible. They need to know that they have something to bring to the table and that they are expected not only to bring it, but to offer it. Given the stakes, we simply cannot delay in involving our young people in meaningful community-centered work.

BENEFITS TO STUDENTS

Involvement in service learning spurs and enriches growth on several different fronts:

Personal Growth applies to the development of the following characteristics related to self-improvement and self-actualization:

- Self-confidence and self-esteem

- Self-understanding

- Sense of identity

- Independence and autonomy

- Openness to new experiences and roles

- Ability to take risks and accept challenges

- Sense of usefulness and purpose

- Personal values and beliefs

- Responsibility for one's self and actions

- Self-respect

Social Growth includes the skills necessary for working with and relating to others in society:

- Communication skills

- Leadership skills

- Ability to work cooperatively with others

- Sense of caring for others

- Sense of belonging

- Acceptance and awareness of others from diverse and multicultural backgrounds

- Peer group affiliation

Intellectual Growth encompasses the cognitive skills necessary to enhance academic learning and acquire higher-level thinking skills:

- Application of knowledge, relevance of curriculum

- Problem-solving and decision-making skills

- Critical-thinking skills

- Skills in learning from experience

- Use of all learning styles

- Development of a positive attitude toward learning

Citizenship refers to the responsibilities of participation in a multicultural society and of citizenship in a democracy:

- Sense of responsibility to contribute to society

- Democratic participation (staying informed, exercising one's voting privileges)

- Awareness of community needs

- Organizational skills

- Action skills (persuasion, policy research, petitioning)

- Empowerment (belief in one's ability to make a difference)

Preparation for the World of Work refers to skills and knowledge that help students gain work experience and make informed choices about possible career directions:

- Human service skills

- Realistic ideas about the world of work

- Professionalism (dress, grooming, manners)

- Ability to follow directions

- Ability to function as a member of a team

- Reliable working skills (punctuality, consistency, regular attendance)

- Contacts and references for future job possibilities

Source: Duckenfield, M., & Swanson, L., *Service Learning: Meeting the Needs of Youth at Risk* (1992), pages 7–9.

COMMUNITY SERVICE AND SERVICE LEARNING

SERVICE LEARNING AND YOUTH AT RISK

> People do better when they love what they are doing than when they are offered a reward or threatened by a punishment to do what they hate. For too many adolescents with a history of academic and behavioral problems, hate is none too strong a word for the traditional classroom and the traditional lesson. We must offer them something more, something different, if we are ever to be able to discard the elaborate behavior-modification systems we build to motivate and control them—and if we are ever to initiate them as active participants into a true community of learners.

Service learning is proving an exciting alternative to behavior-modification interventions for at-risk youth, and we encourage any reader who works with these wonderful and challenging young people to at least explore this potent methodology. We believe it will allow you to take a step away from a curriculum of control and a step toward a curriculum of engagement. We have found that discouraged learners motivate themselves when academic skills become relevant. It is simply much easier for students to learn a 3/4/5 triangle in trigonometry class when they know they will need to apply this new knowledge to build walls on a job site, such as a Habitat for Humanity home, the next day.

We have also found that many a frustrated student is a kinesthetic learner, whose learning style did not mesh well with the instruction offered in a traditional classroom. These individuals learn better and more easily when offered an experiential learning format. Other students simply find school much more enjoyable when it includes physical activity. For many discouraged learners, the school building is associated with years of failure. It can be refreshing for them to sometimes move the classroom off campus.

Service learning often provides another, more personal, benefit for at-risk students. Many times, these youth hail from families who, for generations, have been socialized to be takers—socialized to depend on entitlement programs for their very sustenance. This taking usually has not been without cost. It has been paid for, to varying degrees, with a loss of self-respect, loss of personal competence, and resentment. For such students, one of the greatest benefits of service learning is simply being put in a position to be a giver. Participating in a service learning project offers many of these youth their first-ever opportunity to be on the "plus" side of the equation. The ability to share their knowledge and skills to help others is a powerful self-esteem builder.

To help you build a service learning environment for the at-risk youth you serve, we offer the following basic principles, and the practices that support them.

Principles and Practices for Building Service Learning Environments for At-Risk Youth

Principle	Practice
To be important, you must do important things.	Community service or service learning projects and/or partnerships must address an identified societal need.
Interest equals active learning.	Students must choose to participate based on a desire to help address the identified need and/or an interest in the skills and knowledge to be gained.
Academic learning is relevant to service learning tasks.	Content-area curricula are designed to accompany the service learning environment. The mastering of academic skills leads to competence on the project.
Discouraged learners learn better by doing and do better when they are involved in creating the lesson.	Students and teachers collaborate to identify the skills necessary to complete the task at hand and then decide on the best way to learn those skills. Experiential education has proven to be the most consistently productive methodology.
Discouraged learners do better in programs that stress learning over performance.	Students must be taught to think about what they are doing, not about how well they are doing it. Focus should be on work-group completion of identified tasks as opposed to individual performance.
Self-esteem cannot be given; it must be earned. To help someone else is to help yourself and to build your self-esteem.	Community service or service learning participation must provide first-hand contact with the recipient of the program's work. Opportunities for students to meet and partner with the beneficiaries of their work must be provided.
Reflection does not happen automatically.	Students must be taught techniques and strategies for thoughtful reflection. Regular opportunities must be provided for individual reflection and processing with the community.
There are no contingencies.	Unlike so many high-interest activities/programs, the ability to participate cannot be used as a motivator to encourage other desirable behaviors. The experience itself is the cure. Excluding students who need it most makes no sense.
Everything is built on relationships.	Students and teachers who share a common interest and work outside of the school building build better and richer relationships. Teachers become more effective agents for change.

Adapted from Panico, A. (1998, Fall). Service learning as a community initiation. *Reaching Today's Youth, 3*(1), 39.

For those of you who are new to service learning, we have included examples of service learning lessons. Service learning lessons vary greatly and may be the primary method of instruction (as in our high school example) or enrichment to the existing curriculum (as in our middle school example). If at all possible, we suggest you provide opportunities for your students to partner with volunteers from other organizations and the individuals who will directly benefit from the project. This is what Academy for Learning has done for numerous years with great success.

ACADEMY FOR LEARNING AND HABITAT FOR HUMANITY

Academy for Learning (AFL, formerly PACE High School) is a public school that employs service learning as a methodology for teaching severely behavior-disordered, emotionally disturbed, and general education students who have been expelled from their regular comprehensive high schools. AFL partnered with the Chicago South Region Habitat for Humanity affiliate and together they accomplished much. AFL students participated in the rehab and construction of Habitat for Humanity homes. They traveled from their homes in the southern suburbs of Chicago as far as Homestead, Florida, to offer their energy and apply their skills to Habitat home sites. Because Habitat has a philosophy of providing its families a "hand up" instead of a handout, Habitat families work not only on their prospective home but on the homes of other Habitat families.

This means AFL student volunteers worked beside the recipients of their good deeds. The depth and quality of this person-to-person experience cannot be overemphasized. The change it is capable of provoking in any young person, but especially in discouraged and troubled youth, is nothing short of spiritual. When a 15-year-old gang member accepts the heartfelt thanks of a 35-year-old father of three, the experience can be lifechanging. For a discouraged learner to teach drywall joint taping to a husband and wife anxious to learn is empowering. And for a group of kids from a "tough-guy" school to participate in Habitat's dedication of a home to a family is healing. These tough guys will know the family and will have partnered with them. They will have seen a dilapidated structure become a beautiful home and will have actively participated in the transformation. As a result, some of the tough guys will choose to drop their tough-guy identity. They can now opt for the identity of a significant citizen.

AFL now partners with senior citizens in their local communities to make badly needed home repairs that the citizens would otherwise be unable to afford. Students have also started a recycling program within their school and have created partnerships with a local daycare center, four local schools, and a food pantry.

COMMUNITY SERVICE AND SERVICE LEARNING

In 1999, AFL was named a National Service-Learning Leader School by the Corporation for National Service. It was also named a National School of Character by the Character Education Partnership in 2004. AFL also received the prestigious J.C. Penney Golden Rule Award for outstanding achievement in the area of community service. A Service Learning curriculum developed through an Illinois State Board of Education Grant is available through AFL. For more information, contact Jennifer Avenatti, Assistant Principal, 13811 S. Western Avenue, Blue Island, IL 60406, (708) 597-8862.

Providing time and structure for student reflection is a very important and often neglected part of service learning. It can be easy to focus on getting the job done at the expense of reflecting upon what students are learning. To make sure that reflection is part of the learning process rather than just something you do at the project's end, we suggest you have students keep daily or weekly journals. This sort of structured reflection gives them the opportunity to recognize the changes in themselves and how their work is benefiting the community.

There are also several strategies offered in this book that facilitate reflection of individuals and groups. We specifically suggest the following strategies to help students make connections between their service learning work and their newly acquired skills, knowledge, relationships, status in the community, self-esteem, and feelings of significance.

Strategy	Page
• Crumpled Paper	29
• Talking Circle	29
• Object Pass	30
• Feelings Cards	30
• Postcards	30
• Play Food	30
• Rating Scales	30
• Pick a Photo	30
• Creations	31
• Dyads and Triads	31

SERVICE LEARNING LESSON EXAMPLE

Area of Service/Commitment: To work in partnership with the local Habitat for Humanity affiliate to provide simple, decent housing for those who cannot afford it. We will provide labor to assist in the rehab and/or construction of homes. We will participate in fund-raising activities to raise money for construction materials. We will provide clerical help to assist the affiliate office staff. We will also help prepare for and participate in the dedication of at least one home. Our commitment is for the school year.

Type of Class: High School Construction Trades (Behavior Disorders)

Project Title: Residential Floor Tiling

LESSON 1 (50 MINUTES)

Goal: To become familiar with the materials necessary to tile a floor (such as various types of underlayment and fasteners, mastics, and vinyl tile).

Objective 1: Students will be able to identify three different types of underlayment and explain their respective qualities and applications.

Objective 2: Students will be able to identify four different types of underlayment fasteners and explain their applications.

Objective 3: Students will be able to identify two types of mastics and explain their applications and safety cautions.

Objective 4: Students will be able to identify three grades and two types of vinyl floor tile and explain their applications.

Activity 1: The class is divided into work/study groups, with four students per group. Each group receives a handout and corresponding sample materials for each of the four objectives. Each student is responsible for reading the handout, taking notes, answering the corresponding study questions, and familiarizing him- or herself with the sample materials for one of the four objectives.

Activity 2: Each student teaches his or her objective to the remaining three members of the group.

Activity 3: Groups review individual student answers to the handout study questions and make any necessary corrections. Study questions are turned in and graded (one grade per group).

LESSON II (20 MINUTES)

Goal: To master the procedure for laying out a floor for tiling.

Objective: Students will understand how to clean a floor for tiling and understand the importance of this simple preparation.

Activity 1: The teacher offers a brief lecture on sweeping and cleaning techniques and products.

Activity 2: The teacher demonstrates what happens when tile is laid over a small particle.

LESSON III (30 MINUTES)

Goal: To master the procedure for laying out a floor for tiling.

Objective: Students will understand how to find the center point of a room and divide the room into quadrants.

Activity 1: The teacher offers a brief lecture.

Activity 2: Each student is provided with a "room floor" (a rectangular piece of cardboard and a supply of "floor tiles" (made from colored construction paper). Each student is also provided with a ruler, glue, and a handout that reviews the teacher lecture. Each student must lay out and tile his or her floor.

LESSON IV (50 MINUTES)

*To be conducted in a gymnasium or other large open area.

Goal: To master the procedure for laying out a floor to be tiled.

Objective 1: Students will demonstrate how to find the center point of a room and to divide the room into quadrants (note this is a reteaching objective).

Objective 2: Students will work as productive team (crew) members.

Activity 1: Students work in teams of eight. Each team is given a taped-off area of floor space. The team must compute the area (previously mastered skill) of floor to be tiled and calculate the number of tiles required. The team is provided actual floor tiles per their computations.

Activity 2: The team lays out the floor by finding the center point of their floor space and dividing it into quadrants.

Activity 3: The team lays the tile.

LESSON V (12 HOURS PER WEEK)

*To be conducted on the job site.

Goal: To demonstrate the skills necessary to lay floor tile.

   Objective 1: Students will be able to lay out a floor for tiling.

   Objective 2: Students will be able to apply mastic.

   Objective 3: Students will be able to lay floor tile.

Activity 1: Students lay out and prepare the floor.

Activity 2: The teacher demonstrates applying mastic. Students practice, then apply mastic.

Activity 3: The teacher demonstrates laying floor tile. Students practice, then lay tile.

LESSON VI (90 MINUTES)

Goal: To reflect on the work completed.

   Objective 1: Students will understand the importance of teamwork and communication.

   Objective 2: Students will gain an understanding of the impact their good work will have on a Habitat family.

Activity 1: Students write a 100-word essay explaining how teamwork and communication supported the completion of the job (refer to journal notes).

Activity 2: Students read and discuss a selected excerpt from *The Excitement Is Building* (Fuller & Fuller, 1990).

Activity 3: Students hear from a guest speaker, the Habitat for Humanity construction supervisor. They then complete the "Reflection T-Chart #2" (page 348).

ALIGNMENT OF SERVICE OBJECTIVES AND ACADEMIC OBJECTIVES

Service Project Title: Residential Floor Tiling

Academic Content Area	Academic Objective	Service Objective	Comments
Math	• Measurement • Compute area • Applied multiplica–tion and division • Estimation	• Locate center point of room • Compute necessary materials	• May need to reteach area
English	• Match reading rate to content • Acquire information to communicate in a variety of formats • Read for specific information • Use oral communication precisely	• Read and apply product directions • Explain and discuss product information and directions	
Social Studies	• Understand the role of not-for-profit organizations • Understand the importance of a mission statement to any organization	• Identify community needs • Understand the importance of the work • Realize impact on Habitat family	• Remember excerpt from Gospel of the Hammer • Remind students to refer to their journals
Life Skills/World of Work Skills	• Work as a productive project team member • Use effective communication skills	• Complete floor tile project on schedule • Minimize errors/waste	• Don't throw out ruined floor tile—show to students; compute cost

SERVICE LEARNING LESSON EXAMPLE

Area of Service/Commitment: To work with the teachers in our school to provide a better education for our first and second graders. We will read stories and books and play educational games with small groups of first and second graders so that their teachers can work with other students and do some special testing. Our commitment is for 6 weeks.

Type of Class: Sixth-Grade General Education

Project Title: Work With the Little Kids

LESSON I (35 MINUTES)

Goal: To become familiar with project planning and to develop the necessary skills to plan projects.

Objective: Students will learn to develop project plans.

Activity 1: Students brainstorm all the things that need to be done to prepare for the project.

Activity 2: Students make a list and put the items on the list in the order in which they need to be done.

Activity 3: Students select individuals and groups for specific items/tasks.

Activity 4: Students develop a timeline

LESSON II (35 MINUTES)

Goal: To become familiar with project planning and to develop the necessary skills to plan projects.

Objective 1: Students will learn to develop schedules.

Objective 2: Students will learn to implement a project plan and evaluate their plan.

Activity 1: Students select teams of readers and game supervisors.

Activity 2: Students make a schedule.

Activity 3: Teams begin working with the first and second graders.

Activity 4: Teams meet for 15 minutes immediately after their service to discuss and evaluate the experience. One member of the team serves as a journal recorder. (Note: the whole class will meet once a week to share team experiences and make any necessary plan changes.)

LESSON III (40 MINUTES)

Goal: To realize the importance of their service and the extent of their impact.

Objective 1: Students will reflect on the service experience.

Activity 1: The sixth-grade teacher shares thank-you letters written by the first- and second-grade teachers with the class. The letters include actual comments from the first- and second-grade students.

Activity 2: The three project teams each complete a different Reflection T-Chart: "What We Did/What We Learned," "What We Did/What We Felt," and "What We Gave/What We Gained" (pages 347–349). Teams report to the class, and T-Charts are displayed.

LESSON IV (30 MINUTES)

Goal: To realize the importance of their service and the extent of their impact.

Objective: Students will celebrate their effort and results.

Activity: The principal and parent-teacher organization recognize the students at a school awards assembly.

ALIGNMENT OF SERVICE OBJECTIVES AND ACADEMIC OBJECTIVES

Service Project Title: Working With the Little Kids

Academic Content Area	Academic Objective	Service Objective	Comments
Language Arts	• Discussion skills • Summarizing skills • Knowledge	• Develop a project plan/evaluate plan • Develop a list of specific tasks	
Math	• Computation of time • Using percents and fractions	• Develop a schedule (students/times)	• Student volunteer could do final schedule as an art project—post in first- and second-grade rooms
Higher-Order Thinking Skills	• Prioritize by logical sequence and importance	• Develop a project plan efficiently	
Life Skills	• Use brainstorming as a decision-making process • Use communication skills in group situations	• Select materials (books and games) • Work effectively with younger students • Understand the impact of the project	• Get input/ suggestions from first- and second-grade teachers

The following activities are included to help your students identify possible areas of community service/service learning interest (Activity 93, "I'm a Resource") and to reflect on an actual community service/service learning experience (Activity 94, "Remember to Reflect").

COMMUNITY
SERVICE AND
SERVICE LEARNING

Activity 93
I'M A RESOURCE

FOCUS POINTS

- Help students identify their areas of interest and aptitude.

- Help students identify skills and knowledge they would like to possess.

- Help students make connections between the application or acquisition of interests, aptitudes, skills, and knowledge and areas of social concern.

- Explore areas of possible service learning projects.

PREPARATION AND MATERIALS

A copy of the "Service Learning Profile: I'm a Resource" worksheet for each student (pages 342–344)

DIRECTIONS

Have students complete the "Service Learning Profile: I'm a Resource" worksheet. This can be accomplished by individual students, small groups, or as a teacher-led, whole-class activity.

PROCESSING PROMPTS

- Was it fun to complete?

- Was it easy or hard to complete? Why?

- What connections can we make between our interests, aptitudes, skills, and knowledge and people we could help or projects we could attempt?

EXTENDING ACTIVITIES

- Brainstorm a list of possible projects and make some selections though the classroom community meeting process.

- Brainstorm a list of possible projects and develop a student survey. Administer the survey and use the results to make project selections.

- Brainstorm a list of possible projects. Narrow the list down to several choices and develop a plan for securing more information about the possible choices. Hold a series of classroom community meetings to discuss your information and make your selections.

Name: _____

Date: _____

SERVICE LEARNING PROFILE: I'M A RESOURCE

Completing this exercise may help you identify areas of service you would enjoy and for which you would be well-suited.

Free-Time Activities

When I have free time, I enjoy . . .

Hobbies (such as collecting coins, building model cars, sewing, and painting)

_____   _____

_____   _____

_____   _____

_____   _____

Physical Activities (such as individual sports, team sports, and exercise)

_____   _____

_____   _____

_____   _____

_____   _____

Games (such as board games and trivia games)

_____   _____

_____   _____

_____   _____

_____   _____

Social Activities (such as movies, television, eating out, clubs, visiting with friends, and dating)

_____   _____

_____   _____

_____   _____

_____   _____

Avocations (such as woodworking and public speaking)

_____   _____

_____   _____

_____   _____

Academic Activities

When I'm in school, I can't wait for....

Subjects, Areas of Study, Types of Activities (such as math, English, individual assignments, and small-group work)

_____   _____

_____   _____

_____   _____

Describe yourself in your own words. What do you enjoy doing? What are you good at? What would you like to get better at? What would you like to learn more about? Who would you like to spend time with?

_____

_____

_____

_____

_____

_____

_____

_____

_____

_____

_____

Is there anything that bothers you about your community? Anything you would like to fix? Is there anything you are proud of in your community that you would like to be a part of? Explain.

_____

_____

_____

_____

_____

_____

Where do you see yourself providing service (for example, tutoring younger students, providing craft activities for senior citizens, rehabbing homes, or cooking for the homeless)? Think about a difference you would like to make in someone else's life . . . in your community. Who would you like to help? What skills/talents/interests do you have? What skills would you like to learn? Who or what would you like to learn more about? List some possible areas of service you want to explore.

_____   _____

_____   _____

_____   _____

_____   _____

Activity 94
REMEMBER TO REFLECT: USING REFLECTION T-CHARTS

FOCUS POINTS

- Elicit thoughtful reflection of individual students.

- Elicit thoughtful reflection of the class.

- Help students make connections between their community service or service learning work and their newly acquired skills, knowledge, relationships, status in the community, self-esteem, and feelings of significance.

- Help students make connections between their community service or service learning work and the many benefits to their community, specifically those whose lives they have enriched.

PREPARATION AND MATERIALS

Copies of selected "Reflection T-Charts" (pages 347–349) for each student

DIRECTIONS

The Reflection T-Chart may be used in several ways with groups of students. It can provide a catalyst for meaningful group discussion or can serve as a prompt for individual introspection. Below are some possible applications. You are encouraged to create some of your own applications as well.

- Complete a Reflection T-Chart as a whole-class activity. Elicit a left-hand column response from a student, then have that student or another student provide the corresponding right-hand column response.

- Use a Reflection T-Chart to record a whole-class or small-group brainstorming activity. Simply list as many responses as students can generate for the left-hand column without stopping to evaluate each response or to complete the corresponding right-hand column response. Once the left-hand column is completed, go back and generate right-hand column responses. You may entertain as much discussion as you like.

- Have individual students complete a Reflection T-Chart, then share and discuss responses in small groups or as a whole class.

- Complete a Reflection T-Chart backwards. That is, complete the right-hand column first, then complete the left-hand column. The results can be interesting.

- Have individual students, small groups, or the class as a whole create their own Reflection T-Chart to process their own unique service experience. A Reflection T-Chart without headings has been provided on page 350 for this purpose.

PROCESSING PROMPTS

- What did we do? What did we feel?

- What did we give? What did we get?

- What did we do? What did we learn?

- Was the project fun?

- Was the project frustrating?

- What were we really good at?

- What will we do better next time?

- Did we work as a team?

- What did you learn about yourself? About other people?

- Did any special relationships develop?

REFLECTION T-CHART #1

What I/We Did	What I/We Learned

REFLECTION T-CHART #2

What I/We Did	What I/We Felt

ADVENTURE EDUCATION FOR THE CLASSROOM COMMUNITY
© 2007 Solution Tree • www.solution-tree.com

REFLECTION T-CHART #3

What I/We Gave	What I/We Gained

REFLECTION T-CHART #4

The Road Ahead

I regard it as the foremost task of education to insure the survival of these qualities: an enterprising curiosity, an undefeatable spirit, tenacity in pursuit, readiness for sensible self-denial, and above all compassion.

—Kurt Hahn, German educator and founder of the Outward Bound Movement

We began this journey with the notion that, more than any other single variable, a sense of community will motivate children to do the right thing. We end the journey with the notion that, more than any other single variable, a sense of isolation allows children to visit devastating acts of violence on their peers and in their schools. These acts would have been unthinkable in the not-so-distant past. Today, they are our children's reality.

At its core, this book is our attempt to help you help your students build sound communities—communities that help them identify the many things they have in common while positioning them to celebrate their individual and cultural differences.

We believe that everything we accomplish or fail to accomplish is, to some degree, related to our ability to establish a sense of community. Students in schools and classrooms that are built on a foundation of community are more likely to reach their individual social and academic potential. They are positioned to become critical thinkers and creative problem solvers. They are predisposed to resolve conflict in a nonviolent manner.

Our society, our schools, and our children are faced with the ever-mounting issues of increased economic disparity, poverty, racism, AIDS, drugs, violence, and organized gangs. Our young people are witness to a justice system that, while theoretically blind, surely recognizes the privilege of wealth. They are subject to the hypocrisy of our elected officials, and they are bombarded with media messages that blur reality and sell fantasy. More than ever before, we must teach our commonly held values: honesty, hard work, trust, responsibility, compassion, and acceptance of differences. We should worry less about what is politically correct and worry more about what is truly correct, for we cannot allow political correctness to stifle the truth. Some things are wrong, some practices are destructive, and some myths are disabling. We need to say so. Our children need internal compasses, and we still think it is our job to help develop them.

If you choose to implement the entire curriculum in *Adventure Education for the Classroom Community,* we believe you will instill in your students the lifelong desire to build and live in communities based on commonly held values, while providing them the skills and character necessary to exercise ongoing evaluation of commonly held values in relationship to personal freedoms in the ever-changing context of life.

You will have prepared them to be citizens. What an awesome thing to do.

Appendices

Additional Resources

Benard, B. (2005). *What is it about TRIBES?: The research-based components of the developmental process of TRIBES Learning Communities®.* Windsor, CA: CenterSource Systems, LLC.

Caine, G., & Caine, R. N. (2001) *The brain, education, and the competitive edge.* Lanham, MD: Scarecrow Press.

Caine, R. N., Caine, G., McClintic, C., & Klimek, K. (2005). *12 Brain/mind learning principles in action: The fieldbook for making connections, teaching, and the human brain.* Thousand Oaks, CA: Corwin Press.

Chappelle, S., & Bigman, L. (1998). *Diversity in action: Using adventure activities to explore issues of diversity with middle school and high school age youth.* Hamilton, MA: Project Adventure, Inc.

Frank, L. S. (2004). *Journey toward the caring classroom: Using adventure to create community in the classroom and beyond.* Oklahoma City, OK: Wood 'n' Barnes Publishing.

Gambone, M. A., & Connell, J. P. (2003). *Youth development framework for practice.* San Francisco and Island Heights, NJ: Community Network for Youth Development and Youth Development Strategies, Inc. Retrieved from http://www.cnyd.org/framework/index.php

Goleman, D. (1997). *Emotional intelligence: Why it can matter more than IQ.* New York: Bantam Books.

Huggins, P. (1997). *Creating a caring classroom.* Longmonth, CO: Sopris West.

Kamiya, A. (1985). *Elementary teacher's handbook of indoor and outdoor games.* West Nyack, NY: Parker Publishing Company.

Knapp, C. E. (1992). *Lasting lessons: A teacher's guide to reflecting on experience.* Charleston, WV: Clearinghouse on Rural Education and Small Schools.

Knapp, C. E. (1996). *Just beyond the classroom: Community adventures for interdisciplinary learning.* Charleston, WV: Clearinghouse on Rural Education and Small Schools.

Kovalik, S. (1994). *ITI: The model: Integrated thematic instruction.* Kent, WA: Susan Kovalic & Associates.

Lewis, B. A. (1995). *The kid's guide to service projects.* Minneapolis, MN: Free Spirit Publishing.

APPENDICES

Lewis, B. A. (1998). *The kid's guide to social action.* Minneapolis, MN: Free Spirit Publishing.

Lewis, B. A. (1998). *What do you stand for?: A kid's guide to building character.* Minneapolis, MN: Free Spirit Publishing.

Lieber, C. (1998). *Conflict resolution in the high school.* Cambridge, MA: Educators for Social Responsibility.

Lieber, C. (2002). *Partners in learning: From conflict to collaboration in secondary classrooms.* Cambridge, MA: Educators for Social Responsibility.

Mannix, D. (1993). *Social skills activities (for special children).* Hoboken, NJ: Jossey-Bass.

Marzano, R. J., Pickering, D. J., & Pollack, J. E. (2001). *Classroom instruction that works: Research-based strategies for increasing student achievement.* Alexandria, VA: Association for Supervision and Curriculum Development (ASCD).

Panico, A. (1999). *Discipline in the classroom community: Recapturing control of our schools.* Milwaukee, WI: Stylex Publishing Company.

Purkey, W. W., & Novak, J. M. (1995). *Inviting school success.* Belmont, CA: Wadsworth Publishing Company.

Scales, P. C. (1999). *Developmental assets: A synthesis of the scientific research on adolescent development.* Minneapolis, MN: The Search Institute.

Schoel, J., & Stratton, M. (1990). *Gold nuggets: Readings for experiential education.* Hamilton, MA, and Covington, GA: Project Adventure.

Zins, J. E., Weissberg, R. P., Wang, M. C., & Walberg, H. J. (Eds.). (2004). *Building academic success on social and emotional learning.* New York: Teachers College Press.

Character Education Literature List

CARING

Grades K–3

Bianco, M. W., & Nicholson, W. (1960). *The velveteen rabbit, or, how toys become real*. Garden City, NY: Doubleday.

Bridwell, N. (2000). *Clifford to the rescue*. New York: Scholastic.

Brown, M. W., & Hurd, C. (1972). *The runaway bunny*. New York: Harper & Row.

Carlson, N. S., & Williams, G. (1958). *The family under the bridge*. New York: Harper.

Charlip, R., & Supree, B. (1973). *Harlequin and the gift of many colors*. New York: Parents Magazine Press.

Delton, J., & Maestro, G. (1974). *Two good friends*. New York: Crown.

Freeman, D., & McCue, L. (2002). *Corduroy*. New York: Viking Penguin.

Hoban, R., & Hoban, L. (1993). *A baby sister for Frances*. New York: HarperCollins.

Hutchins, P. (1978). *The best train set ever*. New York: Greenwillow Books.

Korschunow, I., & Michl, R. (1984). *The foundling fox: How the little fox got a mother*. New York: HarperCollins.

Lionni, L. (1974). *Alexander and the wind-up mouse*. New York: Knopf/Pantheon.

Mathis, S. B., Dillon, L., & Dillon, D. (1986). *The hundred penny box*. New York: Puffin Books.

Miles, M., & Parnall, P. (1971). *Annie and the old one*. Boston: Little, Brown.

Mora, P., & Lang, C. (1992). *A birthday basket for Tia*. New York: Maxwell Macmillan International.

Newman, N., & Hafner, M. (1983). *That dog*. New York: T.Y. Crowell.

Sharmat, M. W., & Frascino, E. (1970). *Gladys told me to meet her here*. New York: Harper & Row.

Sharmat, M. W., & Shecter, B. (1976). *Mooch the messy*. New York: Harper & Row.

Silverstein, S. (1964). *The giving tree*. New York: Harper & Row.

Steptoe, J. (1987). *Mufaro's beautiful daughters: An African tale*. New York: Lothrop, Lee & Shepard Books.

Waddell, M., & Firth, B. (1992). *Can't you sleep, little bear?* (2nd U.S. ed.). Cambridge, MA: Candlewick Press.

Williams, V. B. (1982). *A chair for my mother.* New York: Greenwillow Books.

Zolotow, C., & Blegvad, E. (1976). *May I visit?* New York: Harper & Row.

Grades 4–6

Burch, R. (1980). *Ida Early comes over the mountain.* New York: Viking Press.

Burch, R. (1983). *Christmas with Ida Early.* New York: Viking Press.

Burnett, F. H., & Twinn, C. (1976). *The secret garden.* New York: F. Warne.

Cohen, B., & Duffy, D. M. (1998). *Molly's Pilgrim.* New York: Lothrop, Lee & Shepard Books.

Curtis, C. P. (1999). *Bud, not Buddy.* New York: Delacorte Press.

De Angeli, M. (1946). *Bright April.* Garden City, NY: Doubleday.

Estes, E., & Slobodkin, L. (2004). *The hundred dresses.* Orlando, FL: Harcourt.

Fenner, C. (1995). *Yolonda's genius.* New York: Margaret K. McElderry Books.

Gantos, J. (2000). *Joey Pigza loses control.* New York: Farrar, Straus and Giroux.

Holt, K. W. (1999). *When Zachary Beaver came to town.* New York: Holt.

Howe, J. (1983). *A night without stars.* New York: Atheneum.

Jordan, J., & Cruz, R. (1975). *New life: New room.* New York: Crowell.

Miles, B., & Jones, D. (1981). *The secret life of the underwear champ.* New York: Knopf.

Park, B. *Mick Harte was here.* (1995). New York: Knopf.

Perl, L. (1984). *Tybee Trimble's hard times.* New York: Clarion Books.

Rappaport, D., & Collier, B. (2000). *Freedom River.* New York: Hyperion Books for Children.

Robinson, B., Martin, A., & Bloom, J. A. (1988). *The best Christmas pageant ever.* New York: HarperTrophy.

Sachar, L., & Sullivan, B. (1993). *Marvin Redpost: Is he a girl?* New York: Random House.

Shreve, S. R., & De Groat, D. (1984). *The flunking of Joshua T. Bates.* New York: Scholastic.

Skolsky, M. W., & Weinhaus, K. A. (1979). *Carnival and Kopeck and more about Hannah.* New York: Harper & Row.

Sussman, S., & Robinson, C. (1983). *There's no such thing as a Chanukah bush, Sandy Goldstein.* Niles, IL: A. Whitman.

Taylor, T. (1969). *The cay.* Garden City, NY: Doubleday.

White, R. (2004). *Belle Prater's boy.* New York: Dell Yearling.

Winthrop, E., & Watson, W. (1984). *Belinda's hurricane.* New York: Dutton.

Wright, B. R. (1983). *The dollhouse murders.* New York: Holiday House.

Yates, E. (1950). *Amos Fortune, free man.* New York: Aladdin Books.

Grade 7 and Up

Bargar, G. W. (1984). *Life. Is. Not. Fair.* New York: Clarion Books.

Burnford, S. E., & Burger, C. (1961). *The incredible journey.* Boston: Little, Brown.

Greene, B. (1973). *Summer of my German soldier.* New York: Dial Press.

Hamilton, V. (1989). *Willie Bea and the time the Martians landed.* New York: Aladdin Books.

Hiaasen, C. (2005). *Flush.* Waterville, ME: Thorndike Press.

Hinton, S. E. (1967). *The outsiders.* New York: Viking Press.

Hurwitz, J., & Johnson, P. (1982). *The Rabbi's girls.* New York: Morrow.

Jarrell, R., & Sendak, M. (1996). *The animal family.* New York: HarperCollins.

Jones, R. C. (1983). *Madeline and the great (old) escape artist.* New York: Dutton.

Kerr, J. (1971). *When Hitler stole pink rabbit.* London: Collins.

Kullman, H. (1981). *The battle horse.* Scarsdale, NY: Bradbury Press.

Little, J., & Sandin, J. (1970). *Look through my window.* New York: Harper & Row.

Neufeld, J. (1999). *Edgar Allen.* New York: Puffin Books.

Neville, E. (1965). *Berries Goodman.* New York: Harper & Row.

Roberts, W. D., & Sanderson, R. (1988). *Don't hurt Laurie.* New York: Aladdin Books.

Spinelli, J. (1997). *Crash.* New York: Yearling.

Uchida, Y., & Carrick, D. (1971). *Journey to Topaz.* New York: Scribner.

Uchida, Y., & Robinson, C. (1992). *Journey home.* New York: Maxwell Macmillan International.

Wolff, V. E. (1993). *Make lemonade.* New York: Henry Holt.

CITIZENSHIP

Grades K–3

Ackerman, K., & Lewin, B. (1990). *Araminta's paint box.* New York: Atheneum.

Blos, J. W., & Gammell, S. (1987). *Old Henry.* New York: Morrow.

Capucilli, A. S., & Schories, P. (1997). *Biscuit finds a friend.* New York: HarperCollins.

Collier, B. (2000). *Uptown.* New York: Henry Holt.

Cronin, D., & Lewin, B. (2000). *Click, clack, moo: Cows that type.* New York: Simon & Schuster.

Estes, E., & Slobodkin, L. (2004). *The hundred dresses.* Orlando, FL: Harcourt.

Gackenbach, D. (1984). *King Wacky.* New York: Crown.

Levinson, R., & Goode, D. (1985). *Watch the stars come out.* New York: Dutton.

Miller, W., & Ward, J. (1998). *The bus ride.* New York: Lee & Low Books.

Viorst, J., & Cruz, R. (1987). *Alexander and the terrible, horrible, no good, very bad day*. New York: Aladdin Books.

Williams, V. B. (1982). *A chair for my mother*. New York: Greenwillow Books.

Zemach, M. (1976). *It could always be worse: A Yiddish folk tale*. New York: Farrar, Straus and Giroux.

Grades 4–6

Baylor, B., & Parnall, P. (1986). *Hawk, I'm your brother*. London: Collier Macmillan.

Chambers, A. (1983). *The present takers*. New York: Harper & Row.

Cooper, F. (1994). *Coming home from the life of Langston Hughes*. New York: Philomel Books.

Danziger, P. (1974). *The cat ate my gymsuit*. New York: Delacorte Press.

De Jong, M., & Sendak, M. (1956). *The house of sixty fathers*. New York: Harper.

George, J. C. (1988). *My side of the mountain*. New York: Dutton.

Gilson, J., & Wallner, J. C. (1985). *Hello, my name is Scrambled Eggs*. New York: Lothrop, Lee & Shepard Books.

Hurwitz, J., & Hamanaka, S. (1990). *Class president*. New York: Morrow Junior Books.

Isaacs, A., & Zelinsky, P. O. (1994). *Swamp angel*. New York: Dutton Children Books.

Levine, E., & Parmenter, W. (1993). *If your name was changed at Ellis Island*. New York: Scholastic.

Lewis, B. A., & Espeland, P. (1992). *Kids with courage: True stories about young people making a difference*. Minneapolis, MN: Free Spirit.

Myers, W. D. (1982). *Won't know till I get there*. New York: Viking Press.

Myers, W. D., & Myers, C. (1997). *Harlem: A poem*. New York: Scholastic.

Myers, W. D. (2001). *The journal of Biddy Owens: The Negro Leagues, Birmingham, Alabama, 1948*. New York: Scholastic.

Myers, W. D. (2004). *Here in Harlem: Poems in many voices*. New York: Holiday House.

Myers, W. D., & Jenkins, L. (2004). *I've seen the promised land: The life of Dr. Martin Luther King, Jr.* New York: HarperCollins.

Sachar, L. (2002). *Holes*. Austin, TX: Holt, Rinehart and Winston.

Sachar, L., & Wummer, A. (1999). *Marvin Redpost: Class president*. New York: Random House.

Speare, E. G. (1983). *The sign of the beaver*. Boston: Houghton Mifflin.

White, E. B., & Marcellino, F. (2000). *Trumpet of the swan*. New York: HarperCollins.

Woodson, J., & Cooper, F. (1990). *Martin Luther King, Jr., and his birthday.* Englewood Cliffs, NJ: Silver Press.

Grade 7 and Up

Clements, A., & Murdocca, S. (1999). *The Landry News.* New York: Simon & Schuster Books for Young Readers.

Cooney, C. B. (1992). *Flight #116 is down.* New York: Scholastic.

Hentoff, N. (1982). *The day they came to arrest the book.* New York: Delacorte Press.

Merrill, J., & Solbert, R. (1985). *The pushcart war.* New York: Harper & Row.

FAIRNESS

Grades K–3

Bianco, M. W., & Jorgensen, D. (2004). *The velveteen rabbit.* Edina, MN: ABDO.

Bohlken, R., & Veasey, M. (2003). *Listening to the Mukies and their character building adventures.* Maryville, MO: Snaptail Press.

Bonsall, C. N. (1980). *The case of the double cross.* New York: Harper & Row.

Brandenberg, F., & Iki. (1977). *Nice new neighbors.* New York: Greenwillow Books.

Clifton, L., & Grifalconi, A. (1992). *Everett Anderson's friend.* New York: Henry Holt.

Demi. (1997). *One grain of rice: A mathematical folktale.* New York: Scholastic Press.

Freeman, D., & McCue, L. (2002). *Corduroy.* New York: Viking Penguin.

Hoban, L. (1976). *Arthur's pen pal.* New York: Harper & Row.

Hoban, R., & Hoban, L. (1969). *Best friends for Frances.* New York: Harper & Row.

Iwamura, K. (1984). *Ton and Pon: Two good friends.* Scarsdale, NY: Bradbury Press.

Kessler, L. P. (1992). *Here comes the strikeout.* New York: HarperCollins.

Kraus, R., & Aruego, J. (1980). *Leo the late bloomer.* New York: Windmill/Wanderer Books.

Lester, H., & Munsinger, L. (1999). *Hooway for Wodney Wat.* Boston: Houghton Mifflin.

San Souci, R. D., & Pinkney, J. (1989). *The talking eggs: A folktale from the American South.* New York: Dial Books for Young Readers.

Sarnoff, J., & Ruffins, R. *That's not fair.* New York: Scribner.

Viorst, J., & Tomei, L. (1986). *Rosie and Michael.* New York: Aladdin Books.

Yolen, J., & Schoenherr, J. (1987). *Owl moon.* New York: Philomel Books.

Yolen, J., & Young, E. (1988). *The Emperor and the kite* (Rev. ed.). New York: Philomel Books.

Grades 4–6

Christopher, M., & Johnson, L. (1985). *The fox steals home.* Boston: Little, Brown.

Clements, A. (2000). *The janitor's boy.* New York: Simon & Schuster Books for Young Readers.

Curtis, C. P. (1995). *The Watsons go to Birmingham—1963.* Austin, TX: Holt, Reinhart and Winston.

Greenfield, E., & Gilchrist, J. S. (1991). *Night on Neighborhood Street.* New York: Dial Books for Young Readers.

Hiaasen, C. (2003). *Hoot.* Waterville, ME: Thorndike Press.

Konigsburg, E. L. (1996). *The view from Saturday.* New York: Atheneum Books for Young Readers.

Paterson, K. (1994). *Flip-flop girl.* New York: Dutton.

Polacco, P. (1992). *Chicken Sunday.* New York: Philomel Books.

Polacco, P. (1994). *Pink and Say.* New York: Philomel Books.

Spinelli, J. (1993). *Maniac Magee.* Thorndike, ME: Thorndike Press.

Taylor, M. D. (2001). *Roll of thunder, hear my cry.* New York: Dial Books.

Grade 7 and Up

Bloor, E. (1997). *Tangerine.* San Diego: Harcourt Brace.

Cohen, B., & Cuffari, R. (1974). *Thank you, Jackie Robinson* (2nd ed.). New York: Lothrop, Lee & Shepard Books.

Cormier, R. (1988). *The chocolate war.* Boston: G. K. Hall.

Hiaasen, C. (2005). *Flush.* Waterville, ME: Thorndike Press.

Mazer, N. F. (1983). *Taking Terri Mueller.* New York: Morrow.

Myers, W. D. (1981). *Hoops: A novel.* New York: Delacorte Press.

Peck, R. N. (1973). *A day no pigs would die.* Boston: G. K. Hall.

Spinelli, J. (1991). *There's a girl in my hammerlock.* New York: Simon & Schuster.

RESPECT

Grades K–3

Brown, M. T. (1976). *Arthur's nose.* Boston: Little, Brown.

Brown, M. T. (1979). *Arthur's eyes.* Boston: Little, Brown.

Cannon, J. (1993). *Stellaluna.* San Diego: Harcourt Brace Jovanovich.

Cannon, J. (1997). *Verdi.* San Diego: Harcourt Brace.

Carle, E. (1996). *The grouchy ladybug*. New York: HarperCollins.

Cleary, B., & Darling, L. (1968). *Ramona the pest*. New York: W. Morrow.

Clifton, L., & Di Grazia, T. (1980). *My friend Jacob*. New York: Dutton.

Cohen, B., & Duffy, D. M. (1998). *Molly's Pilgrim*. New York: Lothrop, Lee & Shepard Books.

Cohen, M., & Hoban, L. (1971). *Best friends*. New York: Macmillan.

De Paola, T. (1979). *Oliver Button is a sissy*. New York: Harcourt Brace Jovanovich.

Ets, M. H. (1955). *Play with me*. New York: Viking Press.

Flournoy, V., & De Groat, D. (1980). *The twins strike back*. New York: Dial Press.

Freeman, D. (1961). *Come again, pelican*. New York: Viking Press.

Griffith, H. V., & Low, J. (1982). *Alex and the cat*. New York: Greenwillow Books.

Henkes, K. (1986). *A weekend with Wendell*. New York: Greenwillow Books.

Hoban, R., & Hoban, L. (1969). *Best friends for Frances*. New York: Harper & Row.

Hoose, P. M., Hoose, H., & Tilley, D. (1998). *Hey little ant*. Berkeley, CA: Tricycle Press.

Howe, J., & Sweet, M. (1996). *Pinky and Rex and the bully*. New York: Atheneum Books for Young Readers.

Hurwitz, J., & Covington, N. (1997). *Helen Keller: Courage in the dark*. New York: Random House.

Lexau, J. M., & Owens, G. (1979). *I hate Red Rover*. New York: Dutton.

Lobel, A. (1970). *Frog and Toad are friends*. New York: Harper & Row.

Lobel, A. (1972). *Frog and Toad together*. New York: Harper & Row.

Lobel, A. (1976). *Frog and Toad all year*. New York: Harper & Row.

Marshall, J. (1972). *George and Martha*. Boston: Houghton Mifflin.

Marshall, J. (1978). *George and Martha: One fine day*. Boston: Houghton Mifflin.

Ross, P., & Hafner, M. (1980). *Meet M and M*. New York: Pantheon Books.

Rylant, C., & Di Grazia, T. *Miss Maggie*. New York: Dutton.

Sharmat, M. W., & Chartier, N. (1984). *Bartholomew the bossy*. New York: Macmillan.

Siegelson, K. L., & Pinkney, J. B. (1999). *In the time of the drums*. New York: Hyperion Books.

Stanek, M., & Smith, P. (1979). *Growl when you say R*. Chicago: A. Whitman.

Steig, W. (1971). *Amos & Boris*. New York: Farrar, Straus and Giroux.

Stevenson, J. (1977). *Wilfred the rat*. New York: Greenwillow Books.

Turkle, B. (1969). *Thy friend, Obadiah*. New York: Viking Press.

Wittman, S., & Gundersheimer, K. (1978). *A special trade*. New York: Harper & Row.

Grades 4–6

Adler, C. S. (1983). *Get lost, little brother*. New York: Clarion Books.

Beckman, D., & Durell, A. (1980). *My own private sky*. New York: Dutton.

Bianco, M. W., & Nicholson, W. (1960). *The velveteen rabbit, or, how toys become real*. Garden City, NY: Doubleday.

Blume, J. (2004). *Blubber*. New York: Dell Yearling.

Bohlken, R. L., & Veasey, M. (2003). *Listening to the Mukies and their character building adventures*. Maryville, MO: Snaptail Press.

Burch, R., & Negri, R. (1968). *Renfroe's Christmas*. New York: Viking Press.

Byars, B. C. (1977). *The pinballs*. New York: Harper & Row.

Byars, B. C. (1981). *The 18th emergency*. New York: Puffin Books.

Byars, B. C. (1985). *The glory girl*. New York: Puffin Books.

Cleary, B., & Tiegreen, A. (1975). *Ramona the brave*. New York: Morrow.

Coatsworth, E. J., & Turska, K. (1975). *Marra's world*. New York: Greenwillow Books.

Crofford, E., & Nobens, C. A. (1982). *Stories from the blue road*. Minneapolis: Carolrhoda Books.

Conford, E., & Stewart, A. L. (1973). *Felicia the critic*. Boston: Little, Brown.

Dana, B., & Christelow, E. (1982). *Zucchini*. New York: Harper & Row.

Declements, B. (1981). *Nothing's fair in fifth grade*. New York: Viking Press.

Fisher, L. I. (1984). *Rachel Vellars, how could you?* New York: Dodd, Mead.

Fitzgerald, J. D., & Mayer, M. (1971). *Me and my little brain*. New York: Dial Books for Young Readers.

Fox, P., & Lambert, S. (1969). *Portrait of Ivan*. Englewood Cliffs, NJ: Bradbury Press.

Fox, P., & Mackay, D. A. (1987). *The stone-faced boy*. New York: Aladdin Books.

Gaeddert, L. B., & Schwark, M. B. (1984). *Your former friend, Matthew*. New York: Dutton.

Garrigue, S. (1978). *Between friends*. Scarsdale, NY: Bradbury Press.

Greene, B. (1981). *Get on out of here, Philip Hall*. New York: Dial Press.

Greene, B., & Lilly, C. (1974). *Philip Hall likes me*. New York: Dial Press.

Greene, C. C. (1970). *Leo the lioness*. New York: Viking Press.

Greene, C. C. (1970). *The unmaking of rabbit*. New York: Viking Press.

Greene, C. C., & McCully, E. A. (1990). *I and Sproggy*. New York: Puffin Books.

Greenwald, S. (1983). *Will the real Gertrude Hollings please stand up*. Boston: Little, Brown.

Haas, D., & Apple, M. (1984). *Tink in a tangle*. Niles, IL: A. Whitman.

Hansen, J. (1980). *The gift-giver*. New York: Houghton Mifflin/Clarion Books.

Hurwitz, J., & Fetz, I. (1978). *The law of gravity: A Story*. New York: Morrow.

Hurwitz, J., & Tilley, D. (2001). *Superduper Teddy*. New York: HarperCollins.

Hurwitz, J., & Wallner, J. C. (1989). *Aldo Applesauce*. New York: Puffin Books.

King-Smith, D., & Rayner, M. (1984). *Magnus Powermouse*. New York: Harper & Row.

Konigsburg, E. L. (1967). *Jennifer, Hecate, Macbeth, William McKinley, and Me, Elizabeth*. New York: Atheneum.

Lawson, R. (1944). *Rabbit hill*. New York: Viking Press.

Maclachlan, P. (1982). *Cassie Binegar*. New York: Harper & Row.

Maclachlan, P., & Bloom, L. (1980). *Arthur, for the very first time*. New York: Harper & Row.

Mathis, S. B., Dillon, L., & Dillon, D. (1986). *The hundred penny box*. New York: Puffin Books.

McDonnell, C., & De Groat, D. (1984). *Lucky charms & birthday wishes*. New York: Puffin Books.

Miles, M., & McCully, E. A. (1970). *Gertrude's pocket*. Boston: Little, Brown.

Selden, G., & Williams, G. (1990). *The cricket in Times Square*. Santa Barbara, CA: Cornerstone Books.

Stolz, M. (1977). *The noonday friends*. New York: Miller-Brody Productions.

Stolz, M., & Shortall, L. W. (1967). *The bully of Barkham Street*. New York: Harper & Row.

Grade 7 and Up

Armstrong, W. H., & Barkley, J. (2005). *Sounder*. Waterville, ME: Thorndike Press.

Burch, R., & Lazare, J. (1966). *Queenie Peavy*. New York: Viking Press.

Danziger, P. (1974). *The cat ate my gymsuit*. New York: Delacorte Press.

Danziger, P. (1978). *The pistachio prescription: A novel*. New York: Delacorte Press.

Gold, T., Arutt, C., Ward, E., & Pascal, F. (1983). *The hand-me-down kid*. New York: Learning Corporation of America.

Lipsyte, R. (1967). *The contender*. New York: Harper & Row.

Paterson, K. (1980). *Jacob have I loved*. New York: HarperCollins.

Paulsen, G. (1983). *Popcorn days & buttermilk nights*. New York: Dutton.

Philbrick, W. R. (1993). *Freak the mighty*. New York: Blue Sky Press.

Platt, K. (1981). *Brogg's brain*. New York: Lippincott.

Shyer, M. F. (1983). *Adorable Sunday*. New York: Scribner.

Taylor, M. D. (1981). *Let the circle be unbroken*. New York: Dial Press.

Voigt, C. (1982). *Dicey's song*. New York: Atheneum.

Yep, L. (1977). *Child of the owl*. New York: Harper & Row.

Yep, L. (1979). *Sea glass*. New York: Harper & Row.

RESPONSIBILITY

Grades K–3

Berenstain, S., & Berenstain, J. (1985). *The Berenstain Bears learn about strangers*. New York: Random House.

Berenstain, S., & Berenstain, J. (1986). *The Berenstain Bears' trouble at school*. New York: Random House.

Burton, V. L. (1943). *Katy and the big snow*. Boston: Houghton Mifflin.

Cosby, B, & Honeywood, V. P. (1999). *My big lie*. New York: Scholastic.

Gramatky, H., & Burgess, M. (1999). *Little Toot* (Classic Abridged ed.). New York: Grosset & Dunlap.

Lionni, L. (1973). *Swimmy*. New York: Random House.

Perrine, M., & Weisgard, L. (1968). *Salt boy*. Boston: Houghton Mifflin.

Soto, G., & Martinez, E. (1993). *Too many tamales*. New York: Putnam.

Steig, W. (1982). *Doctor De Soto*. New York: Farrar, Straus, and Giroux.

Van Allsburg, C. (1979). *The garden of Abdul Gasazi*. Boston: Houghton Mifflin.

Ward, L. (1952). *The biggest bear*. Boston: Houghton Mifflin.

Wooden, J. R., Jamison, S., Harper, P. L., & Cornelison, S. F. (2003). *Inch and Miles*. Logan, IA: Perfection Learning.

Young, E. (1989). *Lon PO PO: A Red-Riding Hood story from China*. New York: Philomel Books.

Grades 4–6

Armstrong, W. H., & Barkley, J. (1969). *Sounder*. New York: Harper & Row.

Asch, F. (1984). *Pearl's promise*. New York: Delacorte Press.

Ayres, K. (1998). *North by night: A story of the underground railroad*. New York: Delacorte Press.

Bishop, C. H., & Rojankovsky, F. (1992). *All alone*. New York: Viking.

Bulla, C. R. (1980). *Shoeshine girl*. New York: Learning Corporation of America.

Carlson, N. S., & Williams, G. (1958). *The family under the bridge*. New York: Harper.

Carlson, N. S., & Williams, G. (1959). *A brother for the Orphelines*. New York: Harper.

Carrick, C., & Carrick, D. (1983). *What a wimp*. New York: Clarion Books.

Cherry, L. (1990). *The great Kapok tree: A tale of the Amazon Rain Forest*. San Diego: Harcourt Brace Jovanovich.

Cleary, B., & Darling, L. (1990). *Henry and the clubhouse*. New York: Avon Books.

Cleary, B., & Darling, L. (2000). *Henry Huggins*. New York: HarperCollins.

Clymer, E. L. (1967). *My brother Stevie*. New York: Holt, Rinehart and Winston.

Clymer, E. L., & Lewin, T. (1983). *The horse in the attic*. Scarsdale, NY: Bradbury Press.

De Jong, M., & McCully, E. A. (1968) *Journey from Peppermint Street*. New York: Harper & Row.

Delton, J. (1983). *Back yard angel*. Boston: Houghton Mifflin.

Estes, E., & Slobodkin, L. (2001). *The Moffats*. San Diego: Harcourt.

Fox, P. (1986). *One-eyed cat*. Westminster, MD: Random House School Division.

Gardiner, J. R., & Sewall, M. (1980). *Stone fox*. New York: Crowell.

Gile, J., & Heflin, T. (1989). *The first forest*. Rockford, IL: John Gile Communications.

Mann, P. (1966). *Street of the flower boxes*. New York: Coward-McCann.

Rhoads, D., & Charlot, J. (1993). *The corn grows ripe*. New York: Puffin Books.

Sachar, L., & Sullivan, B. (1994). *Marvin Redpost: Alone in his teacher's house*. New York: Random House.

Sauer, J. L., & Schreiber, G. (1994). *The light at tern rock*. New York: Puffin Books.

Grade 7 and Up

Byars, B. C., & Coconis, C. (1970). *The summer of the swans*. New York: Viking Press.

Byars, B. C., & Howell, T. (1990). *The night swimmers*. Santa Barbara, CA: Cornerstone Books.

Cooney, C. B. (1990). *The face on the milk carton*. New York: Bantam Books.

Doty, J. S. (1984). *If wishes were horses*. New York: Macmillan.

Eige, L. (1983). *The kidnapping of Mister Huey*. New York: Harper & Row.

First, J. (1978). *Move over, Beethoven*. New York: F. Watts.

Gerson, C. (1981). *How I put my mother through college*. New York: Atheneum.

Holland, I. (1977). *Alan and the animal kingdom*. Philadelphia: Lippincott.

Hunt, I. (1977). *William: A novel*. New York: Scribner.

Lawrence, L. (1983). *The Dram Road*. New York: Harper & Row.

Lewin, T., & O'Dell, S. (1990). *Island of the blue dolphins*. Boston: Houghton Mifflin.

McHugh, E. (1983). *Raising a mother isn't easy*. New York: Greenwillow Books.

Moeri, L. (1984). *Downwind*. New York: Dutton.

Myers, W. D. (1989). *The young landlords*. New York: Puffin Books.

Paterson, K. (1980). *Jacob have I loved*. New York: HarperCollins.

Paterson, K. (1991). *Lyddie*. New York: Lodestar Books.

Peck, R. (1978). *Father figure: A novel*. New York: Viking Press.

Shyer, M. F. (1988). *Welcome home, Jellybean*. New York: Aladdin Books.

Speare, E. G. (1983). *The sign of the beaver*. Boston: Houghton Mifflin.

Stolz, M. (1974). *The edge of next year.* New York: Harper & Row.

Voigt, C. (1981). *Homecoming.* New York: Atheneum.

Voigt, C. (1982). *Dicey's song.* New York: Atheneum.

Zindel, P. (1968). *The pigman.* New York: Harper & Row.

TRUSTWORTHINESS

Grades K–3

Berenstain, S., & Berenstain, J. (1983). *The Berenstain bears and the truth.* New York: Random House.

Beskow, E. M., Nestrick, N., & Frost, B. (1962). *Pelle's new suit.* New York: Platt & Munk.

Bridwell, N. (2000). *Clifford to the rescue.* New York: Scholastic.

Burton, V. L. (1939). *Mike Mulligan and his steam shovel.* Boston: Houghton Mifflin.

Chorao, K. (1979). *Molly's lies.* New York: Seabury Press.

De Paola, T. (1982). *Strega Nona's magic lessons.* New York: Harcourt Brace Jovanovich.

Havill, J. (1999). *Jamaica and the substitute teacher.* Boston: Houghton Mifflin.

Hoban, R., & Hoban, L. (1969). *Best friends for Frances.* New York: Harper & Row.

Hoban, R., & Hoban, L. (1970). *A bargain for Frances.* New York: Harper & Row.

Monjo, F. N., & Brenner, F. (1970). *The drinking gourd.* New York: Harper & Row.

Peet, B. (1979). *Cowardly Clyde.* Boston: Houghton Mifflin.

Pfister, M. (1992). *The rainbow fish.* New York: North-South Books.

Piper, W., Hauman, G., & Hauman, D. (1990). *The little engine that could.* New York: Platt & Munk.

Sharmat, M. W. (1978). *A big fat enormous lie.* New York: Dutton.

Turkle, B. (1972). *The adventures of Obadiah.* New York: Viking Press.

Wells, R. (1997). *Bunny cakes.* New York: Dial Books for Young Readers.

Yashima, T. (1955). *Crow boy.* New York: Viking Press.

Grades 4–6

Avi. (1994). *Night journeys.* New York: Beech Tree Books.

Bauer, J. (2000). *Hope was here.* New York: Putnam.

Bunting, E. (2000). *Blackwater.* Thorndike, ME: Thorndike Press.

Bunting, E., & Himler, R. (1994). *A day's work.* New York: Clarion Books.

Byars, B. C., & Himler, R. (1974). *After the goat man.* New York: Viking Press.

Curtis, C. P. (1999). *Bud, not Buddy.* New York: Delacorte Press.

Dalgliesh, A., & Weisgard, L. (1986). *The courage of Sarah Noble*. New York: Scribner.

Dicamillo, K. (2000). *Because of Winn-Dixie*. Cambridge, MA: Candlewick Press.

Dicamillo, K. (2001). *The tiger rising*. Cambridge, MA: Candlewick Press.

Fife, D., & Galdone, P. (1977). *Who'll vote for Lincoln*. New York: Coward, McCann & Geoghegan.

Garland, S. (1996). *Letters from the mountain*. San Diego: Harcourt Brace.

Lenski, L. (2005). *Strawberry girl* (Rev. ed.). New York: HarperTrophy.

Little, J., & Lazare, J. (1969). *One to grow on*. Boston: Little, Brown.

Naylor, P. R. (1999). *A traitor among the boys*. New York: Delacorte Press.

Paulsen, G. (1989). *The winter room*. New York: Orchard Books.

Pfeffer, S. B., & Rutherford, J. (1983). *Courage, Dana*. New York: Delacorte Press.

Sachar, L., & Sullivan, B. (1993). *Marvin Redpost: Why pick on me?* New York: Random House.

Sachs, M. (1982). *Call me Ruth*. Garden City, NY: Doubleday.

Sperry, A. (1989). *Call it courage*. Santa Barbara, CA: Cornerstone Books.

Todd, L. (1984). *The best kept secret of the war*. New York: Knopf.

White, E. B., & Williams, G. (2003). *Charlotte's web*. New York: HarperCollins.

Grade 7 and Up

Adler, C. S. (1980). *In our house Scott is my brother*. New York: Macmillan.

Collier, J. L., & Collier, C. (1974). *My brother Sam is dead*. New York: Four Winds Press.

Crutcher, C. (1995). *Ironman: A novel*. New York: Greenwillow Books.

Cunningham, J. (1980). *Flight of the sparrow: A novel*. New York: Pantheon Books.

Greene, B. (1973). *Summer of my German soldier*. New York: Dial Press.

Hall, L. (1984). *Uphill all the way*. New York: Scribner.

Keith, H. (1957). *Rifles for Watie*. New York: Crowell.

Kerr, M. E. (1975). *Is that you, Miss Blue*. New York: Harper & Row.

Kerr, M. E. (1978). *Gentlehands*. New York: Harper & Row.

Lasky, K. (1994). *Beyond the burning time*. New York: Blue Sky Press.

Naylor, P. R. (1991). *Shiloh*. New York: Maxwell Macmillan International.

References

Association for Supervision and Curriculum Development (ASCD). (1998). Moral education in the life of the school. In M. Murphy (Ed.), *Character education in America's blue ribbon schools: Best practices for meeting the challenge* (p. 21). Lancaster, PA: Technomic Publishing Company, Inc.

Benard, B. (1992). Youth service: From youth as problems to youth as resources. In Duckenfield, M., & Swanson, L. (eds.), *Service Learning: Meeting the needs of youth at risk*. Clemson, SC: National Dropout Prevention Center.

Cavert, C., & Friends. (1996). *Affordable portables: A working-book of initiative activities & problem solving elements*. Oklahoma City, OK: Wood 'N' Barnes Publishing.

Cavert, C., Frank, L., & Friends. (1999). *Games (& other stuff) for teachers: Classroom activities that promote pro-social learning*. Oklahoma City, OK: Wood 'N' Barnes Publishing.

Centers for Disease Control and Prevention. (2004). Youth risk behavior surveillance—United States, 2003. *Morbidity and Mortality Weekly Report, 53*(SS02):1–96.

Chicago Public Schools, Office of Curriculum and Instruction, Department of Character Education. (2002). *Chicago Public Schools character education curriculum*. Chicago: Author.

Clayborne, C., Luker, R., & Russell, P. A. (Eds.). (1992). *Called to serve, January 1929–June 1951: The papers of Martin Luther King, Jr.* Berkeley: University of California Press.

Covey, S. (1989). *The seven habits of highly effective people*. New York: Simon & Schuster.

Dale, E. (1993). In T. Jackson (Ed.), *Activities that teach* (p. 15). Cedar City, UT: Red Rock Publishing.

De Tocqueville, E. (1998). *The old regime and the revolution: The complete text* (F. Furet, Trans.). Chicago: University of Chicago Press. (Original work published 1856)

Duckenfield, M., & Swanson, L. (1992). *Service learning: Meeting the needs of youth at risk*. Clemson, SC: National Dropout Prevention Center.

Fenstermacher, G. (1990). Some moral considerations on teaching as a profession. In J. Goodlad, R. Soder, & K. Sirotnik (Eds.), *Moral dimensions of teaching* (pp. 130–137). San Francisco: Jossey-Bass.

Frank, L. (1988). *Adventure in the classroom: A stress-challenge curriculum.* Madison, WI: Madison Metropolitan School District.

Frank, L. S., Christ, J., & Carlin, C. (in press). Foundations of collaborative leadership. Ripon, WI: Collaborative Leadership Institute.

Fuller, M., & Fuller, L. (1990). *The excitement is building.* Dallas: World Publishing.

Gardner, H. (2000). Intelligence reframed: Multiple intelligences for the 21st century. New York: Basic Books.

Gibbs, J. (2000). TRIBES: A new way of learning and being together. Sausalito, CA: CenterSource Systems.

Henton, M. (1996). *Adventure in the classroom: Using adventure to strengthen learning and build a community of life-long learners.* Dubuque, IA: Kendall Hunt Publishing.

Jackson, T. (Ed.). (1993). *Activities that teach.* Cedar City, UT: Red Rock Publishing.

Jensen, E. (1988). *Super-teaching.* Del Mar, CA: Turning Point for Teachers.

Kagan, S. (1992). *Cooperative learning.* San Juan Capistrano, CA: Resources for Teachers.

Kohn, A. (1996). *Beyond discipline: From compliance to community.* Alexandria, VA: Association for Supervision and Curriculum Development.

LeFevre, D. N. (1988). *New games for the whole family.* New York: Perigee Books.

Lewis, B. A. (1998). *What do you stand for? A kid's guide to building character.* Minneapolis: Free Spirit Publishing.

Lickona, T. (1992). *Educating for character: How our schools can teach respect and responsibility.* New York: Bantam Books.

Luckner, J. L., & Nadler, R. S. (1997). *Processing the experience: Strategies to enhance and generalize learning.* Dubuque, IA: Kendall Hunt Publishing.

Murphy, M. (1998). *Character education in America's blue ribbon schools: Best practices for meeting the challenge.* Lancaster, PA: Technomic Publishing Company.

Nansel, T. R., Overpeck, M., Pilla, R. S., Ruan, W. J., Simons-Morton, B., & Scheidt, P. (2001). Bullying behaviors among U.S. youth: Prevalence and association with psychosocial adjustment. *Journal of the American Medical Association, 285*(16):2094–100.

Panico, A. (1997). The classroom community model. *Reaching Today's Youth, 2*(1), 37–40.

Panico, A. (1998). Service learning as a community initiation. *Reaching Today's Youth, 3*(1), 39.

Panico, A. (1999). *Discipline and the classroom community: Recapturing control of our schools.* Mequon, WI: Stylex Publishing Company.

Peck, M. S. (1988). *The different drum: Community making and peace.* NY: Simon & Schuster.

Rohnke, K. (1984). *Silver bullets: A guide to initiative problems, adventure games and trust activities.* Dubuque, IA: Kendall Hunt Publishing.

Rohnke, K., & Butler, S. (1995). *Quicksilver: Adventure games, initiative problems, trust activities and a guide to effective leadership.* Dubuque, IA: Kendall Hunt Publishing.

Schoel, J., & Stratton, M. (Eds.). (1995). *Gold Nuggets: Readings for Experiential Education.* Hamilton, MA: Project Adventure, Inc.

Schoel, J., Prouty, D., & Radcliffe, P. (1988). *Islands of healing: A guide to adventure based counseling.* Hamilton, MA: Project Adventure, Inc.

Schrage, M. (1995). *No more teams! Mastering the dynamics of creative collaboration.* New York: Doubleday.

Toule, P., & Toule, J. (1992). Communities as places of learning. St. Paul, MN: National Youth Leadership Council. As cited in M. Duckenfield and J. Wright (Eds.), *Pocket guide to service learning.* Clemson, SC: National Dropout Prevention Center.

U.S. Department of Justice, Federal Bureau of Investigation. (2004). *Crime in the United States 2003.* Washington, DC: U.S. Government Printing Office.

U.S. Surgeon General. (2006). *Youth violence: A report of the Surgeon General.* Retrieved September 19, 2006, from http://www.surgeongeneral.gov/library/youthviolence/

Van Acker, R., Potterton, T., & Boreson, L. (2003, October). *Blueprints for success: Instructional strategies to promote appropriate student behaviors.* Retrieved from http://dpi.wi.gov/sped/doc/ebdbluepr.doc

Wong, H. K., & Wong, R. T. (2001). *How to be an effective teacher: The first days of school.* Mountain View, CA: Harry K. Wong Publications.

Ziplines: The voice for adventure education. (1998, Summer). Simply paper, *36*, 40–41.

Index of Activities

ACTIVITIES BY CHAPTER

CHAPTER 10

CHAPTER 11

CHAPTER 12

ACTIVITIES BY TITLE

NEED MORE COPIES OR ADDITIONAL
RESOURCES ON THIS TOPIC?

Need more copies of this book? Want your own copy? Need additional resources on this topic? If so, you can order additional materials by using this form or by calling us at (812) 336-7700 or (800) 733-6786 (toll free). Or you can order by FAX at (812) 336-7790 or online at www.solution-tree.com.

Title	Price*	Quantity	Total
Adventure Education for the Classroom Community	$ 39.95		
Building Classroom Communities	9.95		
The Four Keys to Effective Classroom and Behavior Management (video and DVD set)	595.00		
Laughing Matters	9.95		
Teaching Empathy: A Blueprint for Caring, Compassion, and Community	34.95		
Teasing and Harassment	9.95		
The School of Belonging Plan Book	12.95		
Reconnecting Youth (semester-long intervention curriculum)	211.95		
The Resilience Revolution	24.95		
		SUBTOTAL	
		SHIPPING	
Please add 6% of order total. For orders outside the continental U.S., please add 8% of order total.			
		HANDLING	
Please add $4. For orders outside the continental U.S., please add $6.			
		TOTAL (U.S. funds)	

*Price subject to change without notice.

❏ Check enclosed ❏ Purchase order enclosed

❏ Money order ❏ VISA, MasterCard, Discover, or American Express (circle one)

Credit Card No._____ Exp. Date _____

Cardholder Signature _____

SHIP TO:

First Name_____ Last Name_____

Position _____

Institution Name_____

Address_____

City_____ State_____ ZIP_____

Phone_____ FAX _____

Email _____

Solution Tree (formerly National Educational Service)
304 West Kirkwood Avenue
Bloomington, IN 47404
(812) 336-7700 • (800) 733-6786 (toll free)
FAX (812) 336-7790
email: info@solution-tree.com • www.solution-tree.com